INDIAN WOMEN
SOCIETY AND LAW

INDIAN WOMEN
SOCIETY AND LAW

Volume One

DR. ANITA ARYA

GYAN PUBLISHING HOUSE
New Delhi-110002

INDIAN WOMEN
SOCIETY AND LAW
[*Women Study, Law, Sociology*]

ISBN: 81-212-0626-X (Set)
ISBN: 81-212-0689-6

Published in 2000 in India by
Gyan Publishing House
5, Ansari Road
New Delhi 110 002

Laser Typeset at Alphabet, Delhi
Printed at Mehra Offset Press, New Delhi.

Contents

Foreword

I feel great pleasure and honour, while penning down this Foreword for Dr. Anita Arya's first book. I am further happy that this book is on women's studies, which must be the natural forte of a female social activist and a popular leader, which she certainly is.

For years, I have watched Anita Arya growing into a good leader, concerned with basic and vital social issues. She has come a long way from an humble party worker to her present status as Member of Parliament. In between she represented her people in the civic body and rose to become the first citizen of Delhi, as its Mayor. Since her entry in public life, she has never looked back.

It gave me an immense pleasure when I went through her lengthy work: INDIAN WOMEN spread over three volumes. The one thousand or so pages exposed me to a new world, which the women's world is. The way she has treated the subject and handled the material available is really remarkable. What pains she must have taken in collecting material and laying hands upon the original sources over the years, is another story. No doubt, she must be praised for her meritorious work.

Anita Arya, while preparing this book has worked in a large spectrum, which shows her clear understanding of the issues involved and her prowess to overcome the resisting factors whatsoever these were.

The peculiar speciality with Dr. Anita Arya is that she speaks politely, negotiates gently, debates strongly, concludes wisely and acts firmly.

Over a decade or so, I have seen her participating in meetings arguing the matters and making her points assertively. I have always marked her concern for the Indian women. She has her own ideas — based on observations and findings of course — on problems and perspectives, in regard to Indian women, a result of which is the present study.

Here, I take liberty to say that this book by Dr. Anita Arya is a different book on the subject, as it has the support of the experiences of a grassroot worker, practically involved in social activities and mixed up with masses. In this manner, this book has earned a status of a first hand study.

I believe — and quite strongly — that the scholars and readers will find the book thought provoking and eye opening and this is a fact which guarantees her success as an able editor and a good authoress.

As far as I know this gentle lady, known as Dr. Anita Arya, I can say without any fear of contradiction that she will rise steadily in life and career, scaling new heights year after year and achievement after achievement.

I wish her all success and look forward to her vital role as a parliamentarian during the next millennium.

Jagmohan

Preface

Women's world is a world in itself. Similarly, Women studies, as a branch of knowledge has become vast like an ocean. I am proud of being a student of this vital discipline, which has a large room for contribution and work. This effort of mine is a small step in the same direction.

Over thousand of years, our society has changed, a new civilization has replaced the old ones, people have developed culturally, economically and socially but an unfortunate section of the society in the East in general and in our country in particular is still living under the same circumstances, that is women. Their lot is same and they—barring a few fortunate ones—are either shackled, chained and bonded or they are bound to live under the dominance of the men, as ever. Ironically, that's true, in spite of the guarantee of the constitution, protecting laws and all the sincere efforts of various governments over the years. In fact, we cannot change the lot of a community or the whole social system altogether, in one go. Social change has to come from within and it takes its own time.

Throughout my two-decade involvement with women's problems and issues and my search for remedies for them, I have always found it challenging to work in these areas. As a grassroot worker and a down to earth social activist, since my student days, I have felt debted to do some thing for this happless group. I have done only a bit so far but I determine to do a lot in the years to come, in and outside Parliament. I have no illusions and realise that the path is ardous thorny and long enough. However, we have to assert and strive.

As my first humble contribution to women's studies, I am presenting this book of mine. Honestly, I was a bit confused when Gyan Publishing House urged me to compile and edit a book on Women and left the choice of the topic to me only. I had to think for weeks and months, before I decided to bring out a book on Indian women, covering all the concerning aspects. Hence this bulky study, spanning over one thousand odd pages and comprising three volumes. Notably each of these volumes is an independent book in itself.

Study of the prevailing status of women in our society is one of the core areas in women studies today. In order to make the work exhaustive and more comprehensive, I have divided it into three separate volumes, titled: (1) Society and Law, (2) Education and Empowerment, and (3) Work and Development.

The first volume approaches the study of women problems and prospects and the legal aspects have been examined in the socio-cultural settings.

The second volume provides information on women education and empowerment in a historical perspective.

The third volume is designed to provide information on gender and economic participation and the related problems of working women at various levels.

This voluminous book is the outcome of a painstaking research for years and compilation of materials from hundreds of sources, spread all over. In fact, I had begun this project, nearly a decade ago and finished it in over a five year period. So, for the last five years or so it has been lying for a thorough revision of the whole work, an excercise, which I carried out in the previous year only and that too at a fast pace, thanks to my overwhelming engagements in public life. One confession, I wish to make here is that I have not been able to devote my full attention to this work in its last phase and could not collect new data and other latest figure. I am afraid, if I would have opted for it, perhaps this book would not have been able to see the light of the day for another five years. So, I had to make a compromise and I regret for it. Truly speaking, this is the price, we 'politico-academics' have to pay, as public life is always taxing upon one's scholarly pursuit.

I hope this petty contribution of an humble fellows, would at least be able to stir the calm waters, create a sort of awareness among men and women and appeal to those who matter in our political and social system. If this much is done, I should feel honoured and privileged to have played a small role in the continuous process of social change and be apart of an ongoing historic struggle which is slated to be extended to the next millennium.

Dr. Anita Arya

Introduction

Woman is the mother, sister, wife and daughter, all rolled into one. A single woman plays these four roles in her life. First, she is daughter and sister and in that capacity, she serves her father and brothers. In the second phase, she acts as wife, which is perhaps the most important role, she plays. In this capacity she serves her husband and in laws.

In due course, she becomes a mother and brings out her children. A woman normally commands three generations in one life of hers. She is the creator and protector of a family. She gives birth to a generation, develops it and thus forms the society. In fact, society is a product of women.

Ironically, in spite of the importance attached to her personality, a woman is least respected — in the true sense of the word — in society. Over thousands of years, she has not been able to be free of shackles and chains, binding her and confining her to a limited space to move and act.

As far as law is concerned, it has always been there in existence, in one form or the other for the protection of women. All religions give appropriate rights to women, the scriptures have norms for the protection of their rights and personal liberty. But, in fact, the unfortunate lot, known as womenfolk enjoy no rights and no liberty at all. Over the ages, they have been forced to live under the dominance of men. No doubt, women have been in prominence in all eras, but they could at best be termed as exceptions. In an over all manner, the women are 'have nots' and a bad lot is tagged with them.

One point, which all leaders, politicians, thinkers and scholars agree on is that no society, however, well organised, can ever be well oiled and set in motion properly, unless a justified status is granted to women. But, that's all. No one seems to believe in it practically. At least their actions do not depict anything of that sort.

Interestingly, the demand for women's lib or the movement for the protection of their rights is not new. It has been there for years now. However, women's battle for justice got fresh momentum after the independence of the country and it has been in constant motion since then, in one form or the other. The struggle for securing a respectable status for women in the Indian polity and in society, has been on for the last 53 years and the efforts have been made inside and outside legislative bodies, all over the country, the national Parliament, being the natural leader.

Following a long spell of fights and struggles — internal and external — and under the immense pressure of women's lib activists, at the international level, various governments began to act and the result was the creation of a National Commission for Women, besides enactment of a number of laws, protecting women, including some for granting reservation in different elected bodies, in order to provide them with a share in power.

Truly speaking, liberation of womanhood is nothing unnatural or any thing which should be termed as taxing on the males. The right to a personhood is a basic human right of every individual, bestowed upon by humanity and no one can deny it.

One has to believe that the progress of any nation is inevitably linked with the social status of woman in that particular country. But things do not move through papers only. For concrete results, we have to assert and act, with our full might and that's what is needed most.

Empowerment of women can be granted through laws, but for its practical implementation, social response alone is required, which can come from within only. In this study, sincere efforts have been made to bring, the real issues concerning women — in the context of Society and Law — to light and discuss the matter in a logical, convincing and empirical manner. A great effort has been made to study various problems of women in the right perspective, with the legal aspects in view.

Editor

List of Tables

One

Women: Problems and Prospects

Approaches to the study of status of women in India are through many groups of variables, making our investigation, particularly the search for trends and patterns of social behaviour and attitudes, highly complex and difficult. Some of them stem from the characteristic features of our society, others from processes of change effected by modernization and development. Still some others were repercussions of the historical vicissitudes that affected India in the past few centuries, particularly the impact of a colonial regime and exposure to foreign culture. Lastly, they also reflected the influence of the struggle for freedom and social justice.

These variables are closely interrelated. It is imperative to examine the characteristics of our society with its lack of homogeneity within the basic pattern of inequalities, impact of the complex process of socio-economic and political change, instruments of social engineering, degree of social acceptance of desired goals, factors influencing women's progress, varied sources and periodisation, problem of definition and the analysis by categories.

The Preamble to the Constitution of India promises "to secure to all its citizens, justice— social, economic and political; liberty of thought, expression, belief, faith and worship; equality of status and of opportunity; and to promote among them all fraternity, assuring the dignity of the individual and the unity of the nation"

While improvement in the status of women was a pledge made by the Constitution-makers and admitted by the national Government at the very outset as one of the major tasks facing the country, no comprehensive review of the achievements in this direction has been undertaken thus far.

Some laws, attempting to embody the principles underlying the Constitution had, from time to time, passed through the Legislature. Attempts were made to introduce programmes of development, aimed at enabling women to play their role in our national life in an effective manner. Partly as a result of these various measures and partly because of the general processes of social change which have speeded up since independence, the status of women in our country has undoubtedly undergone considerable change.

It is felt that while these changes have been considerable in the urban areas, problems continue to remain virtually unchanged in most of the rural areas. Further, with the changing social and economic conditions in the country, various new problems relating to the advancement of women which had not been visualized by the Constitution-makers and the Government in its earlier days have manifested.

Objectives of the Study

The objective of the study undertaken by the national government to examine the status of women was, in the main—

(a) to assess the impact of the constitutional, legal and administrative provisions on the social status of women, their education and employment, particularly in the rural sector during the last two decades;

(b) to examine the status of women in the changing social milieu; and

(c) to suggest remedial and other measures in the fields of law, education, employment, population policy etc., "Which would enable women to play their full and proper role in building up the nation".

The framework for the study was thus provided on the one hand by the constitutional provisions that have a bearing on the status of women and, on the other, by the clear objective specified, *viz.* enabling women to play their 'full and proper role in building up the nation'.

To attain these national objectives, the Constitution guarantees certain fundamental rights and freedoms such as freedom of speech, protection of life and personal liberty. While these may be termed positive rights, the negative rights are the prohibition of discrimination or denial of equal protection.

Indian women are the beneficiaries of these rights in the same manner as Indian men. Article 14 of the Constitution ensures 'equality before law' and Article 15 'prohibits any discrimination'. There is only one specific provision in Article 15(3), which empowers the State to make 'any special provision for women and children', even in violation of the fundamental obligation of non-discrimination among citizens, *inter alia* of sex. This provision has enabled the State to make special provision for women, particularly in the field of labour legislation like the Factories Act, the Mines Act, etc. These special provisions in favour of women need not be restricted to measures which are beneficial in the strict sense, and therefore, the provision upholding that a man is punished for adultery but not a women was regarded as not being discriminatory.

Article 16(1) guarantees "equality of opportunity for all citizens in matters relating to employment, or appointment to any office under the State". And Article 16(2) forbids discrimination "in respect of any employment of office under the State" on grounds only of "religion, race, caste, sex, descent, place of birth, residence or any one of them". The obligation not to discriminate in matters relating to employment or appointment to any office under the State has thus at least normatively ensured a significant position and status to Indian women. However, the Supreme Court recently dismissed *in limine* a writ petition of a woman lawyer who challenged her being prevented from employment in the Judge Advocate General's office for a 5-year short service commission in the law branch. The reasons given by the government for barring women from applying were that 'they are required to travel by rail, road and river, sometimes for long periods at a stretch; they will have to be present in courts martial where the judge, accused and witnesses may all be males, and that lady advocates are required to study the lives of soldiers (all males) in army units for several months'. The government failed to appreciate the fact that these same grounds also apply to the nursing and medical corps of the Army where women are employed.

In this context we would like to mention that during the tenure of Sri Charan Singh as chief minister, and under his instruction, the Government of the State of Uttar Pradesh attempted a direct violation of this constitutional provision. In reply to a question asked in the Uttar Pradesh Vidhan Sabha on 16 July,

1971, the State Government admitted that "in June 1970, the State Government sent a letter to the Government of India stating that women officers should not be admitted to the Indian Administrative Service. If that was not possible, then at least they should not be sent to this State".

Though this attempt did not succeed, it is a pointer that vigilance is necessary to ensure that the special provision permitted under Article 15(3) is not used to the detriment of women by legislative or executive action.

The Directive Principles of State Policy enunciated in Part IV of the Constitution, embody the major policy goals of a welfare State. They concretize, together with the chapter on Fundamental Rights, the constitutional vision of a new Indian socio-political order. The Directive Principles are declared as non-justiciable; but "nevertheless fundamental in the governance of the country", and the State is charged with "a duty... to apply these principles in making laws" (Article 37). The Directive Principles were made non-enforceable in courts because it was felt that their fulfilment would be spread over a time dimension of a few decades. The constitutional values embodied in the Fundamental Rights needed immediate implementation; but in the case of the Directive Principles, this was not possible save at the cost of the viability of the State.

Juridically, the Directive Principles are a vital part of Indian Constitutional Law. Like the Preamble, they reflect high ideals of a liberal democratic polity; they are meant to be used by all agencies of the State as guidelines to action as major goals of policy; courts can use them as a body of values and standards relevant to the act of judicial choice-making. But the Directive Principles confer no power or legislative competence; nor can they give rise to a cause of action for which remedy is available in a court of law. The principles in themselves do not confer power, bestow rights, or create remedies. At the same time, they cannot be amended, save through the prescribed procedure. Some of them concern women indirectly or by necessary implication. A few are, as it were, "women-specific". In the first category fall:

(a) the omnibus provision of Article 38 briefly directs the State to secure a just social, political and economic order, geared to promote the welfare of the people; Art 39(b) (c) and (f) enunciates the distribution of ownership and control of material resources of the community for the common good, prevention of concentration of wealth and means of production to the common detriment, and protection of childhood and youth against exploitation and moral and material abandonment; Art. 40 lays stress on organisation of village panchayats to promote self-government; Art. 41 specifies right to work, education and public assistance in cases of unemployment, old age, sickness, disablement and other types of underserved wants; Art. 43 spells out provision of work, a living wage, conditions of work ensuring a decent standard of life and full enjoyment of leisure, of social and cultural opportunities, and the promotion of cottage industries; Art. 44 delineates the Uniform Civil Code; Art. 45 provides for free and compulsory education for all children up to the age of 14; and Art. 47 speaks for raising the level of nutrition and the standard of living of the people and improvement of public health.

(b) The Directive Principles which concern women directly and have a special bearing on their status include Art. 39(a) concerning right to an adequate means of livelihood for men and women equally; Art. 39(d) concerning equal pay for equal work for both men and women; Art. 39(e) concerning the protection of the health and strength of workers — men, women and children from abuse and entry into avocations unsuited to their age and strength; and Art. 42 concerning just and human conditions of work and maternity relief.

As previously mentioned, the Fundamental Rights and the Directive Principles are the instruments to attainment of our national objectives of justice, liberty and equality. By adopting the principle of adult franchise, it seeks to establish a democratic republic by giving the adult population direct or indirect share in government.

The special attention given to the needs and problems of women, to enable them to enjoy and exercise constitutional equality of status, along with other specific provisions relating to the hitherto suppressed sections of our society have led many scholars to describe the Indian Constitution as a 'social' document embodying the objectives of a social revolution. There is no doubt that the Constitution contemplates attainment of an entirely new social order by making deliberate departure in norms and institutions of democratic governance from the inherited social, political and economic systems. In doing so the Constitution assigns primacy to law as an instrument of directed social change. It thus demands of the legislature, the executive and the judiciary, continuous vigilance and responsiveness to the relationship between law and social transformation in contemporary India.

Variables in Approach of Study

The field of our enquiry was complicated by many groups of variables, making our investigation, particularly the search for trends and patterns of social behaviour and attitudes, highly complex and difficult. Some of them stemmed from the characteristic features of our society, while others from processes of change released by modernization and development. Still some others were repercussions of the historical vicissitudes that affected India in the last few centuries, particularly the impact of a colonial regime and exposure to a foreign culture. Lastly, they also reflected the influence of the struggle for freedom and social justice.

While all these variables are closely interrelated, for the sake of clarity we may classify them in the following manner :

Characteristics of our society with its lack of homogeneity even within the basic pattern of inequalities

While it is true that the status of women constitutes a problem in almost all societies, and has emerged today as a fundamental crisis in human development, we found that sex inequality cannot in reality be differentiated from the variety of social, economic and cultural inequalities in Indian society. The inequalities inherent in our traditional social structure, based on caste, community and class have a very significant influence on the status of women in different spheres. Socially accepted rights and expected roles of women, the norms governing their behaviour and of others towards them, vary among different groups and regions. They are closely affected by the stage and methods of development, and the position held by the group in the social hierarchy. All this makes broad generalizations regarding women's status unrealistic. It was, therefore, necessary to understand the reality of women's roles and status in the different strata of our society.

Impact of the complex process of socio-economic and political change

The complex processes generally described by broad terms like modernization, democratization, development, urbanization, industrialization, etc., have all affected the status of women in differing degrees. Here again, it would be pertinent to point out that it was not possible to discover any uniform pattern of this impact, since not all sections of women have been affected by these processes in like manner. It is, however, generally accepted that a change in the status of women is a good indicator of the pattern and direction of social change. If the direction of that change is towards a more egalitarian distribution of roles between men and women, in tune with the constitutional directives, then the direction of change is a wholesome one. If, however, the various modernizing forces result in an intensification of inequalities, then we are moving away from the spirit of the Constitution. It was, therefore, important to understand the direction of these changes in order to assess the nature of their impact on different sections of our women.

The issue of social change in India is a complex one. Given the highly complex and heterogeneous social situation in the country, it is not surprising that change takes many directions, some of which are even in conflict with one another. We had to consider only those components of this change which affect the status of women. This brought us face to face with structural changes in the economy as a result of commercialization, expanding markets and technological changes in the methods of production. The combination of these forces with the growth of population has increased both poverty and wealth. Education, urbanization and wider avenues of participation in the social process have both contributed and tried to combat the increase in social inequalities that resulted from this process. We had to examine the extent of their impact on the roles, rights and opportunities open to women in different spheres of social life.

It was also necessary to consider the difference between what are called 'traditional' and 'modern' values, in so far as they affect the life of women. Here again, we discovered that traditionalism and modernity do not necessarily reflect their temporal setting. Traditional values handed down from generation to generation were modelled on the ideal behaviour of the upper classes of our society. Any improvement in the economic conditions of the lower castes or classes has almost invariably led to their adopting these values. An important component of upper caste values was the seclusion of their womenfolk and their withdrawal from work outside the home.

From the point of view of the socially lower groups, adoption of these values enhances their status in the social hierarchy. We could see the impact of this ideology operating among these groups even now. On the other hand, a considerable section of the upper class or the middle class of today has abandoned these values in favour of what is generally regarded as 'modern' ideology regarding equal rights and opportunities of women for participation in the social process. This indicates certain structural changes within the value system and behavioural norms of the middle class under the compulsion of social change. The process of emulation of the traditional values of the upper classes by others, however, though they constitute modernity in the thinking of the latter, is a trend in the opposite direction. It is obvious that the impact of these contradictory forces is bound to give rise to certain ambiguities and confusion in the minds of both men and women in our society.

Instruments of Social Engineering

The period post Independence witnessed the enactment of a number of laws that sought to apply the principles underlying the constitutional guarantees to the sphere of social life. The reforms in personal laws governing marriage and inheritance, in labour laws ensuring humane conditions of work, maternity benefits and welfare of workers, and in social laws seeking the protection of women and children against immoral traffic and exploitation, tried to remove the disabilities that contributed to the low status of women in our society. At the same time, the policies and programmes for economic and social development initiated by the government, attempted positive action to improve and widen opportunities for women to participate in the social processes in a more effective manner. Education, vocational training, health services, family planning, welfare and development programmes, sought to change and improve the conditions of living and the mental horizons of women.

Apart from examining these measures initiated by the government, we had to include under this category, the organised or individual efforts to bring about changes in social attitudes and norms of behaviour that were generated by the community. Most of them had started either as a part of the freedom movement, or dated back to the earlier movement for social and religious reform that developed in the 19th century. Leaders of public opinion and community organisations had sought to mobilize various groups of people to propagate measures for uplift of women's status. The ideology that emerged from these various attempts—governmental and social—have helped to shape the goals and left an impact on the minds of many sections of our society, and have played a significant role in changing the status of women.

Degrees of Social Acceptance of Desired Goals

Indicators of social acceptance of any goals set for the future must include the attitudes of men and women as well as the availability of institutionalized infrastructures that support the attainment of such goals. Examining this group of variables involved discussing the influence, cultural and religious norms, as well as the impact of modern values such as human rights, social justice, equality and participation. It also involved examining the regional differences in the cultural norms that affected women's roles and participation in the social process. This revealed the positive and negative sets of social factors which affected the success or consequent failure of the policies and instruments of social engineering, i.e. institutionalized opportunities as well as disabilities that affect women's enjoyment and exercise of various legal and constitutional rights and their performance of the multiple roles that the goals of our society call for.

Positive Factors Influencing Women's Progress

We had to examine the actual achievements in the fields of education, employment, health, institutionalized welfare facilities and services for development and participation in different levels and spheres of national life. It was also necessary to study the disappearance or removal of certain traditional taboos that had sought to restrict women's life to limited sphere.

Negative Factors Influencing Women's Progress

We had to identify the centres of resistance to the desired change in women's status and roles and the disabilities that still hamper many groups of women at different levels of existence. In the process of this examination, we attempted to identify the lacuna or deficiencies in the instruments of social engineering that have caused the failure to overcome these negative influences.

In order to study the nature and influence of these broad studies of variables we had to depend on various types of indicators. Quantitative indicators provided by vital statistics of birth and mortality rates, sex ratio, rates of participation in economic and political life, literacy and education, provided certain broad measures and trends. None of them could, however, be studied meaningfully without a qualitative appraisal and understanding of their limitations in a field of this kind. For instance the concept of national and State averages normally used for most quantitative analyses becomes meaningless in the context of tremendous socio-economic inequalities and variations in our society. Secondly, there is a wide gap between stated social objectives and achievements, between the legal framework and empirical improvement in education, literacy, life expectancy and political participation. These trends, coupled with the success and the position achieved by a minority of women, could mislead us to think that the status of an average Indian woman was very high. Detailed investigations, however, show that while opportunities had widened immensely at certain levels of society and enabled women to forge ahead in areas which had been completely closed to them in earlier years, this was not true for the other levels of society. The uneven rates of development between regions, communities and sections of our population often make analysis by quantitative methods baffling. It was, therefore, necessary to utilize other methods and techniques to assess these different levels of social reality.

Sources of Data

The sources of data availed of may be broadly classified under three categories:

Basic Documentary Sources

The basic documentary sources are the primary, secondary and tertiary which provide vital statistics and other demographic data, trends of development and decay, and often present the state of affairs in particular areas of life. These included —

(i) census and registration data, their analysis as also comparative studies based on such material, indices worked out from them, etc.; and

(ii) national female surveys and records available with various organisations including government departments and reports of committees and commissions appointed by the government from time to time.

These provided the necessary information on economic participation of women in literacy and education, political participation, and governmental efforts—both legislative and administrative—towards improvement of women's status.

Special Studies based on Literature, using both Published as well as Unpublished Sources

These were prepared at our request by scholars and specialists in the field. The topics mentioned below indicate the coverage attempted in these studies:

(i) Content analysis, relating mainly to understanding the trends in social attitude regarding women; image of women in the various religious traditions of India; status of women in family, kinship, marriage and household; customary marriage institutions in tribal and non-tribal India;

(ii) Status of women among Scheduled Castes and Scheduled Tribes;
(iii) Political roles and status of women since Independence—all-India and State profiles;
(iv) Health and nutritional status of women;
(v) Status of women in different branches of personal and criminal laws governing citizenship;
(vi) Status of women in different professions; women in different industries;
(vii) Protective laws governing women's employment in organised industry.

Material was also Acquired through

(a) Tours of different States and Union Territories. In these tours, we observed and interviewed various categories of people in both urban and rural areas. Factual information and opinions on attitudes and problems were obtained from a cross-section of men and women with greater emphasis on women;

(b) planned empirical studies. These were undertaken by the committee or the task forces or were assigned to research organisations or individual scholars. The important ones were:
   (i) Attitudes towards coeducation and choice of subjects among girl students with a sample from six States;
   (ii) programmes for development and welfare of women from all departments of the Central and State Governments.

(c) The committee invited men and women working in different fields to discuss problems connected with the status of women of diverse categories and socio-economic levels. These included professionals like lawyers, journalists, educationists, doctors and social workers; experts in family planning programme, research and mass communication; representatives of political parties, women's voluntary organisations, trade union organisations and officials from various government departments.

Problems of Study

Problem of Periodisation

Determining the starting point for our enquiry posed a dilemma. The constitutional provisions could provide only a framework of abstract principles. We needed a concrete framework against which the changes and their directions could be measured. At Independence data was available in a concrete form, but it was found that this was not possible in other cases. Trends in population, employment, and changes in social roles, responsibilities, challenges and burdens had begun much earlier than Independence. It was also obvious that any understanding of the motives of the Constitution-makers would be impossible without a background of the freedom and the reform movements that affected the status of women. It was important to look back as well as to future to discern a proper perspective for the study of the present, since a society in the process of rapid transformation cannot be measured except in terms of both past and future.

Problem of Definition

Before going into the diverse aspects of the status of women in India, it is essential to offer an operational definition of the term status and to also consider other allied and interlinked categories. Status refers to a position in a social system or sub-system which is distinguishable from and at the same time related to other positions through its designated rights and obligations. In the pure sociological sense, status does not imply rank or hierarchy but denotes only position *vis-a-vis* others in terms of rights and obligations. But as each status position in a particular structure can be viewed in terms of superiority and inferiority, i.e. in terms of power, privileges, advantages, and disadvantages, the notion of status involves comparison and grading. In assessing the status of women we shall follow the comparative approach as well.

At this juncture we need to adopt a broader perspective and understand that status denotes relative position of persons, groups, social strata, and a range of identified social categories. Men and women acquire their identities through groups, strata, and categories; as such it is imperative to take note of them in assessing women's status in India.

Each status position is expressed in terms of a role. Role denotes a set of expectations and obligations associated with a particular status position within a group or social situation. The expectations and obligations entailed by a role are in terms of activities and qualities. Each individual occupies a number of distinct statuses within a society and therefore he/she performs a variety of roles. Further, around each particular status position centres a role-set.

It is useful to make a distinction between ideal role behaviour, expected role behaviour, and actual role behaviour. Processes of change are responsible for considerable divergence between these three aspects of a role. Performance of multiple roles in varied social situations often leads to a change in the role perception of individuals. Changes in the actual role performance over a period of time influence the expected role behaviour, and gradually there are changes in the ideal role behaviour. But this process is characterized by unreasonable expectations of others and by the incompatibility between the various roles that an individual has to perform in a given situation. This is particularly relevant for women in India.

In respect of some institutionalized disabilities, women as a whole can be compared to men as a whole, for differences between the status of men and women are important in cognitive mapping as well as in ordering interpersonal relations. The presence of ascriptive norms in respect of sex-linked statuses are universal with wide variations in achievement avenues open to them.

As pointed out earlier, a woman, like any person, occupies many status positions at a given point of time and plays a number of roles, such as those in the kinship system, family system, and the wider social system. Her status in society is usually not determined by any one particular status position held by her, but by her composite status which results from the merging of various statuses. To this should be added her consciousness of her own status.

There are multifarious principles of status differentiation operating simultaneously—place in ritual hierarchy, financial position, independent job, education, political participation and so on. A woman of the labour class enjoys a certain degree of autonomy in the house, but she has a low status in the wider setting. Similarly a housewife in a well-to-do home may be enjoying an overall high status, but she may be a distinctly inferior partner in the house. In investigating the position of women, various institutional settings have to be taken into account.

Status is realized through roles. Hence the best way to assess the status of women of any group or category, or in any sub-system is to analyse the roles women are being called upon to play and the manner of their performance. This also brings in the structure of rights and opportunities provided to them by the State and by social and cultural institutions which do not necessarily or always reinforce each other.

Examination of the groups of variables indicated earlier made it clear that the status of women in the Indian context cannot be defined simply. General concepts like equality, role differentiation, legal, social and political rights, dependency or independence, are not applicable to all sections of our population. Since a very large section of our society still continues to be under the influence of traditional standards, we had to juxtapose the role conception, norms and values in all their wide variety in traditional society, against the new dimensions in women's status and roles introduced by the Constitution and the processes of social change.

Traditional India has seen a woman only as a member of the family or a group—as daughters, wives and mothers—and not as an individual with an identity or right of her own. The radicalism of the Constitution and its deliberate departure from the social position or accomplishments, will allow women to function as a equal citizen and an individual partner in the task of nation building.

While motherhood is an important social and biological function, the Constitution implied that this could no longer be regarded as the only significant role for women. A gap between traditional social attitudes and institutions, and the new roles that women are expected to play in the political, social and economic spheres, creates problems and imposes constraints on women's ability to perform such roles. We had to identify the exact nature of these disabilities and constraints.

Analysis by Categories

An examination of the expected and actual roles and the constraints that affect women's performance of these multiple roles made it imperative for us to examine these constraints at different levels of society. Any meaningful analysis of restrictions imposed by social attitudes and norms, possession or lack of necessary equipment, for example, education and other employment skills, political awareness, etc., was only possible by studying women in different categories. Our experience showed that while Indian society can be categorized by castes, communities and classes, for our purpose the most relevant broad categories were as follows :

(a) Women below the subsistence level, whose problems and constraints are radically different in nature from those suffered by women in other sections of society;

(b) Women who move continuously between security and subsistence, and often descend below the subsistence level with the disappearance of their means of earning or livelihood; and

(c) Women firmly above the security line.

Guiding Principles and Criteria

The first of the guiding principles and criteria are the values and goals put forward in the Constitution, namely equality and social justice for all.

Equality is an article of faith in our Constitution and guaranteed by specific Articles. We could, therefore, treat this as a settled fact, for which no discussion was necessary. Our investigation, however, proved that there was still considerable ambiguity as well as ambivalence in the general understanding of the need and implications of sex equality in society and employment in our country.

The history of the discussion on women's rights, both in the Constituent Assembly and in the Central Legislature over the Hindu Code Bill in the period immediately after Independence, indicates that attitudes towards women's equality vary sharply. As long as the discussion was on abstract principles, as was the case during the debate on Fundamental Rights in the Constituent

Assembly, there was no dissenting voice to challenge or even to provoke a discussion on this historic decision. When it came to applying the same principles on established preserves of traditional male privileges, such as the right to property and the unchallenged dominance of the husband in family life, the reactions of the same body were very different. One group accepted both the concept of equality and its implications for society. The second group accepted the concept in theory, but was not prepared to practise, or follow up its implications. The third group rejected the concept outright as totally inapplicable and undesirable for Indian society. It is believed :

1. Equality, of women is necessary, not merely on the grounds of social justice, but as a basic condition for social, economic and political development of the nation;
2. In order to release women from their dependent and unequal status, improvement of their employment opportunities and earning power has to be given the highest priority;
3. Society owes a special responsibility to women because of their child-bearing function. Safe bearing and rearing of children is an obligation that has to be shared by the mother, the father and society too;
4. The contribution made by an active housewife to the running and management of a family should be admitted as economically and socially productive and contributing to national savings and development;
5. Marriage and motherhood should not become a disability in women's fulfilling their full and proper role in the task of national development. Therefore, it is important that society, including women themselves, must accept their responsibility in this field;
6. Disabilities and inequalities imposed on women have to be seen in the total context of a society, where large sections of the population: male and female, adults and children, suffer under the oppression of an exploitative system. It is not possible to remove these inequalities for women only. Any policy or movement for the

emancipation and development of women has to form a part of a total movement for removal of inequalities and oppressive social institutions, if the benefits and privileges won by such action are to be shared by the entire women population and not be monopolised by a small minority.

7. If our society is to move in the direction of the goals set by the Constitution, then special temporary measures will be necessary, to transform *de jure* into *de facto* equality.

REFERENCES

1. Anju Vyas and Sunita Singh, *Women's Studies in India*, New Delhi, 1993.
2. Archana Parashar, *Women and Family Law Reform in India*, 1992.
3. Asha Goel v. Union of India.
4. Basu, *Commentary on Constitution of India*.
5. Raju Ramachandran, *From Mythology to Contemporary Politics*, New Delhi, 1995.
6. Seema Alavi, *Tradition-Modernity Divide*, Delhi, 1994.
7. Tanika Sarkar, *Analysing Substantive Socio-historical Processes*, Delhi, 1995.
8. Towards Equality, A report by the Government of India, New Delhi, 1974.
9. Upendra, Baxi, "Constitutional Provisions relating to Status of Women—An Analytical Examination", a paper prepared for the Committee on the Status of Women in India.
10. Vasudha Dhagamwar, *Law, Power and Justice*, New Delhi, 1992.
11. Yusuf v. State of Bombay.

Two

Women and Socio-Cultural Problems

An enquiry into the status of women cannot be conducted outside the social framework. We have thus studied the problem keeping in mind diversities and inequalities prevalent in our society through the ages.

Therefore, the images of women in our religious traditions, the role of social reform movements, the descent, marriage and family in the various provinces of India, changing milieu and role of women and their special problems like prostitution, women in prison, aged and destitute women have been discussed in order to understand the status of women in the Indian society and their prospects in proper perspective.

Any attempt to assess the status and problems of women in a society should start from the social framework. Social structure, cultural norms, and value systems are important determinants of women's roles and their position in society. They influence social expectations regarding behaviour of the two sexes, both as individuals and in relation to each other. Social traditions are a major influence in shaping attitudes as well as behaviour patterns of human groups; emerging trends of society cannot be viewed in isolation from them.

The response of the structural forms to the forces of change in other sectors of life is not easy to predict. Social structure can stimulate certain trends of change, but at the same time it can also prove to be an impediment in their path. Changes in the normative structure and in the organisational forms of society do not take place in unison; the difference in their pace often creates a hiatus.

Thus we find that reforms in law and educational policy do not always make the desired impact because of the normative and structural unpreparedness of the society to accept their goals and means. In respect of the status that is accorded to women by law and by the Constitution we notice that there is a gap between the theoretical possibilities and their actual realization.

Religion, family and kinship, roles and cultural norms delimiting the spheres of women's activities obstruct their full and equal participation in the life of the society and the achievement of their full potential. The new role and responsibilities and status visualized for Indian woman will thus have to relate to the living realities of the social and cultural contexts of their present position. Therefore, our main endeavour will be :

1. To analyse the institutional complexes and basic conceptions which would be helpful in explaining the present position of women belonging to various categories, groups, and strata operating in various spheres;
2. To examine some of the myths about the natural capacities and disabilities of women and, in consequence, about the roles suited to them; and
3. To discuss some features of our social order which reflect and affect the status of women. This would include dowry and other avoidable marriage expenses, prostitution, female suicide, female infanticide and destitution in female population.

These are essentially social phenomena which are directly related to the position of women in our society and hence constitute our important concerns. We propose to examine them in their social and cultural contexts and suggest lines of action wherever possible.

In this chapter the terms upper or higher castes, middle level castes, and lower castes are used. This has been done to conform to Indian social reality in which there exists a ritual hierarchy of castes. Although this hierarchy is not a clear cut one, in terms of closeness of status and a broad commonality of customs and practices, it is possible to conceive of three levels of castes.

In many ways the necessity of changes in role relationships and in the treatment of women in various subsystems indicates a positive need for attitudinal changes. Hence, it is necessary to think of ways and means to bring about these changes in values and attitudes and perceptions of the people.

It is obvious that for an adequate description of the social and cultural scene and for an assessment of their social status, women of India cannot be treated as a homogeneous group. Broadly speaking, in our highly complex and extremely diversified society, women in different religious groups, caste levels, economic strata, and those belonging to tribal, rural and urban areas merit separate consideration. Differences in customs and norms and in conditions of their operation across groups and categories make it imperative for us to adopt this approach.

In an effort to grasp and portray the social and cultural reality and arrive at a cogent understanding of the present status of women in India, we take note of what is present in the people's consciousness as also of what is indicated by the logic of sociological understanding.

In the first section we examine the influence of religion in shaping and sustaining certain images of women. The second section deals with the forms of social organisation that exert the greatest pressure on women's roles and status, namely descent and kinship systems, marriage, and family organisation. The third section examines some of the constraints on women because of the distinction between men's sphere and women's sphere such as, those springing from division of work and seclusion and segregation of women, and the problems of adjustment that arise due to processes of social change. These are connected with the multiple role of women as home makers, wage earners, and participants in the wider society. The fourth section discusses certain special problems of women such as prostitution and suicide.

Images of Women in Religious Traditions

Indian society consists of communities professing diverse religious faiths. Because of the secular character of the polity and criminal and civil laws, the State does not make any distinction on the basis of religion, but because of the continuation of various systems of personal law, and special protection for minorities provided in the Constitution, religion does receive some recognition.

In starting with a discussion on religious traditions it is not implied that religion is of paramount importance in understanding the relative statuses of men and women or that all categories of social facts which need to be understood in this connection are rooted in religion. That religion itself is born and nurtured in a certain type of social structure cannot be denied; nor can it be denied that religion imparts legitimacy and is functional to sustaining certain kinds of social structures.

At the same time when a religion is superimposed on the substructures of certain sections of a society, it calls for and necessitates many compromises and adjustments. Religious systems and principles of social organisation cut across each other. For analytical purposes only, therefore, discussion of religion is separated from social structure and the various social institutions.

Religion provides ideological and moral bases for the accorded status and institutionalized roles of women in a society. The social restrictions on women, and also the people's notions about their proper roles in the domestic and extra-domestic spheres, are largely derived from the religious conceptions of a woman's basic characteristics, her assumed 'virtues' and 'vices', her proverbial strengths and weaknesses, and the stereotypes regarding her nature and capacities. Each religion has a treasure of myths and legends which through descriptions of events and activities emphasize certain values.

Religion has a definite role to play in the crises of life, i.e. the points of transition in an individual's life such as birth, initiation, marriage, and death. The social and religious aspects of these occasions are intermingled in all communities. It is an accepted fact that there are definite social mechanisms which help an individual to internalize the values, norms, and behaviour patterns rooted in religion.

A continuity of conceptions regarding women's status and roles is assured in the process of socialization in which women play a prominent role. A comparison of the fundamental notions regarding women in the major religious traditions reveals a direct conflict between them and the idea of the equality of sexes which is one of our guiding principles.

It is true that scriptures and sacred texts provide scope for diverse interpretations and value emphasis at the hands of different authorities and at different periods of time. Religion has a dynamic character and is shaped and reshaped by historical processes and the interaction with popular religion. In India, Islam and

Christianity had to compromise with local customs since their followers remained under the influence of pre-conversion social and religious traditions. Similarly, Hinduism has always absorbed both the "Great Tradition" and the "Little Traditions". According to Refield (1956) :

"In a civilisation there is a great tradition of the reflective few and there is a little tradition of the largely unreflective many. The great tradition is cultivated in schools or temples, the little tradition works itself out and keeps itself going in the lives of the unlettered in their village communities. The tradition of the philosopher, theologian and literary man is a tradition consciously cultivated and handed down; that of the little people is for the most part taken for granted and not submitted to much scrutiny or considered refinement and improvement. The two traditions are interdependent. Great tradition and the little tradition have long affected each other and continue to do so."

Through different periods of history orthodox Hinduism has produced strong reactions and has resulted in the establishment of new religions or sects, such as Buddhism, Jainism, Sikhism, Veerasaivism, and Vaishnavism, and the nineteenth century reform movement like the Brahmo Samaj and Arya Samaj. These have to be viewed in the context of the direct or indirect effect that their preachings and activities have had on the status of women.

Hinduism

Hinduism has a long history and many facets. During the centuries of its existence, the image of women has undergone many changes. It is said that women in the Vedic period enjoyed a high status. They had the right to study the Vedas and to offer sacrifices and enjoyed considerable freedom in marriage. There was no bar on the remarriage of widows or women remaining unmarried.

This is not, however, true of Hindu women today. The women of the later ages pictured in the epics, the *Puranas*, and the *Dharmasastras* have travelled a long way and can be seen in some ways even in the modern age. The image of women is not consistent and coherent, but her expected rights and duties are fairly clear. It is not our intention to trace and analyse the deterioration or ups

TABLE - 2.1
DISTRIBUTION OF POPULATION BY RELIGION 1971

Sl. No.	Total	Hindus		Muslims		Christians		Sikhs		Budhists		Jains		Other Religions and persuasions		Religions not stated	
	Population	Population	%age	Population	%age	Population	%age	Population	%age	Population	%age	Population	%age	Population	%age	Population	%age
1	2	3	4	5	6	7	8	9	10	11	12	13	14	15	16	17	18
INDIA	547949809	453292086	82.72	61417934	11.21	14223382	2.60	10378797	1.89	3812325	0.70	2604646	0.47	2184556	0.40	36083	0.01
STATES																	
Andhra Pradesh	43502708	38119279	87.63	3520166	8.09	1823436	4.19	12591	0.03	10035	0.02	16108	0.04	995	N	98	N
Assam	14957542	10625847	71.04	3594086	24.03	667151	4.46	12347	0.08	45212	0.30	12917	0.09	62	N	-	-
Bihar	56353369	47031801	83.46	7594173	13.48	658717	1.17	61520	0.11	4806	0.01	25185	0.04	976997	1.73	170	N
Gujarat	26697475	23835471	89.28	2249055	8.42	109341	0.41	18223	0.07	5469	0.02	451578	1.69	18781	0.07	9547	0.04
Haryana	10006808	8956310	89.23	405723	4.04	9802	0.10	631048	6.29	845	0.01	31173	0.31	5	N	1902	0.62
Himachal Pradesh	3460434	3324627	96.08	50327	1.45	3556	0.10	44916	1.30	35937	1.04	626	0.02	319	0.01	128	N
J & K	4616632	1404292	30.42	3040129	65.85	7182	0.16	105873	2.29	57956	1.26	1150	0.02	8	N	42	N
Kerala	21347375	12683277	59.41	4162718	19.50	4494089	21.05	1284	0.01	605	N	3336	0.02	562	N	1504	0.01
Madhya Pradesh	41654119	39024162	93.68	1815685	4.36	286072	0.69	98973	0.24	81823	0.20	345211	0.83	836	N	1357	N
Maharashtra	50412235	41307287	81.94	4232023	8.40	717174	1.42	101762	0.20	3264223	6.47	703664	1.40	80023	0.16	5079	0.01
Manipur	1072753	632597	58.97	70969	6.61	279243	26.02	1028	0.10	495	0.05	1408	0.13	83167	7.75	3846	0.36
Meghalaya	1011699	187140	18.50	26347	2.60	475267	46.98	12262	0.12	1878	0.9	268	0.03	318168	31.45	1369	0.43
Mysore	29299014	25332388	86.46	3113298	10.63	613026	2.09	6830	0.02	14139	0.05	218862	0.75	380	N	91	N
Nagaland	516449	59031	11.43	2966	0.58	344798	66.76	687	0.13	179	0.04	627	0.12	108159	20.94	2	N
Orissa	21944615	21121056	96.25	326507	1.49	378888	1.73	10204	0.04	8462	0.04	6521	0.03	91859	0.42	1118	N
Punjab	13551060	5087235	37.54	114447	8.84	162202	1.20	8159972	60.22	1374	0.01	21383	0.16	355	N	4092	0.03
Rajasthan	25765806	23093895	89.63	1778275	6.90	30202	0.12	341182	1.33	3642	0.01	513548	1.99	4339	0.02	723	N
Tamil Nadu	41199168	36674150	89.02	2103899	5.11	2367749	5.75	4355	0.01	1148	N	41097	0.10	6080	0.01	690	N
Tripura	1556342	1393689	89.55	103962	6.68	15713	1.01	318	0.02	42285	2.72	375	0.02	-	-	-	-
Uttar Pradesh	88341144	73997597	83.76	13676533	15.48	131810	0.15	369672	0.42	139639	0.05	124728	0.14	423	N	742	N
West Bengal	44312011	34611864	78.11	9064338	20.46	251752	0.57	35084	0.08	121504	0.27	32203	0.07	194126	0.44	1140	N

UNION TERRITORIES																
Andaman and Nicobar Islands	1115133	70134	60.92	11655	10.12	30342	26.35	865	0.75	103	0.09	14	0.01	1264	1.10	756	0.66
Arunachal Pradesh	467511	102832	21.99	842	0.17	3684	0.79	1255	0.27	61400	13.13	39	0.01	296674	63.46	785	0.17
Chandigarh	257251	184395	71.68	3720	1.45	2504	0.97	65472	25.45	92	0.04	1016	0.39	47	0.02	5	N
Dadra and Nagar Haveli	74170	71075	95.83	740	1.00	1918	2.58	3	N	73	0.10	303	0.41	21	0.03	37	0.05
Delhi	4065698	3407835	83.82	263019	6.47	43720	1.08	291123	7.16	8720	0.21	50513	1.24	527	0.01	241	0.01
Goa, Daman and Diu	857771	550482	64.18	32250	3.76	272509	31.77	885	0.10	260	0.03	556	0.06	269	0.03	560	0.07
Laccadive, Minicoy and Amindivi Islands	31810	1545	4.86	30019	94.37	239	0.75	4	0.01	-	-	-	-	3	0.01	-	-
Pondicherry	471707	400793	84.97	29143	6.18	41296	8.76	51	0.01	21	N	237	0.05	107	0.02	59	0.01

*Only an abridged schedule for 297,853 persons was canvassed at the 1961 Census instead of all-India schedule, hence the religion break up for 1961 Census is not available.

N stands for negligible.

and downs in the position of Hindu women through the various periods of history. What we are primarily concerned with is to identify the traditions which continue to affect the status of Hindu women in modern times.

Hindu society, with its well-defined strata, cannot be said to have nurtured to the same degree and at all levels, the values, ideals, and norms propounded by a religion having a continuity of thousands of years. There has been a continuous interaction between the Great Traditions of the literati and Little Traditions of the masses, and the percolation of the ideals, models, and values contained in the corpus of religious literature of Hinduism.

This work has been carried out through the rendering of myths and legends in regional languages and by institutions like Hari Katha, Ramlila, Kirtan and Bhagavat.

In Hinduism a woman is described by a multitude of derogatory attributes. She is called fickle-minded, sensual, seducer of men; given to falsehood, trickery, folly, greed, impurity, and thoughtless action; root of all evil; inconsistent; and cruel.

She must not study the *Vedas* or perform any sacrifices; knowledge of the *Shastras* is forbidden to her. There is no provision for a woman to become a regular *Sanyasin*. A woman is grouped with the *Sudra*, and along with them is called *Papayoni*, i.e. of sinful birth or one preordained to a low station in life.

There are exhortations that a woman should be kept under control. "In childhood a woman must be subject to her father, in youth to her husband, and when her lord is dead, to her sons. A woman must never be independent." This dictum of Manu along with Tulasidas's well-known stanza in which he groups women with drums, morons, *Sudras* and cattle as objects fit to be beaten have influenced the attitude of the Hindu masses towards women.

There is no overall appraisal of a woman's personality in the lore of Hinduism. She is viewed only in specific roles. With the conception of marriage as the true destiny of a woman and with her important obligation to bear a son, the roles of wife and mother emerge as the proper roles for a woman.

The cult of the mother-goddess, whether accepted as an important trait of the pre-Aryan matrilineal cultures or borrowed from the tribals, seems to have had some influence on the status of women. A woman in mother's role has been elevated to a very high position in Hindu religious literature. She has been given high praise and a son has been asked to give respect to her.

The *Mahabharata* says that mother excels in her greatness ten fathers and even the whole Earth. There is no guru like the mother. A *sanyasi* is supposed to go beyond any kinships, and if he happens to come across his parents, the biological father touches the feet of his *sanyasi* son, but even this *sanyasi* is expected to touch the feet of his mother.

The close and sustained association of the child with the woman's body is emphasized in a number of ways. By idealising the quality of sacrifice in a mother and by eulogising her motherhood, religion binds a woman to the home and to her role of creating and nurturing. A young virgin before the onset of menstruation and the mother of a son are the two images which evoke veneration.

There are numerous laudatory references to the female sex in these roles in the religious texts which are hardly in consonance with her limited rights laid down in the *Dharamashastras*. Under the impact of images created and sustained in Hinduism, women are regarded, on the one hand, as the embodiment of purity and spiritual power, while on the other, they are viewed as being essentially weak and dependent creatures who are in need of constant guardianship and protection of men.

There is strong emphasis on a faithful and uncomplaining wife. The ideal woman is the devoted wife who is willing to suffer all kinds of adversities for the sake of loyalty to her husband. The dominant characteristics of well-known characters of Hindu mythology — Sita, Savitri, Ahalya, Draupadi, Gandhari, Mandodari, Damyanti to name a few are loyalty to their husbands, steadfastness and chastity. This has been the essence of a woman's role as wife. Her husband is her lord and master. She has no separate existence. As *Ardhangini* she is her husband's partner in *Dharma*, *Artha* and *Kama*.

As a part of *Dharma* she has to respect and look after her parents-in-law and other members of her conjugal family, look after the home and take care of guests and servants. As the statement of Draupadi runs, "the husband is a woman's God; it is through her husband alone that a woman, obtains progeny, enjoys comforts and luxury, attains fame in this world and heaven in the next. She serves her husband and performs *Vratas* for his welfare. She gives up cosmetics when her husband is away." Bhishma in *Mahabharata* states the following attributes as the best feminine virtues: fidelity, forgiveness, absence of guile, piety, and truthfulness. These virtues please Laxmi and bring rewards. Parvati says that there is no other God for a woman but her husband, and by serving him she attains heaven. She must be kind even to an unkind and irrational husband and obey him.

Thus not only marriage but the services rendered to one's husband are of paramount importance to a woman. So much so that it is said that for women there is no other religious rite but to serve their husbands. It is testified in the *Puranas* that a woman by serving her husband in thought, word and deed secures with much less trouble the same spiritual and heavenly worlds that her husband does with great effort and trouble. Expectation of immolation on the deceased husband's pyre (*Sati*) by the widow was the extreme limit of the notion that a woman's worth is nil without her husband.

For *Moksha*, women are grouped with *Sudras* and uneducated Brahmins. *Devi Bhagavata Purana* states that since women and Sudras, are unable to study the *Vedas*, the *Puranas* are compiled for their benefit. The *Bhagavata Purana* states that the *Mahabharata* was composed for women and Sudras, who are debarred from listening to the *Vedas*.

After the emergence of *Bhaktimarg*, the path of devotion which did not need complicated knowledge and elaborate rituals, some women attained eminence and it provided an honourable way of partial asceticism, sometimes even complete asceticism for women.

In Hinduism, a strong patrilineal social structure along with features like the giving away of the girls in marriage, importance of the son for continuity of the line, authority and superiority of the male, significance of virginity, etc., have been sanctified with the help of *Sanskaras*. The significant ideas contained in the Vedic or Puranic texts used for *Sanskaras* have their influence in varying degrees at various levels of Hindu population.

***Vratas* or fasting for Women**

Marriage and motherhood are the most honourable and religiously valuable achievements for a Hindu woman. The critical significance of marriage, of the continuity of the married state, and of motherhood for a woman is dramatically expressed and emphasized in the observance of special *Vratas*. They are observed for ensuring long life and welfare of the husband, for the realization of the culturally coveted goal of getting married and of getting a suitable partner for life, and for securing special protection of sons.

Their content in terms of the type of worship, the nature of fasting may differ from region to region; but a degree of self-denial, invocation of some deity or sacred object, commemoration of the ordeals of some mythological female figure constitute their core features. Renewal and distribution or exchange of objects which serve as diacritical marks of the married state such as vermilion, glass bangles, and black beads is also customarily done on such days.

Some *Vratas* are meant to be observed throughout life, some for a particular period; some by unmarried girls; some by married women. To mention a few: a special worship of Goddess Laxmi on particular days; yearly commemoration of the steadfastness of Savitri who followed the God of Death and brought back her husband alive; annual worship of Parvati who performed difficult penance to win the heart of Siva; *Varalaxmi puja* prevalent in the South; *Karwa Chauth* observed in North India; *Jayaparvati* observed in Gujarat; *Mangala Gaur* or worship of Goddess of Tuesday in the month of *Savan* in Maharashtra, a special *Vrata* in Bundelkhand called *Suhagle* (observed for the sake of *suhag* or *Saubhagya*, i.e. the good fortune of having one's husband alive). Some of these have their sanction in the great *Sanskritic* tradition while others are rooted in regional beliefs.

Most of the *Vratas* observed by a mother for the welfare of her children are meant to be observed by those who have a son. Women having only daughters do not observe them. The differential value of son and daughter is apparent.

Internationalization of values of steadfastness, self-effacement, service and playing a secondary role is effected through these *Vratas*, which are observed even by many educated and sophisticated women. This may be either because of the strength of their beliefs; or because of their socialization which they cannot shake off or because of the expectations of the family for whom this is an inalienable aspect of a wife's or a mother's role. Tremendous importance is attached to these observances for newly married women.

The converse of this notion of marriage as women's destiny and the married state as the most desirable, is the idea of inauspiciousness and loss of the right to full participation in socio-religious life associated with widowhood.

In contrast, a Hindu male has no fasts to observe for the wife's long life and welfare. The husband wears no distinctive marks signifying the married state and does not incur any inauspiciousness at the death of his wife. Religion, as a system of beliefs and rituals, undoubtedly accords an inferior and dependent status to Hindu woman. The common blessing to a woman 'May your husband live long' is self-explanatory.

Although the strict code of conduct prescribed for widow is no longer operative in its most restrictive and oppressive aspects, there are certain disabilities associated with widowhood. She is debarred from active participation in auspicious occasions. Besides the items of decoration associated with the married state, she is expected also to discard colourful clothes, glass bangles, wearing of flowers and attractive jewellery. Plain white colour is associated with widowhood, and by implication is forbidden traditionally for the *Sumangali*, i.e., one whose husband is alive.

The widows of Bengal, who abstain from fish and the Kammas and the Reddy widows of Andhra Pradesh who give up meat are not yet extinct. Among the Brahmin and also among such non-Brahmin communities who do not have the custom of widow re-marriage, there are a number of ways for restricting the life of a widow so that she gets little pleasure out of life and her natural desires are suppressed. A distinct contrast between the status of a widow and a *Sumangali* is characteristic of India as a whole.

Even among such groups which traditionally allow widow remarriage, the disabilities associated with widowhood are present though not in same degree of severity. In Hindu and tribal India a woman is entitled to marry with full rites only once in her life. Her subsequent unions, though approved by society, are solemnized by a very simple ceremony or may often be given recognition after a simple feast.

Women with such secondary unions suffer from a few specific disabilities in regard to performance of particular roles in the rituals of marriage and worship of deities. This again indicates the significance of marriage for a woman and the vulnerability of her purity. No such disability characterizes a man; he can marry a virgin any number of times with full rites and ceremonies. Even though the Widow Remarriage Act was passed in 1856, Hindu society still has not come to accept widow remarriage without reservation. For the majority, widowhood continues to be associated with the handicaps.

Grave impurity is associated with menstruation and child-birth. Severe restrictions over menstruating women in respect of association and participation in domestic, extra-domestic, and religious activities found in the texts have been strong among the Brahmin and upper caste groups, but have been operative among other sections especially in the sphere of religious ceremonies.

This notion of periodical impurity of women is one of the important bases for the conception of inferiority of the female sex as compared to the male. A woman is usually in charge of routine domestic worship; but nowhere is she found to be in charge of worship at the shrines and temples. Even Kali and other female deities are to be worshipped by a male priest. It should be noted that this exclusion of women from officiating at community worship is not a direct result of their lack of knowledge of rituals which may be needed for worship, since in many kind of worship no such knowledge is required. Periodical impurity appears to be the basis for the exclusion of women from this role.

The Bhakti Movement

The *Bhakti* movement which arose during the medieval period, denounced complicated rituals, and asserted that God could be worshipped not only through knowledge and rituals, but also by devotion. The devotional hymns composed in the languages spoken by the people brought this movement close to women, whose ignorance of Sanskrit had often deprived them from sharing the religious practices and experience of the men. This movement placed God within the reach of all, irrespective of caste or sex.

The history of the *Bhakti* movement reveals that it brought great solace to women and presented an alternative way of life to many individual women. Some even attained sainthood. Meerabai, Muktabai, Janabai, Vishnupriya are well known names in *Bhakti* literature whose compositions are popular to this day. For widows and neglected women, devotion provided an austere way of life and a certain justification for living. Neither a Brahmin nor a husband is needed to reach God.

Veerasaivism (Cult followed by the Lingayat Community in Karnataka)

Combining work and Bhakti, *Veerasaivism* was, at the time of its inception, a democratising movement. The corpus of religious lore of *Veerasaivism* consists of *vachanas* (sayings) of 200 to 300 saints. Out of these about 50 are women.

Marriage, which is not strictly a religious ceremony, is not considered as an obligatory ritual nor is it regarded as a hindrance in the path of devotion. Divorce and remarriage were allowed. *Veerasaiva* saints emphasize harmonious relations between husband and wife and frown upon the violation of martial fidelity by either of the two. A sin is not considered indispensable. Spiritual attainment and higher level of religious experience are possible for women also. They are known to have participated in philosophical discussions and missionary work. They are, however, not allowed to become *Gurus*.

Islam

In their relationship with the divine, men and women stand on a footing of equality in Islam. Woman, like man, is an individual who can pray to the Almighty, and can hope for redemption. A non-ascetic religion, Islam does not consider woman as an impediment in the path of religion, nor does it consider her as the root cause of man's downfall. The *Quran* is replete with injunctions aimed at bettering the lot of women who in the pre-Islamic societies had held a very inferior and servile position.

However, in spite of the fact that Islam provided a much

higher status to women than was commonly recognized in earlier societies, the social standards of the time were very different from those accepted today, and therefore the Muslim Shariat Law as it has developed over the centuries, places women in a disadvantageous or an inferior position in many respects.

Many of these disadvantages arise from interpretations of the Quranic verse or the sayings of the Prophet in the light of the cultural norms prevailing in medieval times. Sometimes, traditions of the Prophet were even invented to validate later cultural norms which were being adopted under various types of influences. A few examples may be mentioned here.

In regard to witnesses, it was said that if a second man is not available, two women should be called so that if one errs, the other will remember. This was perhaps a safety device in view of women's extremely limited understanding of financial, commercial, and trade relationships, but it was also used for curtailing the women's right to a minimum in respect of offering evidence in criminal and civil cases.

In Islam a woman is as much a believer as a man, and (except in certain bodily conditions such as menstruation) has an equal right to undertake religious duties like praying and fasting. But a woman cannot be priest, nor can she lead the prayers. She has no place in the formal religious organization and legal affairs of the community. She cannot be appointed a *Kazi*.

Modesty, decorum and chastity were emphasized in the *Quran*, and the women were advised not to display their ornaments of beauty. This led to conflicting viewpoints about the veiling and seclusion of women. It was thought proper to keep the women away from the gaze of outsiders.

Among Indian Muslims, *burqa* and use of covered vehicles have been common devices for keeping women away from the gaze of outsiders. The matrilineal Muslim women of Lakshadweep and Kerala have however moved about without a *burqa* but with the head covered. It appears that the veil and seclusion of women have been more characteristic of the upper and middle strata of society, more so in urban areas.

The *burqa* is now becoming more of a lower middle-class phenomenon and a status symbol amongst the working classes to indicate a rise in their social status. It is otherwise decreasing due to a number of factors such as education, economic pursuits, and the forces of modernization generally. But it still continues to be a social reality and much religious feeling is associated with it.

Women's seclusion in Islam made them lose one of their important privilege that is participation in communal prayers. It also lent extra support to a series of restrictions — women should not converse with other men, they should not talk loudly, letting their voices be heard by other men, they should not receive guests without the permission of the husband, and so on. Women can join in the prayer at the mosque for which there is a separate and secluded area reserved for them.

Marriage in Islam derives its legitimacy from the Shariat and is a contract. There is no ban on widow remarriage and divorce is allowed. Marriage is not religiously obligatory for a woman. But the contract of marriage gives unequal rights to man and woman.

Besides, the prevailing social customs are much more powerful in determining the social attitudes towards marriage, widow remarriage and divorce than the religious injunctions. As an example, religion provides for the free consent of both parties in the *nikah*, but in practice, it is a mere formality, so far as the girl is concerned. Similarly, widow remarriage and divorce are generally frowned upon, especially among the middle and the upper classes, even though they are permissible in Islam.

The rights of repudiation of the marriage contract is with the husband. Polygamy is permitted in Islam. A wife, therefore, has a distinctly inferior status. The institution of marriage-guardian (details of which differ according to different schools of law) places a woman in a subordinate position. Religion makes the husband the family head and expects the wife to obey and serve him.

Mehr (dower) is meant to be a security for the wife against the possibility of divorce at the husband's free will. It is doubtful, however, as to how many women are in a position to assert their claims to *mehr* in the event of a divorce or widowhood, particularly in the communities among whom the marriage contract need not be in writing.

Women's rights to inheritance, provided in Islam, are

significant especially in view of the fact that they were meant for a patrilineal social structure. Islam introduced shares for wife, daughter, mother, sister and grandmother, the general rule being that the female was to inherit half of what the corresponding male would inherit. However, the women's right to hold or inherit property, is not often upheld in practice. This is largely due to their seclusion, absence of education, and the prevalence of customs and conventions which, in the Indian cultural setting, go against women's rights.

With regard to education, although Islam has made acquisition of knowledge an obligatory duty for every Muslim, in the case of women, it is largely restricted in practice, to enable them to offer prayers and to recite the *Quran*. Only the girls of the elite class have had access to some private instruction.

It is to be noted that in India, towards the end of the last century, Maulana Abdul Hayy-Lakhanavi was requested for a juristic opinion based on the Shariat whether a Muslim girl should be allowed to learn writing. Though it was supported with the help of a tradition of the Prophet, a diffused kind of feeling against women's education has continued and has received strong support from such customs and norms as seclusion of women, the desirability of their subordination to male authority, and the insistence on their performing assigned tasks in the domestic field.

The two practices that have been most detrimental to the status of women in Islam have been *Talaq* or unilateral divorce and seclusion of women. It is largely seclusion that has kept women backward in respect of education and health and prevented their participation in economic and social fields and has been a hurdle in the way of realizing their property rights. It has made them heavily dependent on men for the business of living and hence also for achieving any progress.

Christianity

In India, Christianity is represented by communities of various denominations. In each of these communities the practice of the tenets of Christianity has been influenced, in varying degrees, by historical and contemporary sociocultural factors. This has resulted in overshadowing, suppressing, or reviving and bringing into focus the essence of the teachings of Christianity regarding the status and role of women.

The myth of creation which says that Eve was created after Adam to act as his companion and help-mate accords a secondary place to woman in domestic and social life. She has to be subordinate first to her father and then to her husband. The mythic image of Eve as one who tempted Adam to eat the forbidden fruit has put a permanent stamp over women as tempters and seducers and has given the husband the right to control the wife.

The Indian Christians believe that the wife belongs to the husband and it is because of this notion, with its roots in religion, that among some dowry-giving Christians a man is supposed to have a right over ornaments and property received by his wife from her parents.

Marriage in Christianity, however, lays emphasis on the establishment of a mutual relationship between husband and wife and on their duty towards each other. This is powerfully expressed in the following pronouncement which forms a part of the marriage rites:

> "Man shall leave his father and mother and shall cleave to his wife; and they shall be one flesh."

These words are interpreted to mean that the nucleus of family organisation is the mutual relationship of husband and wife; the ultimate authority and responsibility is not placed in the extended family or the patriarch. This outlook accords a better status to the wife than the others which regard marriage as an alliance between two families and transfer of the girl from one family to another.

Our investigations show that even in some Indian Christian communities, like the various groups of Syrian Christians of Kerala and Catholic Christians of Mangalore who practise joint family system to some extent, the daughter-in-law is not relegated to the background. She can move about with her husband and it is recognized that her primary relationship is with her husband. Her status is much better than the status of a daughter-in-law in patrilineal families of the upper caste Hindus. Though the father is the recognized head of the family, the mother has her own sphere of work and influence. Although the central authority in the home is vested in the male, mutual responsibility of husband and wife is recognized.

Christianity forbids polygamy. The establishment of monogamy stands out as the one enduring factor which has raised the status of women in Christianity. However, the concept of permanency of marriage which is considered a divine sacrament with no place for divorce has affected the women's status in both ways among the Catholics and some other groups. Along with the security of home and the certainty of not being separated from her children, she also has to be subjected to the husband's authority and is deprived of legal rights and independent existence. Divorce is recognized by the other groups, and is permitted according to the Indian Divorce Act of 1869.

The *Bible* lays great emphasis on the image of woman as a strong and steady influence for the good. Her notable qualities are: capacity to work with hands, kindness, wisdom, love and charity for the needy outside the home, and capacity to run her household in a manner that children get care and affection and the husband finds relaxation and peace.

In Christianity, both men and women are believed to have been created by God in his own image. Thus a woman is as much entitled to strive for her salvation as man. In fact every other role in her life is subordinated to this role. She is a spiritually sovereign human being and this right vested in her may not be violated in marriage. She has an individual moral independence and responsibility.

In Christianity women have been entitled to study and learn religion and to attend and participate in all religious ceremonies. She has a right to become a nun. Thus, in one aspect of life, viz., in matters pertaining to the spirit and the practice of religion, Christianity accepts equality between men and women. Everybody is baptised in the name of Christ. However, women have never been given full ecclesiastic responsibility in the Church organization. Even in those Churches where women hold subordinate offices, ordination of women was not permitted till recently.

Today the situation varies all the way from Churches like those of the Syrian Christian who do not permit women to hold any office in the church, to the Methodist Church which accepts the ordination of women to complete priesthood.

The acceptance of the notion, common to all Christians, that by helping each other one can attain salvation and the emphasis laid on the virtues of service, love and charity provide a women honourable careers other than marriage. Marriage is not a woman's sole destiny although socially it is most desirable.

We do not find the practice of child marriage among Christian communities, and widowhood is not a curse. A woman is not confined to the home. Her participation in congregational prayers, absence of *purdah,* no rigid insistence on segregation of sexes, monogamy, emphasis on husband-wife relationship, value of charity, and service to others - all these features of Christianity place women in a relatively better position than in other religions.

There is little wonder that in India in the later nineteenth and early twentieth century, Christian girls were way ahead of others in education and employment. The first educational and vocational institutions for women were established by Christian missionaries and though many of them were open to non-Christians they gave special concessions to Christian girls.

The Christian girls, not subjected to many injunctions and taboos, were in a better position to derive benefit from these institutions. As there was no taboo against their working outside the home, some of them also took up jobs. It is generally known that in the late nineteenth and early twentieth century women teachers, inspectresses of schools, doctors, and nurses in India were largely from among the Christians.

Some of the teachings of Christianity are found to be overshadowed or misused by the customs and values of particular converted groups to the detriment of women's status. However, the basic notion of inferiority of women not softened by any distinct elevation of her sex-linked roles has left Christian women to fight against the slavery of the home and against their large-scale confinement to less prestigious jobs in the men's world.

Jainism

Except in Kerala and parts of Karnataka, the Jains are patrilineal and are governed by the Hindu personal law. Kinship ties and joint family living are strong. Because of recruitment from diverse culture areas the Jains internally differ in their customs and practices, which often overshadow or even override religion.

As a way of life Jainism lays great stress on self-denial, restraint of passion, and a life of renunciation for both men and women. As a socio-religious organisation the *sangh* comprises both monks and nuns as well as both male and female lay followers.

A woman has a legitimate position in the congregational life. She can occupy a position of leadership in which she deals with matters of practical concern and not with instruction. But the female ascetic appears to have suffered from certain handicaps in scriptures. By and large religious learning and renunciation are allowed to women who have a full right to aspire for *Moksha.*

The sects differ in their view of whether a woman can attain liberation as a woman or her soul has to be reborn as a man (as women have certain physical disabilities and mental weaknesses) in order to attain liberation. However, since according to Jainism no one is likely to attain liberation in the present age, this controversy does not have much practical significance.

In the religious context it cannot be ignored that in ascetic manuals and sermons there is severe condemnation of a woman who is looked upon as a tempter and seducer and is called tricky, deceptive, hypocritical, fickle, untrustworthy, and treacherous. This has been done with the specific purpose of warning a monk to keep himself away from women so that he is not swayed from strict celibacy in word, thought and deed. No such derogatory characterization of man is needed to keep women on the path of self-restraint in Jainism.

Jainism prescribes suitable patterns of moral conduct for ascetic as well as domestic life. Although actual customs and practices of the Jains often depend on their environmental setting and thus manifest differences between north and south, east and west, certain basic features of the faith have definite influence on the status of women. As there is no religious obligation of *Pinda-dana* to ancestors in Jainism there does not appear to be any premium on the birth of son.

In the patrilineal setting, however, boys have been claiming superiority over girls in respect of the right to inheritance and succession. For a daughter it has been customary to get *Kanya-shulka* or some kind of compensation. Nor is marriage obligatory for a girl in the same sense as it is in Hinduism, for the religious path is open for her. Marriage is not a religious institution and so the customs differ from area to area, but basically a wedding is a simple ceremony. Jain women also use diacritical marks to denote their marital status. Marriages are arranged by the parents and they tend to do so in restricted circles which are something like sub-castes.

Polygamy is not forbidden. There is no sanction for widow remarriage, for a life of self-restraint is generally valued. Divorce and widow remarriage are, however, found customarily practised among certain sections. But a widowed woman does not easily lose her position. She can lead a pious life of *Shravika* within the family setting. A widow is obliged to lead a simple life but with the adoption of a pious way of life she could become an object of reverence. She could also become a nun. Thus widowhood is not exactly a curse in Jainism. But differential treatment of the sexes in this respect is clear.

In the context of the family, chastity in women is greatly valued and several stories in Jain scriptures are woven round this theme. Motherhood is respected but a childless woman does not find her future absolutely dark.

In Central and North India, the Jains follow a certain degree of segregation of sexes. Kinship ties are strong and women have constraints comparable to those of their high caste neighbours. The brunt of maintenance of regulations related to purity and to food falls on women. In the changing milieu, the religious prescriptions are mainly observed by women.

Buddhism

Buddhism recognized broad parity between man and woman in matters of religion; both the sexes being charged alike with the duty of upholding *Dharma*. Women are allowed to become nuns. *Nirvana* is possible for both men and women.

Thus, Buddhism as a liberal reaction against orthodox Brahmanism elevated the status of women. But after a modicum of equality, the scales have been tipped in favour of the monk.

This is clear from such evidence as : a statement that the merit accruing from a donation to the *Sangh* of monks is more than that accruing from a donation to the *Sangh* of nuns, the rule that cannot preach to the order of monks, and the rule that a *Bhikumi*, even though older, should bow down even before a younger *Bhikhu*.

Buddhism does not consider woman as evil or as one solely responsible for sensuality in the world. Yet she can be an obstruction in the path of deliverance. Woman is physically weak and dependent, but mentally as good as man.

A girl can remain unmarried by becoming a *Bhikhuni*. From widowhood also there is a respite in renunciation. However, the ideal propounded for women in society is not materially different from the one upheld by the orthodox Hindu view. She has to serve the man. Mother as a self-sacrificing and benevolent figure is very much present in Buddhist thought. Despite her intellectual parity, woman is definitely considered as inferior to man in the monastery as well as in society.

In Ladakh, Lahaul and Spiti where Buddhism prevails, at least in theory, men and women are considered mentally on a par with one another. But in practice the position is quite different. Of the two types of nuns in the Buddhist order the *Bhikhuni* (with 300 rules of conduct and treated more or less equal to male counterparts) and the *Samenara* (with only ten rules to obey)—today, we find only the *Samenara* who generally live with their families, and are treated like honoured servants. They are given higher seats, but their job is to perform household chores. In this area there are very few nunneries. Even senior nuns are considered inferior to monks.

Because of the prevailing practice of polyandry in these regions, girls are often forced to become nuns. Since the communities in these regions practice the customs of bride-price as well as divorce and remarriage the Buddhists also follow them.

The birth of a boy is not specially felicitated. This is presumably so because the girl is a productive worker and brings gifts at marriage. Because a son is not needed by the parents for the last rites and *Pindadana*, in the same way as the Hindus, girls are not lower in status than the boys.

The position of women in these areas appears to be better

than that of the women in the plains, but it is difficult to ascribe this to Buddhism as such. The main reason perhaps lies in their participation in the economy. Buddhism leaves most of the areas of worldly life to be managed by the people according to their customs and traditions.

In the newly emerging areas of activity like education, medical service, and political participation men are coming forward more than women. The preaching and organization of religion is in the hands of monks.

Sikhism

Sikhism condemns formal ritual, idolatry, and superstition, and emphasizes simple devotion to God. In the pursuit of religion both men and women have a place as individuals. "That tongue alone is blessed, that utters words of God's devotion". Sikhism emphasizes the householder's ideal and demands respect for woman as men's helpmate and sharer in his domestic life. It does not look upon woman as an agent of sin and evil; nor does it regard her as an object of pleasure.

Guru Nanak asks women to have a pure way of life and not indulge in extravagances of wealth. Association of impurity with the cosmic natural processes like birth is condemned. Man is exhorted not to condemn woman who is his companion and of whom are born great men and all men.

For the purposes of devotion there is no difference between men and women. In social life, however, Sikhism did not concede equality for women. Her kinship and domestic roles are emphasized. She has important roles to play as wife, mother, sister and daughter. The qualities that women are asked to develop are love, obedience, contentment, and sweet temper. A woman should be in harmony of temper with her husband. Mother's role and wife's roles are brought into relief in the tales of the wives of the Gurus.

Sikhism was adopted by people belonging to different Hindu castes mainly in the Punjab. In this religion, there are several clearly defined rules regarding personal habits, but not many well-laid out injunctions covering institutions like marriage and family that could have imperatively changed people's staunch beliefs and actions.

We, therefore, find that social customs defining woman's roles and constraints over them are not common to all the Sikhs. In this respect there are important differences from territory to territory and from group to group. The differences in the rural and urban settings are also significant. The Jat Sikhs continue to follow their original Jat customs.

In matters such as divorce, separation, remarriage, widow's position, women's rights of ownership and inheritance and seclusion of women, people generally tend to follow the customs and practices of their original caste or regional culture.

Importance of kinship and of the family ties, with the idea of the transfer of the girl in marriage from one family to another, have a prominent part in shaping role relationships in the family. The Sikhs are governed by the Hindu Personal Law which exists side by side with the customary law of particular groups.

Zoroastrianism

In India there are less than 100,000 Parsees, who follow Zoroastrianism—one of the oldest religions of the world. Migrating to India over 1300 years ago, the Parsees adopted Gujarati as their language, and while retaining most of the customs and elements of their religion, they could not escape some influence of the indigenous populations. After the coming of the British, they were among the first to take to the Western style of life and to English education.

Zoroastrian women enjoy a position of honour in the family and in the society. The evils of polygamy and child marriage, which had crept in under Hindu and Muslim influence, were fought and removed by the Parsee Panchayat in the 19th century. The Parsee Marriage and Divorce Act and the Parsee Succession Act were passed with the strong support of the leaders of the Parsee community.

In Zoroastrianism women are entitled to both religious and secular education. Boys as well as girls go through the investiture rites. Marriage is solemnized and sanctified by a religious ceremony, but it is a contract. It is always monogamous. Consent of both the boy and the girl is essential for marriage. Religious tradition does not approve of child marriage, and today, as in ancient days, the minimum age of marriage for girls is fifteen. If circumstances demand, a girl can marry against the wishes of the parents. Dissolution of marriage, for proper reasons, is allowed. The practice of remarriage has always been there. A Zoroastrian woman is an equal partner in marriage and family, and enjoys respect as mother and wife. Parents of both the bride and the bridegroom contribute to the setting up of a new household. A woman has inheritance rights both in her capacity as a daughter and as a wife. A widow does not have to forego the inheritance of husband's property if she remarried.

Zoroastrianism traditionally imposed menstrual taboos demanding segregation and non-participation in religious activities. Though no longer stringently practised these restrictions are operative in the context of rituals. Women can preach but they cannot became priests. Only since 1935, the Parsee Panchayat has started admitting women into it as members.

There is one disability which women suffer compared to men, but it is more a function of patriliny, combined with a non-proselytizing religion. The child of a Parsee father and a non-Parsee mother, whether in wedlock or out of it, can be initiated into Zoroastrian faith by the *Naojote* ceremony. But neither by religion nor by law can a child of a Parsee mother and a non-Parsee father be received as a Zoroastrian.

The dwindling numbers of the community are to some extent due to this discrimination as marriages between Parsee women and non-Parsee men are on the increase. The community is unable to stop such marriages, for girls have great freedom of movement, but it certainly has tremendous reservations and resentment so far as their marrying outside the community is concerned. Conversely, a Parsee boy's marriage with a non-Parsee girl is accepted with greater grace, although the non-Parsee wife is never accepted in Zoroastrianism, which is not a proselytizing religion. Parsee girls marrying a non-Parsee by the Special Marriage Act are claiming a right to remain a Parsee and visit the fire-temple but the Parsee Panchayat has not yet decided the issue. It may, however, be mentioned that these girls do not lose their inheritance rights in intestate succession.

Tribal Religions

Tribal religions in India do not constitute a homogeneous system. What is attempted here, therefore, is to identify some significant elements of these faiths and examine the place of woman in respect of them.

The percentage of tribal population to the total population is 6.87% according to the 1961 Census which records 2,98,79,229 people as tribals. It is obvious from the table of distribution of population by religion that all tribals are not included in the state-wise figures stated in the column "Other Religions and Persuasions". This will be clear if we have a look at the state-wise distribution of population. Conversion to Christianity accounts for a large section of the tribal population. For instance in Manipur 26.03% population is Christian and in Assam 46.28% population is Christian. The Christian population of Bihar and Orissa (6,58,717 and 3,78,888 respectively) also comprises tribals on a large scale.

Another factor is the presence of Buddhism in some tribal population such as the tribals of Himachal Pradesh. Further, the people of Lakshadweep who are Muslims have been declared as Scheduled Tribe and Jaunsari people now included in Scheduled Tribe are Hindus.

Moreover, in States like Madhya Pradesh, Bihar, and Orissa many tribal groups who have been influenced by the neighbouring Hindu population return themselves as Hindu. There is a substantial proportion of tribal population in these States, and if all of them had declared themselves as belonging to tribal religion, figures in the column of 'Other Religions' would have been different.

It is, however, important to note that those tribals who return themselves as Hindu or Christian do not completely discard their tribal customs. Majority of them hold their beliefs, worship the tribal deities and conduct rituals, etc., according to tradition.

The social structures and cultural systems of the tribes are reflected in their system of beliefs and ritual practices. Tribal religion is matter-of-fact and materialistic. The purpose of propitiation or homage and of manipulation of supernatural powers is mostly to avert misery and destruction in interpersonal relationship and maintenance of structural principles.

Religious activities can be classified into (a) of the family, (b) of the group, and (c) of the village. Women have a role only in the first set. They may be responsible for keeping the domestic fire kindled and for routine looking after of the place assigned for gods and ancestors in the house; but in the periodical or special worship of lineage ancestors or deities and clan deities, women have no place; at the most they play the role of helpers in making preparation for rituals.

Matrilineal communities like the Khasi are an exception; among them the youngest daughter has an important role to play in relation to lineage ancestors and deities. The Garo also have priestesses. However, it needs to be mentioned that even in many of the matrilineal communities priestly functions and handling of matter pertaining to transgression of taboos are in the hands of men. In most tribal communities priesthood is a male prerogative. Knowledge of ritual formulae rests with men. In a few tribes like the Saora of Orissa, and the Irula and the Paniyan of Kerala, women function as *shaman* (diviner and curer), but female priesthood is almost absent.

Horror of menstrual blood is universal in tribal India and leads (a) to exclusion of women from holding any positions of ritual importance, and (b) to their association with malefic supernatural powers. Witchcraft, which is considered dangerous, is largely associated with women, in both tribal and rural India. It is believed to be some kind of an unavoidable malefic power which gets transmitted from another person, commonly one's mother in some vulnerable circumstances. During the periods of menstrual flow, pregnancy and post-natal impurity, women are held to be specially vulnerable.

Rites of passage are definitely male weighted. So also are the sacrifices and various devices for increasing the fertility of the soil and cattle, and rites to please the elements of nature.

In some tribal communities women suffer from severe disabilities in the religious sphere. The Toda debar their women from having anything to do with the buffaloes and their products. Their rituals are centred round the buffalo and women are completely excluded. Among the Kota also women are strictly forbidden to associate themselves in any way with the funeral and other rituals. Santhal women are also not allowed to participate in communal worship nor can they eat sacrificial meals. In fact, a Santhal woman is not considered a full-fledged member of the society.

In the maintenance of community discipline and public morality which is the function of the Panchayats or Tribal Councils, women have no role. Even the Regional Councils set up after independence in some tribal areas, have resisted the efforts of few women to obtain any position on these bodies.

While their position in religion and rituals is definitely lower than man, women's participation and contribution in economic activity results in considerable freedom in norms of social behaviour. The average age of marriage is higher among tribal women than among other communities. In choice of partners, rules of divorce and remarriage most tribal women enjoy greater freedom, though the influence of Sanskritisation has reduced this in some communities.

Social and Religious Reform Movements of the 19th and 20th Centuries

The broad aims of these movements in the social sphere were specially emphasizing caste reform or caste abolition, and improvement in the rights and status of women and generally against social and legal inequalities. It involved an attack on certain social institutions and practices like child marriage, position and treatment of widows, seclusion and the denial of women's rights to property and education, the roots of which lay in the religious traditions of different communities.

The impact of British rule, English education and Christianity propagated by missionaries resulted in a number of movements for social change and religious reform in the 19th century. According to Gopal Krishna Gokhale in Rao & Singh (1934) :

> The first impact of Western teaching on those who received it was to incline them strongly in favour of the Western way of looking at things and under this influence they bent their energies, in the first instance, to the re-examination of the whole of their ancient civilization or their social usages and institutions, their

religious beliefs, literature, science, art as also in fact their conception and realization of life.

Leaders of the reform movements therefore realized that it was difficult to separate social reforms from religious reforms. Though some of the earlier leaders like Ram Mohun Roy had believed that it was possible to reform all religions together, bringing out the basic unity that underlay all religious faiths, such attempts met with resistance, not only from the orthodox sections of different religious communities, but also from the policy of the ruling power which believed that the security of British supremacy in India depended on keeping the different religious communities separate from each other. This policy was particularly aided by the existence of different systems of personal law, closely related to the religious and customary traditions of the communities and castes which the British helped to perpetuate.

Historians of the Indian social system have always emphasized a characteristic feature of this stratified society which, while retaining its basic framework of inequalities and divisions, had by and large displaced considerable capacity for adapting itself to processes of social change. Much of this process of adjustment and adaptation took place because of regional diversity in cultural norms and the realization by religious and community leaders that without such adjustment it would not be possible for their particular traditions to survive in the Indian context.

Different religious faiths like Islam and Christianity compromized with existing sociocultural traditions in different regions and communities. The British system of recording and providing official recognition to principles and practices of social organisation at a period of time however introduced an element of resistance to this process of natural adjustment and change.

It was therefore inevitable that the movement of social reform should develop within the folds of each religion rather than as a unified movement for the transformation of the society as a whole. The most important of these movements that developed within the Hindu society were the Brahmo Samaj, Prarthna Samaj and the Arya Samaj.

The Brahmo Samaj

Brahmo Samaj was founded by Ram Mohun Roy in 1825. Concerned with religious issues, it opposed the dogmatic structure of religious tradition. It also attempted to remove certain restrictions and prejudices against women rooted in religion. These included the abolition of child marriage, seclusion of women, limited inheritance rights, polygamy, etc. The Samaj emphasized the need for educating women as the best instrument to improve their position.

Under the leadership of Keshab Chandra Sen, the Brahmo Samaj became more concerned with improving the position of women. Provision was made for educating women at home and government assistance was enlisted for this purpose. A new magazine was started to publish articles of special interest to women and to provide an opening for their literary aspirations. In 1862 an inter-caste marriage was solemnized under the auspices of the Samaj. Opposition of orthodox Hindus to the legality of such marriage resulted in the passing of the Native Marriage Act (popularly known as the Civil Marriage Act) in 1872 which permitted inter-caste marriage and divorce, prohibited polygamy and prescribed 14 and 18 years as minimum age of marriage for a girl and boy respectively.

The Act facilitated the sweeping social reform advocated by Keshab Chandra Sen, particularly the abolition of caste distinction.

In 1879 the more radical section of members founded a separate wing — the Sadharan Brahmo Samaj. They started a women's association in which key positions were held by women. They propagated education and social interaction between men and women and careers for women outside the home.

It is generally believed that the influence of the Brahmo Samaj was confined mainly to Bengal and North India, but there is evidence to show its extension to South India also. At the end of the 19th century coastal districts of Andhra Pradesh were exposed to the influence of the Brahmo Samaj. But it was primarily a reform rather than a religious movement. As these districts had seen a great deal of missionary activity, and the conversion of caste Hindus to Christianity, Brahmoism expectedly gained the greatest ground here. This was because the Brahmo Samaj was not a proselytizing movement. Rather, it sought to integrate the untouchables within the Hindu fold. Brahmo leaders were active in providing education and in inculcating a social consciousness.

Venkatratnam Naidu adopted girls from the Scheduled Caste and arranged their marriages to high caste boys. Other leaders included K.V. Pantulu, Unnavalaksh Minarayana, Ramjee Rao and Chilakamarthi Lakshmi Naresimhan.

The Prarthna Samaj

Founded in 1867 the Prarthna Samaj remained principally a movement of western India. It propounded belief in one God, supported *Bhakti* and opposed idolatry. While as a body it did not take any formal stand on social reform except sponsoring education for women, some of its leading members were active in the women's cause. Talang was a founder member of the Bombay Widow Reforms Association which arranged the first widow remarriage in 1869. Ranade and Bhandarkar were among the participants when Shankaracharya was challenged to a public debate to decide whether or not the *Shastras* sanctioned widow remarriage.

Ranade acted as the spokesman of the educated people and moderate reformers strengthened the hands of the government in passing the Age of Consent Bill in 1891. Founding of the National Social Conference in 1887, with the specific purpose of bringing together annually the representatives of various associations, was a big achievement of Ranade in the women's cause. Two leading Prarthna Samajists, Bhandarkar and Chandavarkar, agreed to be Vice-Chancellors of the Women's University started by Karve in 1916.

Both these movements made a forceful effort to prove that Hindu religious tradition was certainly not the source of legitimacy for the pitiable condition of women. Under the influence of liberal thought of the West, they recognized the individuality of women. But essentially they aimed at making women better wives and mothers and were keen to bridge the gap between the levels of understanding of the males (both husband and son), who had the benefit of modern education, and the women of the family.

The Arya Samaj

While the Brahmo Samaj and Prarthana Samaj were the products of the reaction of a section of urban, western educated elite, influenced by Western liberalism, the Arya Samaj was a dissident religious movement which rejected Hindu medieval religion with its idol worship and the post-Vedic caste society. This was founded in 1875 by Dayanand Saraswati. Essentially revivalist in character, the Samaj also stood for the reform of the caste system and tried to raise the status of women in several ways. It advocated revival of the Vedic society in its pristine form. Its influence spread mainly in the Punjab and United Provinces among the middle and higher castes. Though mainly an urban movement, its influence extended to semi-urban and rural areas also.

Dayanand Saraswati emphasized compulsory education of both men and women and spoke of *purdah* as an evil which came in the way of courage, learning and broadmindedness. He propagated prohibition of child marriage by law and approved the remarriage of child widows. He was, however, opposed to divorce or to remarriage of widows in general. While he prescribed similar education and religious initiation for boys and girls, he emphasized the need to maintain sex distinction in schools and among teachers, prescribing a minimum distance of 3 miles between boys' and girls' schools. This emphasis on education was continued by the Samaj even after his death, and a number of institutions were established. The Arya Kanya Pathshalas, which gradually developed into colleges have contributed greatly to the cause of women's education. In the later years, leaders of the Samaj broke away from his disapproval of widow remarriage and contributed to improving the position of widows. The Samaj did not make any distinction in marriage rites of virgins and widows.

Its repudiation of the caste system, however, did not extend to demanding its abolition, nor did the Samaj mount a campaign against untouchability. The followers of the Arya Samaj tended to follow the pattern of arranged marriages for their children as well as the rules of endogamy. While there is no objection to intercaste marriage, most families tend to establish marital connections within the caste group, sometimes with *Sanatani* families of the same caste. In consequence, the reformist character of the movement has tended to recede. On the other hand, the emphasis on the home making roles of women, whose primary duty is to love and serve their husbands, and children in the traditional way has limited its contribution to the cause of women's emancipation.

The Muslim Reform Movement

Like the parallel movements among the Hindus there were movements of reform within the Islamic community too. Regarding the position of the women, however, reforms were delayed, partly because modern education entered the Muslim community much later, and partly because the seclusion of women was defended by leaders of the community more persistently. "The practice of polygamy, however, registered a marked decline due to prevalence of modern ideas and decline in material prosperity."

A progressive movement to improve women's educational opportunities began to develop from the last years of the 19th century, under the leadership of a few visionaries like the Begum of Bhopal, Sheikh Abdullah in Aligarh, Justice Karamat Hussain in Lucknow and others of their ilk; a large number of books and journals appeared which carried enlightenment to the newly educated Muslim women.

Many reformers tried to revive widow remarriage, which had become strictly taboo among the respectable classes, due perhaps to the prevailing social ideas. Criticism also started against the custom of denying to the daughters a share in their fathers' property as a violation of the tenets of Islam. Failure to eliminate seclusion, however, defeated many of the aims of these reformers and the status of Muslim women still remained far from one of equality in spite of these reform movements. Among the urban educated middle-classes, however, these ideas contributed to some change in the position and treatment of women within the family.

Similar movements to improve the position of women emerged among other communities and different regions. Behramji Malabar was the main spirit behind the Age of Consent Act of 1892. The depressed condition of women in all communities made it difficult for them to fight for their own rights. A few outstanding exceptions faced great opposition from their communities. Pandita Ramabai, having incurred the wrath of the orthodoxy by marrying out of caste, ultimately turned to Christianity to aid her campaign to improve the condition of women. Dhan Korbai suffered great hardship for marrying after widowhood. Vidyagouni Neelakant faced bitter opposition to obtain education.

The changes envisaged by these reformers were only partial. They aimed to change the position of women within the family and the domestic framework and did not foresee any radical change in the social structure. Education, raising the age of marriage, widow remarriage, the abolition of seclusion and rights to property were essentially attempts to improve the woman's position within the family framework and to ensure for her a degree of dignity and independence.

None of these movements aimed to make the woman an equal partner of man in the societal roles outside the family. The movements were also limited in their appeals; while the Brahmo Samaj and Prarthna Samaj appealed only to a limited section of Western educated urban Indians, the Arya Samaj, Ramakrishna Mission and other revivalist movements appealed to a wider group, including the urban lower middle-class. The general impact of all these movements has been most pronounced on the urban middle-class. Some of the ideas projected by them, namely disapproval of child marriage and ill-treatment of widows, education and better treatment of women within the family, ensuring to them a position of greater dignity, have become a part of the general cultural heritage of this section of Indian society.

Being elitist in character and limited in approach, they have never tried a proper investigation of the problems that weighed on women outside the middle-class. Education, though valuable, could not reach the masses. The universal oppression on all women however lay in their subordinate and subjugated position in society, which sanctioned such treatment. Its removal called for a restructuring of the social organisation which the reform movements, by and large, did not aim for. The two social ideas which really threatened the basic structure of Indian society during this period were 'women's emancipation', and 'mass education'. Since the reform movements were not prepared to identify themselves with such extreme, radical ideas, their efforts to emancipate women, could be only limited in effect.

It has to be remembered that the most towering personalities in the movement for improving the lot of women came from individuals who were indifferent to the religious aspects of the reform movements. Iswar Chandra Vidyasagar and Jotiba Phule wanted to free Indian society not only from religious superstitions, but from the social inequalities that oppressed all the weaker sections, including women. It was however left to Mahatma Gandhi and, the freedom movement to place the movement for women's emancipation in its proper perspective, as a part of the larger movement for social transformation.

REFERENCES

1. Rehana Gha Lialley edited, *Women in Indian Society*, 1988.
2. Saradamoni, K., *Finding the Household*, 1992.
3. Sriniwas, H.N., *Social Change in Modern India*.
4. Susanne Thorbek, *Gender and Slum Culture in Urban Asia*, 1994.

Three

Descent Family

Descent systems

Modes of descent, types of family organisation, and the nature of the institution of marriage provide the major contours of the sociocultural setting in which women are born, brought up and live their lives. These features of social organisation are related to the economy in such a way that while their roots often appear to lie in the economic system, even large-scale changes in the latter are not able to carry along with them parallel changes in these areas. The lag between the two is a matter of serious concern. These institutions in the Indian society have implications for the status of women.

Matrilineal Descent

India has only a limited number of matrilineal communities which are concentrated in the south-western and the north-eastern regions of the country. Kerala has been the stronghold of matrilineal culture. The Nayars and Tiyyars of North Kerala, and several temple servant castes, occupational castes, and some forest tribes have followed this mode of descent which governs group placement, property rights and successions of authority. Matriliny is found in parts of Karnataka and Tamil Nadu also. The legal systems of these communities have undergone drastic changes since the close of the last century. Muslims following matriliny are Moplahs of northern parts of Kerala and the inhabitants of the Union Territory of Lakshadweep. The latter are classified as Scheduled Tribes. They have all along followed their customary laws for inheritance of matrilineal property and present an example of a rare kind of organisation which is characterized by absence of the institutionalization of the unit of husband, wife and children as an independent entity or as one embedded in larger entity, and which has struck a remarkable compromise with Islam. Of all the matrilineal systems in India, the one found in Lakshadweep islands is so far the least affected by the processes of change.

In the north-east, the matrilineal pattern is represented mainly by the Garo, the Khasi, and the Pnar in the States of Meghalaya and Assam. At least 44% of the Khasi and 30% of the Garo population is Christian, but adoption of a new religion has not drastically affected their patterns of kinship and marriage.

Since the last few decades of the nineteenth century, the matrilineal cultures in both the corners of the sub-continent have been exposed to processes of change brought about by introduction of market economy, opportunities for education and mobility, diversification of occupational structure, and changes in the legal framework. They have introduced differences in patterns of marital residence and composition of operative units, bases of economy, constituents of property, rules of inheritance, and authority structure.

Thus, the Nayars have functioned as an integral part of the larger caste system of Kerala and have mostly been landlords or non-cultivating tenants in the feudal system. The main occupation of men was military service while the women were bound to home and hearth. Cultivation was supervised by the elder among the males. Through hypergamous marriage, women were perhaps helpful in establishing favourable political connections for their own kin-groups. The traditional residential unit was groups of matrilineal kin in which the husbands were outsiders. Whereas among the Nayars and Tiyyars of North Kerala, the woman customarily went to live with the husband, and through her also her children, retained her right in the natal property.

The Moplahs have been principally traders and have tended to accommodate the sons-in-law as resident members. The Khasis and the Garos have flourished in a hoe culture in which actual use of land and not absolute ownership has relevance. In the traditional land tenure system clans or matrilineages have commanded certain territories to be taken under cultivation by their members. Marital residence is predominantly uxorilocal in which the husband comes to live with the wife's people or in the wife's land.

Such differences notwithstanding, it is possible to view these matrilineal systems in relation to the status that they accord to their women. This is only to bring into relief the institutions and groupings based on patrilineal descent ideology which tends to view women in a different way. There is also another valid reason for their consideration. It is the opinion of many scholars that matriliny was widespread in India in pre-Aryan days, on which the Aryan patriarchal culture was superimposed. The ambivalence in attitudes to women, a manifestation of which may be seen in the low status of women in the same community which also worship the goddess mother in various forms as a benevolent matriarch, a destroyer of demons, as an indignant goddess demanding attention and respect, is attributed to the matrilineal base of Indian culture.

In a matrilineal system the genetic line is continued through women, but power does not usually vest in women. For this reason we should not confuse matrilineal systems with matriarchal systems. In the matrilineal systems political power, including social control and decision making in matters of land and other property, vests in men; in matriarchy this power should vest in women. Matriliny has been associated with such economic systems in which women are not really dependent on men and can manage most of the business of living themselves. Men render some help; they engage in hunting, fishing, trading and warfare. Simple agriculture, without the use of the plough, is suited to matriliny. The Garos have taken to plough cultivation only in the past few decades. The matrilineal communities in the south-west — the land-owning Nayars in particular — are an exception, for their women do not engage in any productive work but they still enjoy full property rights and serve as links for inheritance and succession.

In matrilineal systems the woman is the perpetuator of the line. Children owe to the mother their social placement and it is through the mother that they acquire their right in movable as well as immovable property, and men succeed to positions of authority. It may, however, be noted that the status of a woman does not depend on her proved fertility. As fertility is not subservient to the continuity of a male line, she does not have to prove her worth by giving birth to children or by producing children of one particular sex. She is a full member of her matrilineal group and cannot be alienated from the natal group on marriage. Among the Khasis the youngest daughter gets the major share of the ancestral property, for she is responsible for the rituals of the house, death rites, propitiation of ancestors, and care of the aged parents. The Garo parents select one of the daughters to be the heiress. The Nayar girls are co-sharers of property with the male members.

Among these groups there is no premium on the birth of a male child. In fact among the Garos the birth of a daughter is more welcome for among them there prevails a feeling that a son is brought up only to work in the fields of his in-laws and not of his parents.

Where there is a greater concern with the maintenance of group boundaries and the retention of the status of the group, we find greater constraints on women because of her biological function of child bearing. For example, the Nayars living in the complex caste society would not allow their women to contract unions with men of groups lower than their own. Proper paternity used to be ensured by men of the lineage by having a control over the marital unions of the women and by the requirement of the payment of delivery expenses by the father of the newborn. In contrast, in this respect there appears to be much less rigidity among the Khasis. The children of informal unions with outsiders do not have a problem of group placement. The Garo women operate under greater restrictions as compared to the Khasis. This is because among the Garos the household-based on the bond between husband and wife is the unit through which relationship between two lineages continued over generations and the husband has full managerial powers over the property of the wife. Among the Khasis and the Nayars, however, the maternal uncle or elder brother is the manager of ancestral property.

The degree of freedom of movement and operations is also directly related to the contribution of women to the economy. The Khasis, the Garos, and the Lakshadweep islanders stand in a better position compared to the Nayars. However, in all these communities division of labour between the sexes emphasizes differential rights and expectation. A Khasi proverb says, "war and politics are for men, while property and children are for women". Modesty is a female virtue. Muscular strength of men is recognized. As noted earlier, political organisation is in the hands of men. Rulers, chiefs, and elders are all men. Managers of property too are men—either matrilineal kin or in some cases husbands. Only for some matrilineages in Kerala and Karnataka women were entitled to headship. In the pattern of family living of the Garos and the Khasis, each generation sees the establishment of separate households of non-heiresses in which the women can hold considerable initiative and authority.

Women in matrilineal systems seem to fare better as members of kin groups and in dyadic (interpersonal) relationships. Husband's position *vis-a-vis* the wife is considerably different from that prevailing in the patrilineal systems. He is not her supporter, nor does she gain her status through him. She can, therefore, hold her own in this intimate relationship. She does not lose her children on divorce. The mother commands genuine respect from the son. Among the Nayars, the mother's curse is believed to be very powerful. Between brothers and sisters, age is important for guiding their behaviour, but there is a feeling of awe and sacredness about the sister. The mother's brother is an authority figure, but on the whole, a woman is fairly secure in her natal home. Her rights give her a certain dignity; her consent is necessary for property transactions. She cannot, therefore, be ignored.

A comparative status evaluation of women in matrilineal communities with the help of indicators like economic power, religious responsibilities, degree of constraint at home and outside, and decisiveness and value of female roles shows that where a woman has an active role in the economy and besides subsistence, production also participates in handicrafts and marketing outside, and she enjoys better status and greater influence.

Matriliny is not a mirror image of patriliny. There is a certain inherent conflict in this system that authority is in male hands while group placement is in female hands. A husband is not incorporated in the wife's group; he is still needed in his mother's group for positions of authority and for taking decisions about the lineage land and other property. He is insecure because of minimum rights over his wife, hardly any rights over his children, and only right of use in the ancestral property. There is much suppression of fatherly inclination in a matrilineal system. It is based on the principle of the unity of matrikin and their collective control which cannot be sustained under the processes of change. With opportunities for education, new avenues of livelihood, and geographical mobility, a man can gain some control over his wife and children but this certainly disrupts the matrilineal system as such.

The disintegration of Nayar Taravads has come about because of political and economic changes and passing of new laws which changed the implications of marriage and conferred on individual members the right of demanding their shares. The Taravad still continues in its name which is used by its members for identification and in rituals. Within smaller kinship and domestic units, the matrilineal ideology still persists. The Nayar woman was home-bound and did not contribute to the economy, but as a property holder and as a perpetuator of the line, she has enjoyed respect. The study of Taravads over generations tells us that Nayar girls used to receive education at home at the hands of a teacher. They are now taking advantage of educational opportunities offered to them. Old values and norms and their share in property help them to enjoy some status even in the new kind of family—husband, wife, and children which is becoming common because of diversifications of occupations and spatial mobility. However, to the detriment of women's status, the Nayars have also moved towards Sanskritic rituals like those associated with marriage and are already settling marriages with the help of dowry.

Patrilineal Descent

The overwhelming majority of the Indian population follow the patrilineal systems of descent. Though the influence of this system on institutions of family, marriage, or the place and role of women vary between religions, regions, castes and socio-economical levels, there are some common underlying principles and patterns.

Patriliny is used for the formation and continuation of discrete kin groups, for example, clans which are often based on putative kinship and lineages of different orders. These have an important role to play in occupation of territories, use of ownership of land and other economic resources, and political and religious organisation of a community. Innumerable tribal groups of India and caste groups like the Jat and the Rajput may be mentioned here. Even where there are no corporate kin groups with a depth of a number of generations, recognition of patriliny variously known as 'Vansha', 'Kula', 'Khandan' is most common. Patriliny is emphasized with the help of a common name, a common place of origin, ancestor worship, common deity and rituals, pollution observed on death of patrikin, and such other means. Family in India is embedded in this patrilineal setting for patriliny is used as the framework for family grouping, big or small.

This has direct relevance to the place of woman in society. A boy is the perpetuator of the patriline; he will continue the family name. By contrast, a girl is of no use in this respect. Her contribution in this sphere will have to be made in some other house. "A bird of passage," "another's property", "a guest in parents' house", "a thing to be preserved for an outsider", or "a thing which has to be given away" are some of the common descriptions of a daughter. Such notions may be overtly expressed or covertly held. In the urban areas even those parents who do not think in this manner are made aware of it on various occasions. Educated girls revolt against this notion, but most of them have to remain reconciled to it.

This transferability of the girl from the parents' house to the husband's house is a poignant reality of Indian society. *Bidai, Rukshati,* and *Doli* signify a sorrowful goodbye to the daughter after her marriage. We would like to emphasize that this cannot be dismissed as a mere stereotype for it seriously affects the daughter's jural rights and her socialization and training. There was no tradition of daughters having a right of inheritance from the father except among the Muslims. There is ample evidence to show that among the Muslims daughter's rights have often been ignored. This is true to tribal India also. An Angami Naga may give his daughter fields to use during her life time after which they have to be returned to the patrilineal kin. A Mizo daughter gets her mother's weaving apparatus. Such examples can be multiplied but they only indicate inferior rights of daughters. Besides her right of maintenance as an unmarried girl and the right of being married off in an appropriate manner, a daughter basically has only a moral right to be invited to the natal house periodically and to receive gifts. By way of residual, contingent rights in her parental house she is customarily entitled to return there and seek support in the event of desertion, divorce and widowhood. But essentially this also is only a moral right, which is being eroded through the process of socio-economic change. Many widowed and deserted women whom we met during our tours told us that they could expect support and shelter from their family only as long as their father was alive.

The custom of retaining a daughter in the house by a son-less father by having a resident son-in-law, who should look after the property and would provide male progeny to be the rightful heirs of the maternal grandfather, does not alter the situation regarding daughters in general. Even today the provision of the daughter's share in her father's property in Hindu law is not fully implemented. Many daughters give up their rights of their own accord or may not fight for it. A common argument is that such insistence is likely to destroy the affection of brothers who at present feel morally bound to make appropriate contribution for her marriage and to give gifts to the sister and her children on various occasions such as festivals, weddings, child birth, etc.

In the patrilineal and patrilocal kinship system, a son is looked upon as the father's natural apprentice and successor and supporter of the parents in old age. Sons are supposed to build up family prestige and prosperity. A father believes that he will continue to live in this world through the son. All this imparts a special value to the son.

A son is necessary for performing the prescribed rituals of his parents when they die. Even in domestic rituals a daughter cannot take the place of a son. Although ritual considerations are less compelling among the lower castes, the relative importance of the son has become generalized throughout Hindu society.

A daughter cannot effectively take the place of a son. Her loyalties change at marriage. As a popular saying in Telugu puts it, "Bringing up a daughter is like manuring and watering a plant in someone else's courtyards", for her services and affections are to go to others. A daughter is an easy source of disrepute for the family, particularly before marriage and also after marriage for she is always referred to as the daughter of such and such family. Since marriage of a daughter is a matter of anxiety and expenditure, daughters mostly are not welcome. People complain that daughters have to be educated as well as married off. This puts a double burden on parents.

According to our survey 44.57% of the respondents said that people react differently to the birth of a girl and a boy, whereas only 35.41% said that they do not react differently. It is commonly seen that in hospitals the menial staff asks for a larger tip at the birth of a son. In villages and towns the midwife expects twice as much gift at the birth of a son than at the birth of daughter. At the birth of her first baby, the mother gets better gifts from elders if the new-born is a male. A first son, whether born as a first child or later, invariably gets a warm welcome. It is no wonder that while striving to get a son, a family may come to have a number of daughters.

Reaction to the birth of a particular girl depends on the socio-economic culture of the family and her place in the sibling group. The act of "giving away" a daughter is believed to earn special merit; her contribution in terms of domestic work and affection is also valued. Without a daughter a household is not really complete. And yet it is often remarked that whereas a couple miss something if they do not have a daughter, they are also saved from much worry and trouble.

Discrimination between sexes in the allocation of scarce sources in various fields such as nutrition, medical care, and education is directly related to the greater desirability of the son and transferability of the daughter. In most families girls are taught to see that brothers get more and better food. This attitude is internalized by girls often without being conscious of it; but a conscious effort is also made so that the girls inculcate the cultural norms which legitimize a differential treatment between girls and boys. In educated families we may not find so much of discrimination. Among tribal and other groups for whom a girl is an asset, as a help in domestic and productive activities and as a bringer of gifts and cash by way of bride-wealth, such discrimination is somewhat less. But discrimination in giving modern education at all levels is certainly related to the distinction between the rules of male and female children. According to conventional thinking, parents cannot expect economic support from the daughter, once she is married. Many still considered it improper to accept such support, even if it were offered. While the process of economic and social change is driving many families out of this pattern of thinking, the resistance of the in-laws still prevents many daughters from giving such support to parents, even when it is needed.

In her husband's house also a woman does not acquire rights comparable to those of the male members. Though ceremonially welcomed there with symbolic expressions of her future role as a contributor of prosperity and fertility, she is an inferior partner, and has to make a place for herself by establishing a relationship with the husband's kin, by learning the traditions of the family, and by producing progeny. The degree of incorporation expected of a woman in her husband's group differs in different communities and socio-economic levels.

Even in tribal and rural areas her rights to property are extremely limited. Men are the possessors and inheritors of land and its resources. In the cognitive map of the people the wife works on her husband's fields and lives in her husband's house. Where divorce or separation are permitted she may have to leave if she does not satisfy and she may leave if she is not satisfied. Wife beating, which still prevalent in our society, cannot be explained away only by the superior physical strength of the husband. The notion of the wife being a possession of the man is also responsible for it. Whether a widow has a right of usufruct on husband's land or whether she can inherit his land and other property, these rights are subject to her not remarrying. Children do not belong to the mother. In the event of divorce or separation small children may accompany the mother to be returned to the husband when they grow up. Even in those areas where a woman's contribution to the economy is substantial and she has considerable leeway, the cultural notion that her role is only supportive has to be traced to patrilineal descent and patrilocal residence.

However, it is not the fact of patriliny by itself but its association with joint property, and joint family household and certain rules and patterns of marriage which lead to greater constraints over women and affect their position in an adverse way.

Family Organization

Family in India largely exists in the framework of patrilineal descent, but differences in its form, function, and process are crucial to the position of women. A common image of the Indian patrilineal patrilocal family is that of three generational, commensal and co-residential group formed by close male patrikin with their wives and unmarried daughters. This group has a common budget, common residence, and common hearth. Joint landed property, a family business or family craft are conducive to this type of family as they require pooling of their skill, labour and resources.

In common parlance such a family has been described as "joint family". While the fundamental feature of a joint family according to Mitakshara law is a corporate group of companies parceners i.e. patrilineally related males who have a joint right to property for our purpose of examining the role and status of women, coresidence and commonality are immediately identifiable characteristics of a joint family household. Such a consideration would also accommodate family patterns of those areas which have followed Dayabhaga law and of Muslims and other communities. It would also accommodate family which hardly have anything by way of ancestral or immovable property but which may comprise more than one couple related through patrilineal links, i.e., father and sons along with wives and children, or brothers and their wives and children. This type of joint living is observed in all parts of the country, though its incidence is variable, depending on :

(a) the culturally patterned time of break-up which differs across caste, community and area;

(b) on demographic profiles based on such factors as average life expectancy, average age of effective marriage, average number of children born per couple, age of father at the birth of various children, etc.; and

(c) on influence of education, spatial mobility and diversification of occupation.

The findings of anthropologists and sociologists about the familial patterns in India tell us that among the tribal groups of India, nuclear household is the most common and culturally approved form of domestic group. It is common for sons to have separate hearths as they get married or as they come to have one or two children. But the sons tend to have their houses close to their father's residence. In terms of locality the marital residence is largely patri-virilocal viz., where on marriage, a woman comes to live in the house or in the locality of her husband's father. Moreover, at any point of time, there may be some family units of husband, wife, and children with additional members like an aged parent of the husband or his unmarried brothers and sisters. In some tribes like the Bhils in Rajasthan at least one of the sons is expected to live with parents. Only a few tribal groups like the Tharu, the Rabha, and some Gonds have joint family living during the lifetime of the father as the cultural norm. We would thus like to conclude that by and large, family organization among the Indian tribes does not impose as much constraint on the women as amongst non-tribal groups particularly the upper and middle strata. Joint family living appears to be more characteristic of land-owning and trading classes and of upper castes in general, though Brahmins are not at the top in this respect. It is least characteristic of Scheduled Castes. There are also regional differences, the Gangetic plains show higher incidence of joint families. One significant finding is that although the majority of households are nuclear, majority of people may live in joint and supplemented nuclear families. There is something like patterned rearrangements of family structure through time. There are definite group and regional differences in the customary time of break-up of the joint family and these differences appear to correlate with the incidence of joint families at any point of time.

Indian patri-virilocal family has to be viewed in terms of its developmental cycle. It develops into a joint family after the marriage of a son and coming of a daughter-in-law. After the death of the father, brothers generally separate. In the villages of Andhra Pradesh for example, sons are expected to stay together along with the parents till all of them are married, after which they tend to separate, the parents generally choosing to live with one of the sons. Thus, joint family is broken into one relatively smaller joint family household and perhaps a few simple households. It is common to find an aged parent and dependent siblings living with a man and his wife and children. The role configuration of such households is undoubtedly different from that of a simple family. This type of household is found also in urban areas, though it is being subject to severe strains. Lack of adequate housing facilities sometimes leads to a break-up, or it may, contrarily, compel a family to remain joint. Changing attitudes, aspirations and norms of different generations, however, imposes a constant strain on joint families and often results in a break-up. Occupational mobility of individual members have contributed to this process, and break-ups in such cases take place without any serious overt tensions in the family.

An understanding of this family organisation entails recognition of degrees of jointness such as (a) jointness of property, income or production and domestic grouping (b) jointness of property and income or production but not of domestic groupings and (c) jointness of property alone.

Another feature of Indian family organisation is the recognition of a kind of oneness between the father's and the son's households, or between the brothers' households. A son's family is in a sense an extension of the father's family. In fact they are one 'family'. It is in this 'family' that the incoming wife has to be incorporated. There is always the contingency of younger siblings or aged parents of the man coming to live with his simple family household. Parents may divide their time between various sons. Vicinage and common business or property interests are conducive to the continuation of this sense of unity. Formal obligations towards relations by marriage and towards the daughters of the house are expected to be shared by this 'family'. Each generation experiences weakening of the ties between brothers, usually after the death of parents, and a growth of their own respective branches.

There is great emphasis on adjustability in the socialization of girls. In their training for sex-linked roles, they are made aware that they are girls and constantly reminded of the pitfalls they must avoid and of the uncertainties they must face. In urban educated families, there may be little discrimination between boys and girls in regard to food, medical attention and even education, but notions about the appropriate spheres of men and women are implicit in the general distribution of household work and in the concessions and freedom of behaviour permitted to the boys. In middle-class families girls receiving education does not undermine their femininity. Even for young boys and girls of urban areas socialized in the sixties and seventies, the need for reallocation of work and responsibility within the family is not emphasized. In joint living, discrimination tends to be more pronounced. Even where girls are exempted from onerous tasks and a rigid routine, it is often with an expression of the feeling that since they will have to do all this after marriage, they should at least have some comfort and freedom in the parent's house.

Very few women start their married life independently in a simple household. Even when the husband is working away from his parents, a girl 'enters' as daughter-in-law in the house of the parent-in-law or husband's elder brother. In the first few years of married life her behaviour is to be governed by the norms of a subordinate and submissive role appropriate for a daughter-in-law. She has very little hand in any kind of decision making, and has to start her new life under severe restrictions. These are more onerous in certain regions and in the well-to-do and middle-classes than in poorer sections. Norms of segregation and seclusion of women, marriage rules, degree of distinction between bride givers and bride-takers, as well as the extent of contribution of the woman to family earning are responsible for these differences.

Among the Muslims the prevalence of marriages between close kin, including children of two brothers, does not allow a sharp distinction between bride-givers and bride-takers, and where such marriages have taken place, rules of avoidance between a woman and her husband's kin may not be as rigid as among the Hindus of North India. But by and large similar rules of avoidance operate in Muslim families of particular regions and socio-economic levels. A distinct notion about women's subordinate role, general segregation and seclusion of women, and conception of patrilineal and patrilocal family have their effect on the status of the Muslim women in general.

In the authority pattern of a joint family the daughter-in-law is directly subordinate to the mother-in-law. According to a Telugu proverb, 'good and bad scorpions both have their sting; the difference is that one uses it more than the other'. A woman is at the peak of her life when her daughters-in-law are young and her husband is an active provider. It is only gradually that a daughter-in-law's position in her husband's family improves. In the words of Mandelbaum, "A young wife, of any Jati or region, usually has the lowest status in the family and is given the more onerous chores. Whatever goes away, she is apt to be called the culprit. Whenever the finger of blame is pointed, it somehow swings to her."

With a long standing in their husband's family and as mothers, old and experienced women in the middle-classes enjoy considerable authority and respect in the family and have a say in the decision making. They may even be consulted by men in matters of land, property and business.

Our survey however reveals that the women members of the family as a whole have a marginal role to play in decision-making. The only decision in which the woman takes an active part is in buying the foodstuffs. Male dominance in decision making is more pronounced in rural areas and among lower caste groups.

Decisions such as those about educational career to be pursued, about jobs and marriage, are collectively taken by the family, as revealed by low percentage of respondents saying that the children take these decisions 'himself/herself'. A higher percentage of respondents said that the 'sons' take their own decisions about the job they want to take and educational career. Though the overall percentage of female participation in such family decisions is lower it is slightly higher for decisions affecting the daughters, whereas the male members of the family were instrumental in deciding about the sons. On these issues again the major part in decision-making is that of the male members. Decisions about marriage of sons and daughters are mostly collective in nature.

A woman's authority is reflected directly in her control over the daughter-in-law, but it would be a mistake to view the position of a mother-in-law as indicative of the status of women in general. For, the same woman's status may decline with old age, widowhood, and with the daughter-in-law's coming into importance as mother and as the wife of the principal provider.

Besides her kinship status, a woman's status in the family is also influenced by her husband's social position and his contribution to the family economy. Thus, her own efforts by themselves may often not be able to bring her status. In middle and upper classes the amount of dowry a daughter-in-law has brought and the gifts that her parents send also contribute to her status in the family. With greater diversification of occupations in urban areas, the husband's status becomes more relevant for the woman's status.

With the authority of the mother-in-law or elder sister-in-law, little contact with the husband, and a general expectation of subordination, a woman's position in a joint family can be miserable. In this social milieu, it is difficult for a woman to evoke a balanced relationship with the husband and have a role in decision-making. Many of the critical decisions of her life remain beyond her control, such as planning one's family, further training or education, taking up or continuing a job.

Our survey attempted to obtain first-hand data on the observance of rules of avoidance with the husband's kin by asking whether *purdah* was observed in the presence of the father-in-law, mother-in-law, husband's elder brother and husband's elder sister. The findings reveal that in the presence of the father-in-law purdah is observed in the case of 44.04% Sikhs, 40% Muslims, 39.19% Jains and 32.08% Hindus. Distribution by States reveals that such avoidance is highest in the Northern States in the following order: Haryana (72.61%); Rajasthan (62.18%); Delhi (60.78%); Himachal Pradesh (51.19%); Uttar Pradesh, M.P. and Gujarat follow. Manipur also has a high incidence of avoidance. Figures for *purdah* in the presence of father-in-law are as follows : Kerala (4.29%), Tamil Nadu (4.93%), Mysore (5.44%) and Andhra Pradesh (9.40%). Maharashtra has a little higher incidence. In Goa *purdah* is wholly absent. Obviously this is a cultural difference, and indicates a major area of constraints for women in North India.

A simple family allows a greater scope for a woman to have less restricted roles and greater part in management and policy decisions. As has often been pointed out, in a simple family a woman is subordinate to no other woman. The husband is dependent upon her for running the house, rearing of children, and management of social relations. Depending on the personalities of the couple and personal equation, a woman can truly be the mistress of the house. If she is educated and enlightened, she acquires a personality and a dignity of her own.

Thus situated a woman has much greater initiative to have sustained contacts with her own kin, not only as prescribed by custom (and mainly on formal occassions) but on a basis of equality in which both mother as well as father are equally relevant for reckoning kinship ties. It has been found that those away from the patrilocal village and settled in urban areas have greater freedom to choose their contacts.

With the absence of large-scale joint family, greater freedom of association and movement, and economic contribution of both husband and wife towards living, a woman gets a better status in the family. This is largely true of small-scale agriculturists and artisans, but it is the women of the lowest category who seem to be more equal to their husbands: "...in certain senses women whose fortune it was to be poor enjoyed higher status than those who were rich". Participation in extra-domestic economic activities does not give these women status in the larger context because the work they do is of low prestige.

REFERENCES

1. Altekar, A.S., *The Position of Women in Hindu Civilisation*, 1938.
2. Chunge, G.S., *Caste, Class and Occupation.*
3. Hutton, J.H., *Caste in India.*
4. Uma Ramaswamy, Self Identity among Scheduled Castes: A Study of Andhra Pradesh, *Economic and Political Weekly* Vol.IX No.47.

Four

Marriage

Many problems of major importance for women are linked with marriage. Various issues like age at marriage, procedures for contacting and executing marriage, customs of dowry and bride wealth, patterns of presentations between the wife's and the husband's kin groups, multiplicity of spouses, divorce and separation, widowhood, and remarriage are vitally relevant for assessing women's status.

In a patrilineal society, marriage signifies a transfer of the woman from her natal group to her husband's group. This is associated also with the notions of male superiority and secondary importance of the female in the continuity of the line. The 'seed', people believe, is more important than the 'field'. Concern with paternity tends to become stronger in a patrilineal system, and paternity can be approximately assured only by controlling women's sexuality. Another way adopted by some tribal groups is to establish definite rules for assigning the children born to an unmarried girl.

By and large insistence on low age of marriage for girls is related to avoidance of unclaimed progency. Notions of vulnerable purity of women, value of virginity for girls at marriage, and a clear differentiation between primary marriage and secondary marriage for women, in castes which have the institutions of divorce and remarriage also follow from this. Widespread prevalence of child marriages in the country has its roots in this feature of human biology coupled to a concern for ascertaining paternity. The custom of mock marriage, in which a girl is ritually married to some object like a spear, an arrow, a pestle or *Mahua* tree, before she attains puberty also reflects the group's concern for the purity of women.

Existence of caste in Hindu society which traditionally limits marriage contacts within certain groups, rules against marrying within *gotra*, clan and lineage. Regulations about not marrying certain types of close blood relations, and customs which enjoin or indicate reference for marriage between certain types of relatives or groups, make arranged marriage the most desirable form of marriage. Among Muslims and other religious groups also there are either certain socio-economic categories or groups and sections within which marriage is restricted. Where inter-group marriages are approved, they are mostly on hypergamous basis, daughters being accepted from lower groups. The concept of purity of blood among Muslims seems to be responsible for preference for marriage between close relatives, particularly between children of siblings and for exchange marriages. Many Muslim groups in North and Western India, consider marriage between the children of two brothers as most desirable. A common explanation for this preference is offered in terms of the desire to keep the property within the family since, according to Islamic law, girl is also entitled to a share in her parental property.

In the south there has been a preference for marriage of a girl with her father's sister's son, and less generally with her mother's brother's son or with her mother's younger brother. Some castes practice direct exchange also. In the matrilineal communities marriage with mother's brother who belongs to the same lineage as the sister's daughter is unthinkable.

Marriage cannot be left to the young if these restrictions and preferences are to work. The institution of arranged marriage thus fits well with the social structure. Only in subsequent marriages one's own choice can be exercised.

In urban areas there is a trend towards ignoring for the sake of marital relations, the differences between caste groups which belong to the same generic category or are closely situated in hierarchical grading. Education, travel and liberalization of ideas have contributed to this trend. In the salaried sections economic considerations and status also play an important part in ignoring these distinction.

Patterns of selection of marriage partner have become varied, particularly in urban areas. Between one's own choice at one end and the selection by parents without any consultation with the marriageable son/daughter at the other end, we find self-choice with parent's consent and parent's choice but with the approval of the marrying parties. Another intermediate pattern is one in which boy's wishes are given weight but it is not considered necessary to consult the girl with any seriousness. The position in which the elders alone decide is more prevalent among those who have little or no education.

However, the young who want to take their own decision in this area of life are not many. Respect for parents and desire to avoid uncertainties are behind this attitude. In many surveys of the attitude of college girls towards marriage, an interesting combination of approval of greater mixing between boys and girls and preference for arranged marriages under parental guidance has been revealed.

The studies made in the pre Independence phase and those made in the post Independence period highlight certain interesting points in selection of partners. Merchant, who had made his study when romanticism was emerging in the young boys and girls found that 79.2% of his respondents opted for self-choice of the partner. This romantic approach to marriage does not last long and in G.B. Desai's period i.e. 1945, more respondents (68.2%) favour marriages arranged by parents. Perhaps in absence of any opportunity for free-mixing, the younger generation might be finding it very difficult to make independent choice, and hence basks under parental security. It is for this reason that we find Raj Mohini, Kaker and Ramanamma's data indicate younger generation in favour of arranged marriages. The major change noticeable is that with the impact of urbanization and education, individuals would like themselves to be consulted before the match is finalized.

Another aspect of arranged marriage, is the humiliation that a girl has to face when she is obliged to present herself repeatedly before marriageable boys and their relations and friends. In a few sophisticated families the two parties may be treated on an equal footing as genuinely trying to assess each other's suitability. But in the middle-class families, by and large this situation is most humiliating for a girl. Inter-caste marriages today are not common and inter-religious marriages are even rarer. The freedom movement which also included a rejection of social taboos, propagated inter-caste as well as inter-religious marriages. At that stage such marriages were regarded as not only progressive but also as patriotic. But the momentum of this ideology seems to have receded in the years since Independence.

In a study done in 1969, only 24 out of 1036 i.e. 2.31% women had been married in castes other than their own. In the survey of affinal and consanguinous marriages conducted in 569 villages during 1961 Census operation, only 966 of 1,33,775 marriages i.e 72% have been reported to be across castes. The percentage of such marriages is 0.82 among the Hindus and only 0.01 among the Muslims. In another study made in 1972, it was found that 60% of respondents did not approve of inter-caste marriages.

In the actual rituals and ceremonies of marriage the unequal status of man and woman becomes apparent. In a Christian marriage the bride has to be ceremonially given over to the bridegroom and the bride is exhorted to promise that she will love and obey her husband. In a Muslim marriage, the parties to the contract are in a sense the husband and the bride's 'wali', though with her formal consent. In many parts of India, a Muslim bride duly decorated and sitting with a modest demeanour, is actually lifted by the bridegroom and put in the vehicle which is to carry her to his home.

Like language forms, rituals and ceremonies not only reflect the unequal treatment accorded to the sexes in a social system but by repetition emphasize and perpetuate the same inequality of status. Marriage is essentially a social affair and therefore succeeds in indoctrinating coming generations in the ideology implicit in it. It is because of this conservative attitude, particularly among women that in order to enjoy the rights given by the Constitution or law, women have to assert themselves. It is women who exercise the greatest vigilance over the members of their own sex regarding the observance of norms rooted in tradition.

The rites of Hindu marriage stress male primacy and superiority. Kanyadan is a gift of the virgin daughter for purposes of *Dharma*, *Artha* and *Kama*. The parties to the transaction are father of the girl (accompanied by his wife) who is the giver and the bridegroom who is the receiver. When the bridegroom accepts the bride he tells her that union with him is bringing her prosperity, cultivation, and auspiciousness. In fact marriage is the first major *Sanskara* for a Hindu woman. Promises made by the two during the rites like circumambulation of fire, walking seven steps, or the bride's changing over from the right to the left side of the groom are also worth noting. While emphasizing life, friendship and partnership for the two, they exhort the bride to follow the husband, to act according to his wishes, to remain steadfast in the loyalty and love. The bridegroom promises to protect and support the bride. He asks her to serve the elders of his family, be affectionate to the young, and not to be lazy. There is a special significance of the rite of showing the polar star (or Sun or Atar of Arundhoti) to the bride and of making her stand on a stone. She is to be steadfast like a stone and the polar star, not deviating from the right path and be calm and ready to suffer in silence.

The basic rituals of Hindu marriage are not confined to the so-called twice-born castes but are enacted with some variation among other castes also. The process of acculturation has resulted in the lower groups inviting the Brahmin priest who recites the "mantras" and helps his clients to enact the Sanskritic rituals. The lowest groups in the Hindu hierarchy, who operate without a Brahmin priest and also very many tribes, are seen to imitate some of these rituals — *Kanyadan* being the most popular among them. It is perfectly congruent with their notion of transfer of the bride.

While it is true that *kanyadan* relegates the status of the woman, in accepting the bride, the bridegroom has to make the following promise to the bride's father—*Dharme arthe Ca kame Ca naticarami* (i.e. I will not transgress in the attainment of duty, wealth and desire). There is also no doubt that the bride is given a warm welcome in the husband's house and is referred to as Laxmi (Goddess of prosperity). Her future role as home-maker is associated with great prestige. She is one who will give him progeny to continue the line, to free himself of his debt to ancestors, and to support him in old age. However, a close examination reveals that the rites of Hindu marriage stress male primacy and superiority. It is worth noting that the Brahmo Samaj had made special efforts to rationalize the ceremony of marriage and to drop those rites which perpetuated low status of women; the content analysis of Bengali and Marathi magazines and newspapers in the thirties and the forties of the present century show that there were strong reactions against these rites and "mantras" in some regional languages like Marathi and Bengali.

One important aspect of marital alliance in Hindu society, except in some parts of South India, is the unequal status of bride-givers and bride-takers. Just as woman is inferior to man, and bride is inferior to bridegroom, bride-givers are inferior to bride-takers. The son-in-law and his kind are to be respected. Marriage automatically establishes the lower status of the bride-givers. This distinction between bride-givers and bride-takers is far more pronounced in the northern States, but it is also very much there in central and western India. In the south because of common patterns of marriage among close kin which involves direct exchange or delayed exchange, systematic differences in the status of givers and takers do not emerge. In the context of a particular marriage because of the symmetrical relation between husband and wife, slight distinction of status between wife's kin and husband's kin may be there; this is particularly so among the Brahmins with their emphasis on Sanskritic rituals. But the overall pattern creates an ethos of near-equality between bride-givers and bride-takers. Marriages in the south tend to be contracted within a limited group and thus the girl is not thrown in with strangers. There is a regular to and fro movement and contact between the wife's family and the husband's family so that the girl is not left alone to face a hostile environment. Rules of behaviour are not as stringent for a daughter-in-law in the south as they are in the north where the contrasting norms of behaviour for the daughter and the daughter-in-law tend to make the life of woman alternate between freedom and restrictions, between harsh and soft treatment, and certain restrictions which do not allow her to become a freer person. She has roles but no personality. It is well-known that in western U.P., where marriages are arranged outside the village, daughters-in-law were not sent to the literacy classes while the daughters of the village could go in groups for election campaigning but the daughters-in-law were not permitted to do so.

The distinction between bride-givers and bride-takers is made harsher by the pattern of unilateral gift-giving. The son-in-law, and his parents are entitled to receive gifts from the girl's parents on different occasions but the latter are not even supposed to accept any food at the son-in-law's house. Common people in the north observe this rule strictly. These differential norms of behaviour are likely to be more pronounced in rural areas where the village is a kind of in-law village, or paternal village, and particularly in such castes and communities whose women do not work outside the home. These norms of behaviour operate in urban areas too. It is not uncommon to encounter a girl in her parents' house in a modern outfit and the same girl in her in-laws house in traditional clothes, partially veiled.

Hypergamy

Practice of hypergamy, i.e. marriage between man of higher and woman of lower groups, brings down the position of women. Within a caste, groups are ranked as the relatively high or low status. Practice of hypergamy is found among such groups as the Rajput and the Jat of North India, Anavil Brahmin and Patidar of Gujarat, Maithil Brahmin of Bihar, and among the Kanyakubj Brahmin and Sarayupari Brahmin to some extent. In hypergamy, clans and lineages are of unequal status; gotra and families among the Brahmin may also be of unequal status. As women in hypergamous marriages are treated as of inferior status, their incorporation in the husband's family is a painful process. Female infanticide among the Jat and the Rajput was partly a consequence of hypergamy, for the girls of the highest groups had very little choice for marriage as boys of these groups could marry lower down. Dowry is generally high in hypergamous communities.

Polygamy

Both the variants of polygamy, viz. Polygyny (plurality of wives) and polyandry (plurality of husbands) are found in India.

Polyandry is confined to tribes like the Toda in the Nilgiri, groups, like the Khasa in the Jaunsar Bawar area of U.P. and the people of Kinnaur and Lahul and Spiti in Himachal Pradesh. Some of these, like the Khasa, belong to the Hindu fold and are divided into castes. But today all these polyandrous groups of the Himalayan region are declared as Scheduled Tribes, and hence do not come under the limitations imposed by Hindu Law regarding monogamy. They practice fraternal polyandry. This group is numerically insignificant. But among the higher castes of Jaunsar-Bawar there is now a tendency of taking as many wives as there are brothers but there appears to have grown a vested interest in polyandry, particularly since they have been declared as a Scheduled Tribe with all its privileges. However, from the point of view of women's status it is worth noting that these are patrilineal and patrilocal groups and a woman has absolutely no right over her children and property. Polyandry in patrilineal setting far from being a privilege, is an obligation for a woman to allow sexual access to the rightful share.

Social reaction against polygyny as an indignity offensive to the status of women was one of the most marked features of the 19th Century Reform Movement. While the acceptance of monogamy as a necessary principle for civilized living became widely prevalent among the educated classes, there was a difference of opinion regarding the action necessary for eradication of this practice. While leaders like Iswar Chandra Vidya Sagar and the Brahmo Samaj and Christian Missionaries wanted legislative action to prohibit the practice, others believed that it would die a natural death with the spread of education. Partly as a result of this social reaction and partly due to declining material prosperity, among the classes which had earlier practised polygyny, the prevalence of this practice declined considerably over the last hundred years. The demand for legislative action against polygyny gained momentum under the influence of Gandhiji and made women's organisations increasingly vocal, resulting in legislative measures in different provinces and in the princely States even in the pre-independence period. The Hindu Marriage Act Introduced the principle of monogamy in 1955. As already mentioned, it is only in Muslim Law that plurality of wives is still permitted.

A study undertaken by the Census of India in 1961, however, found polygyny to be still prevalent among most communities to a certain extent, though its incidence had declined over the decades. Tables 4.1, 4.2 and 4.3 give us incidence of Polygynous marriages among tribals, Hindus and Muslims respectively according to the 1961 census. The survey was based on a total sample of nearly 1 lakh marriages. 5,911 marriages in the sample were found to be polygynous. If the time when these marriages had taken place is ignored, then the incidence was found to be the highest among the tribal communities (15.25%), Buddhists 7.97%, Jains 6.72%, Hindus 5.8% and Muslims 5.7%. As, however, the marriages covered were not selected on random sampling basis, the Census authorities observed that it would be risky to draw any quantitative generalization from this data. But at the same time, it has to be kept in view that the size of the sample is fairly large and hence until more valid quantitative data are available, one would be justified to question the validity of the prevailing notions in this matter. The most interesting finding of the Survey was regarding the trend of change in incidence.

TABLE - 4.1
INCIDENCE OF POLYGYNOUS MARRIAGES AMONG TRIBALS

State	*1931-40*			*1941-50*			*1951-60*		
	Total	*No.*	*Percentage*	*Total*	*No.*	*Percentage*	*Total*	*No.*	*Percentage*
Orissa	22	3	13.64	16	2	12.50	59	7	11.86
Arunachal Pradesh	324	30	9.36	463	82	17.71	664	123	18.52
Total	346	33	9.53	479	84	17.53	723	130	17.98

Source: Census of India 1961 (Incidence of Polygynous Marriages in India)

TABLE - 4.2
INCIDENCE OF POLYGYNOUS MARRIAGES AMONG HINDUS

State	*1931-40*			*1941-50*			*1951-60*		
	Total	*No.*	*Percentage*	*Total*	*No.*	*Percentage*	*Total*	*No.*	*Percentage*
Gujarat	810	21	2.59	1089	36	3.31	1340	15	1.11
Jammu & Kashmir	165	11	6.67	257	11	4.28	365	15	4.11
Madhya Pradesh	652	49	7.52	1021	83	8.13	1313	62	4.72
Madras	3134	225	7.18	4188	383	9.15	5571	380	6.82
Maharashtra	1043	83	7.96	1725	144	8.35	1899	179	9.43
Mysore	4619	272	5.89	6686	368	5.50	8369	298	3.57
Orissa	356	14	3.93	536	26	4.85	630	26	4.13
Rajasthan	558	18	3.23	834	33	3.96	1086	41	3.78
Uttar Pradesh	882	23	2.61	1233	24	1.95	1363	11	0.81
Delhi	16	2	12.50	17	1	5.85	15	3	20.00
Himachal Pradesh	1062	202	19.02	1525	289	18.95	1635	191	11.68
LM & A Islands	-	-	-	1	-	-	1	-	-
Manipur	92	2	2.17	137	9	6.57	169	3	1.78
Pondicherry	189	18	9.52	231	14	6.06	296	12	4.05
Tripura	352	7	1.89	519	10	1.93	548	9	1.64
Arunachal Pradesh	14	-	-	45	4	6.89	50	4	8.00
Total	13944	947	6.79	20044	1435	7.15	24659	1249	5.06

Source: Census of India 1961 (Incidence of Polygynous Marriages in India)

According to the data, the highest incidence, (7.15%) in the Hindu Community was found for marriages performed between 1941 to 1950, after which it declined to 5.06% in 1951-60 and the frequency declined steadily. Among Muslims, the highest incidence was found between 1931-1940 (7.29%) after which it declined steadily coming to 4.31% in 1951-60. Among the Jains the highest incidence was recorded between 1931-40(13.63%). As for Buddhists, the highest incidence (10.93%) is recorded between 1911 and 20. Incidence during 1951-60 was 8.13%. Amongst the tribal community, however, the trend has been markedly different. The lowest incidence 0.68% was between 1921-30 and the highest 17.98% during 1951-60.

Most tribal groups in India permit polygyny. Those not permitting it are very few; most of them either follow matriliny or recognize both the mother's and the father's line. The most important culturally accepted motivations for polygyny are barrenness of the wife, economic advantages accruing from plural marriages, and gain in prestige. Entanglements culminating in bringing another wife are also accepted by the society. Tribal groups like the Bhil in Rajasthan, the Bagata, the Raj Gond, and the Birdugond, see economic advantage in polygyny in two ways. Wives can contribute to the agricultural and other economic activities by their own labour and by producing sons who would supply the needed labour for working in the fields, tending cattle, and building houses. In a patrilineal setting where land and other economic resources belong to the men and where women's contribution to the economy is substantial, this can prove to be a strong incentive. Another incentive is that of prestige. Where bride price is high, it needs resources to obtain more than one wife and having more wives adds to one's prestige. The chiefs and village headmen, as also such other important men prefer to have more than one wife. During our tour of Arunachal Pradesh, we were informed by many that polygyny was mainly practised by chiefs or headmen. Similar was the case in Nagaland. It is interesting to note that such marriages among Christian Nagas still receive customary sanction though they are not permitted by the Church.

Even though a particular society permits polygyny, it is only a few people who can take advantage of it, and it is seen that only men of some means and power can avail of it. In many tribes it is feared that the coming of a second wife would lead to clashes among the wives and the first wife might leave and go to some other man that acts as a deterrent. A temporary phase of polygyny is also not uncommon.

TABLE - 4.3
INCIDENCE OF POLYGYNOUS MARRIAGES AMONG MUSLIMS

State	*1931-40*			*1941-50*			*1951-60*		
	Total	*No.*	*Percentage*	*Total*	*No.*	*Percentage*	*Total*	*No.*	*Percentage*
Gujarat	153	12	7.84	172	17	9.34	273	16	5.86
Himachal Pradesh	14	2	14.29	23	2	8.70	24	1	4.17
Jammu & Kashmir	639	55	8.61	1012	69	6.82	967	43	4.44
Madhya Pradesh	16	2	12.50	20	1	5.00	36	2	5.46
Madras	191	11	5.75	242	16	6.61	286	9	3.14
Maharashtra	15	-	-	29	2	6.90	36	-	-
Mysore	651	23	3.53	962	48	4.99	1125	42	3.73
Uttar Pradesh	198	10	5.05	325	19	5.84	367	14	3.81
Rajasthan	55	1	2.00	63	4	6.35	78	4	5.13
Delhi	18	1	5.56	38	2	5.26	49	-	-
LM & A Islands	368	41	11.14	613	53	8.65	775	37	4.77
Tripura	122	20	16.39	201	29	14.43	208	14	6.73
Total	2440	178	7.29	3710	262	7.06	4224	182	4.31

Source: Census of India 1961 (Incidence of Polygynous Marriages in India)

Among the essential social reasons, the most important are infertility of the wife, her prolonged sickness and the lack of a son. In some communities, the custom of marrying one's elder brother's widow, sometimes results in polygyny. Another social reason, which has become increasingly important in recent years, is the cultural and communication gap that often results when the wife is illiterate and uneducated and the husband receives modern education. Most of these cases result from child marriages. With the changing aspiration, pattern of social needs of the educated husband, finding their first wife a social handicap they turn to a second marriage in many cases. Many of them do this not without serious misgivings. In some of these cases their offers of divorce to the first wife are rejected by the latter, who finds herself unable to face the consequences of a divorce, because, the status of a deserted wife is better than that of a divorcee. Married status gives them certain rights in their in-laws' home which would be denied to them if they were divorced. In most of these cases their reluctance for divorce lies in their social and economic dependence and absence of the necessary equipment for earning. Resistance from their family may also be an added reason for their preparedness to put up with the indignity and unhappiness rather than seeking a divorce.

An important motivation of polygyny, however, is economic gain. Where women are not a burden but are self-supporting and contribute substantially to productive activity like cultivation and handicraft, they are real assets and a man can gain by having more than one wife. (Its long term implication that more hands will be available for work also has its temptations for some). Thus polygyny in Manipur clearly indicates that sometimes women's worth as productive workers may become a hindrance to their unopposed status in the family. Economic motivation for polygyny also operates among artisan groups, both Muslim as well as Hindu. Religious allowance for a man to marry as many as four wives at a time proves useful for the Muslim inhabitants of a district in Karnataka engaged in lacquer work, for what they gain by having extra hands to work is much more than what they have to spend on their keep. This, certainly, is a form of exploitation of women.

While the census study indicates that the incidence of polygyny among Muslims is not as high as it is believed to be, there is no doubt that the prevalence of legal sanction for polygyny caused widespread resentment among the women of this community. During our tours, we met many groups of Muslim women in different parts of the country, who expressed their unhappiness and resentment at the continuation of this situation. We met many, such women who had been abandoned by their husbands as a consequence of a second marriage. Still many others had to acquiesce to the second marriage because of their economic dependence. They also expressed a view that a protest against this institution from them had invariably resulted in acute oppression against which they obtained no protection from society. While it is a fact that changes in law alone cannot eradicate the prevalence of this practice, it is our view that continuing sanction by the law in a way perpetuates it. The role of law in such social matters in our country has usually acted as a norm in order to arouse the public conscience. We cannot appreciate the denial of similar support to Muslim women in their struggle against this social injustice.

Even though it is nearly 20 years since the law was passed banning polygyny for Hindus and making it a criminal offence, we regret to admit that the practice has not been eradicated altogether. Apart from the findings of the census study in 1961, the committee, during its tours, heard large number of complaints from women that their husbands had married again. Their lack of knowledge about their legal rights and social acceptance of the situation make the position of these women deplorable. In Andhra Pradesh, the Committee was told about the prevalent practice of wives being compelled to sign a document giving their permission to the remarriage to their husbands. Dependence on their husbands, both socially and economically and inadequate social condemnation of their deeds are the causes of the wives' acquiescence. Most of them believe that signing such a document deprives them of their legal right of redress. Education, economic independence and fuller knowledge of their legal rights can ultimately free society from the stranglehold of these traditions. We feel strongly that women's voluntary agencies should launch a campaign against this type of marriage by ostracising the men who commit bigamy and by mobilizing public opinion, particularly among women, to resist this practice.

Bride-price and Dowry

Bride-Price

Solemnization of marriage is a social occasion. In the Indian context it signifies the creation of a bond between two individuals and also between their families. It involves, with a few exceptions, the transfer of the wife to the husband's family. Two major types of transfers of material wealth accompany marriage: in one the wealth travels in the opposite direction of the bride and in another it travels along with the bride in the same direction. The former is bride-price; the latter is dowry. These need to be considered as components of marriage because of their implication on the status of women.

The patrilineal tribal groups of the Indian subcontinent customarily pay bride-price. The form and amount of bride-price vary from region to region and from tribe to tribe. Some pay only in cash, while others make the payment in kind, and still others pay the bride-price in both cash and kind. The second category, i.e., payment in kind, includes a wide range of subjects such as clothes and ornaments, tools and implements, liquor and grain, and cattle and goats. The *Uraon* of Chhotanagpur take sets of clothes for the bride's relatives, while the *Ho* and *Munda* concentrate on heads of cattle; so also in Arunachal Pradesh where *mithun* is the customary bride-price. The *Ao* Naga give baskets of paddy and an indigenous dagger. *Bhumias* of Orissa have to offer some cash, five to six sarees, and three goats as bride-price. Bargaining for bride-price is common. A survey of recent information indicates that in many tribes bride-price has increased manifold. Table 4.4 will give some idea of the trend:

TABLE - 4.4
BRIDE-PRICE CHANGES OVER TIME IN TRIBES

Name of Tribe	*Traditional Bride-price (in rupees)*	*Present Bride-price (in rupees)*
Irular (Tamil Nadu)	0.25	100
Sounti (Orissa)	3.00	40
Mahali (Orissa)	5.00	80
Mullukurumbe (Kerala)	5.50	100 onwards
Mal Paharia (Bihar)	12.00	20-50
Kurumba (Karnataka)	32-80	200-210
Binjhal (Orissa)	60-100	400
Bhil (Rajasthan)	60-100, 120	300-1000
Panchcha Maleyelee (Tamil Nadu)	10.50	100-300

Many castes on the lower rungs of the hierarchy and some on the middle rungs also have a tradition of bride-price. As they come under the influence of Sanskritic values they tend to give up their custom and instead adopt the custom of dowry. Table 4.5 gives the SC, ST and non SC giving bride-price in different regions.

TABLE - 4.5
SOME TRIBES AND CASTES PAYING BRIDE-PRICE IN DIFFERENT REGIONS

Zone	*Scheduled Tribes*	*Scheduled Castes*	*Non-Scheduled Caste Hindus*
Southern	29	36	49
Eastern	45	7	2
Northern	3	9	9
Western	34	5	5
Central	5	2	—
	116	59	65

Analytically speaking, payment in cash and kind to the bride's father by the bridegroom's father is made in exchange for the authority over the bride which passes from her kin group to the bridegroom's kin group. The idea of compensation for the loss of a productive worker is also implicit in it. This lends some status to a daughter. Data show that so far as the girls' status in her natal group is concerned, in the communities which follow the custom of bride-price, a daughter is not regarded as a burden, and parents do not have to dread the time when she will have to be married. At her departure a daughter is likely to bring some material wealth. Birth of a daughter is, therefore, not regarded as some kind of a calamity. However, there is a custom of buying a wife in the transaction of bride-price. The fact that wealth has been spent to bring her home is not easily forgotten. When a woman leaves her husband and goes to another man, in the settlement of the amount of compensation to be paid by the latter, a reference to the amount of bride-price paid by the former husband comes into the picture too. This certainly speaks for the relatively low status of the woman *vis-a-vis* man. In spite of it, in these societies the woman has some bargaining power in regard to her relationship in the husband's house. The man cannot drive her too hard or else she will leave and he will have to pay bride-price to bring another wife. The compensation that he will get for her will not be the same as the bride-price that he will have to pay.

Among the underprivileged sections, the custom of bride price often places a man and his family in debt. It has been responsible for pushing many tribal and caste groups into the clutches of moneylenders. It is well known that in South India the landless farm labourers owed their almost permanent servitude to particular landowning families for generations because of debts incurred during marriage and death. It is reported that among some Scheduled Castes of Uttarkashi region a wife may be sent for prostitution to clear the debt incurred in her own marriage.

Both from the point of view of improvement in the condition of life of the people and for changing the conception of woman as someone's possession, the custom of bride-price needs to be eradicated. In fact the law aimed at prohibition of dowry is directed against bride-price also.

With a raise in social status by economic prosperity or regular wage earning and under the influence of the high prestige groups who practise dowry, many castes of the lower and middle rungs and even some tribal groups are shifting towards dowry. When it is adopted by the well-to-do families in the caste, the poorer ones also succumb to this change for it becomes a trend in the marriage market. The peasants of the village in Karnataka have changed over from bride-wealth to dowry over the last fifteen years or so. In Andhra Pradesh, the Golla or the caste of cowherds and nomadic Lambadas have been gradually changing to dowry. This was also confirmed by our tour of the Himachal Pradesh. Various villages studied by individual scholars and the Socio-Economic Survey Division of the Census of India have reported this trend. Whereas the people changing over to the form of dowry consider this a matter of prestige, the result of it is to make the daughter a liability. A girl's value to her husband and the in-laws is enhanced when she is accompanied by a substantial dowry. Epstein's study of the social life of peasants of Karnataka clearly shows that withdrawal of women from productive activities along with absence of training of girls in agricultural work is one of the potent factors contributing towards a change over from bride-wealth to dowry.

Dowry

Technically, dowry is what is given to the son-in-law or to his parents on demand either in cash or in kind. There are baffling regional variations in people's understanding of dowry. From the point of view of women's status the custom of dowry has to be looked at as constituting (1) what is given to the bride, and often settled beforehand and announced openly or discreetly. The gift, though given to the bride, may not be regarded exclusively as her property; (2) what is given to the bridegroom before and at marriage; and (3) what is presented to the in-laws of the girl. The settlement often includes the enormous expenses incurred on travel and entertainment of the bridegroom's party.

In the continued relationship between the two families, gift-giving characterizes the occasions of visits, fasts and festivals, and ceremonies like those associated with marriage, childbirth, initiation, etc., particularly in the first few years of marriage. It is a matter of general observation and experience that in such gift-giving, the bride's family is under compulsion and heavy pressure. These subsequent expenses are often regarded as making up for the deficiencies in the dowry and can cause severe hardship to the girl's parents. In the first few years of marriage, the girl's treatment in her husband's house is linked to these gifts. Thus according to Goody and Tambia in *Dowry and Bridewealth*: "Dowry is not one isolated payment but one array of gifts given over time. But it is also clear that amongst the ways of payment that constitute dowry, that given at the time of marriage is most important and conspicuous."

Dowry is linked with a number of social and cultural elements which sanction, justify or explain the practice. It has been viewed as a kind of premortem inheritance of the daughter who has to leave her natal family to join another but has some rights over the former. Dowry thus stresses the notion of female property and female right to property.

Both among the Hindu and the Muslim communities, this notion of dowry as the realization that daughter's right is prevalent. It is commonly expressed that claim to dowry takes care of a daughter's right to inheritance given by *Islam*. In Hindu law, a daughter's claim to maintenance in the joint property included her marriage portion with the help of which she could be married properly. An important ingredient of *Stridhan* are the gifts given to her by the bride's relatives during and after marriage. In many communities in the South and Maharashtra, such as Mangalorean

Christians, Tamil Brahmins, *Deshasth* Brahmins, the bridegroom's parents customarily buy the ornaments to be given to the new daughter-in-law out of cash received from her father.

A daughter should have something to fall back upon in times of crises, and also for setting up her house. This aspect is so deep-rooted in the minds of the people that ornaments, particularly of gold are regarded as "security". Ornaments impart to a girl a special position in the in-law's house. The bride's parents associate their own prestige with these valuables. In the upper castes of Tamil Nadu and Karnataka, diamond eartops constitute the most prestigious item of jewellery to be given along with a pair of gold bracelets and maybe a gold necklace.

It is not considered odd for the bridegroom's mother or other relatives to examine the jewellery on the person of the bride and comment on it. All over India, jewellery (gems, gold and silver) is given importance. There is a new trend in more sophisticated urban families to give cash or savings certificates, but jewellery remains the most accepted form of security, since it also has an exhibitive value.

Among the landowning castes of Andhra Pradesh like the Reddy and the Kamma, or the Paganeri, and the Ambalakkareu of Tamil Nadu, a father may give to the daughter land and jewellery. The cash has to be given to the bridegroom's father or the bridegroom himself, but land is registered in the name of the daughter. During our tour of Andhra Pradesh, we received two points of view. One group supported the practice on the ground that while cash or movables can be disposed of by the in-laws, land remains as secure property of the woman. The other group felt that as the land was looked after by the father or the brother, the income from it that reaches the woman depends on the whims of the former. This often reduces the woman's share, particularly after the father's death.

Pots and pans and cots and beddings are important items included in bridal gifts. These are mostly regarded as belonging to the couple. In the matter of utensils, however, customs differ. In North India, where there has been a tradition of large utensils being given at the time of marriage to the daughter, they are generally in the control of the in-laws.

Living in the social milieu of inequality, there is a genuine desire on the part of parents to see their children well-placed. "It was a matter of preserving the status of a daughter as well as the son. Sons might inherit all the productive capacity but the daughters had to be assured of marriage that would provide them with the same (or better) standard of life to which they were accustomed". The daughters thus have to be endowed with some property, generally moveables. Transfer of wealth at the time of marriage enables a girl to enter into a desirable match. Hypergamy is based on consideration of status by birth. We find that caste groups following hypergamy have had a high incidence of dowry.

In the past few decades there has been a diversification of occupations within endogamous groups, and a sharp rise in economic and social inequality between their members. This has been one of the most important inducements for dowry, and operates at all level of the society. The amount of wealth that is involved may range from a few hundreds to lakhs of rupees but its weight on the persons is not substantially different. This motive is often expressed in the form of a fond desire of the parents to see that their daughter is not placed in conditions to which she is not accustomed. Whether it is about working in the fields and carrying water, cooking and washing clothes, or being accustomed to the use of a refrigerator, car, and air-conditioner, similar arguments operate. Desire for special mobility for the daughter and indirectly for the parental family is also very strong.

The most common rite associated with Hindu marriage is *kanyadan*. It is recommended in the *Shastras* that she be duly adorned with jewellery and then gifted. This is related to the desire to obtain security and good status for the daughter. Increasing the value of the girl with jewellery and household goods is especially prevalent in these sections of Indian society. Irrespective of religion, in which women are homebound and do not contribute to the economy of the family in terms of gainful work.

According to Hindu *Shastras* the meritorious act of *Dana* or ritual gift remains incomplete till the receiver is given a *Dakshina*. So whenever a bride is given over to the bridegroom, he has to be given something in cash or kind. This *Vardakshina* has assumed enormous proportions. The bridegroom and his kin group are believed to have done a favour by accepting the girl in their fold, for marriage with an appropriate person in the path of honour for a girl. They, therefore, deserve to be honoured with gifts. They are higher in status by virtue of their being bride-takers. In the south of India and in Maharashtra, there is some exchange of gifts between the two parties. In Bengal, close women relatives of the girl are honoured with some presents. But nowhere are the parties equal, the proportion of the gifts for the bridegroom and his people being much larger. Non-Hindu communities also tend to manifest these regional variations.

In North India, what the bridegroom's parents bring for the bride is supposed to go into the bridegroom's family because the bride is joining his family. In the South, traditionally there is greater respect for *streedhan* which includes also what has been represented by the husband's family. But in groups which have the custom of divorce/separation and remarriage the general custom is to deprive the women of the valuables that she has received from her husband and his people, in case the marriage breaks up. Only if the husband is proved to have been at fault would the situation be different.

In actual practice it is difficult to locate the principles enumerated above in a reasonable form. As regards premortem inheritance, in dowry there is hardly any consideration of rightful share for the girl. It is demanded and given without regard to the actual wealth of the girl's father; it is also not equal for all the daughters and its payment often plunges the girl's father and brothers into debt.

This fact was brought to our notice in practically every State. The financial burden on the family worsened, with increasing rates of interest for such loans, which ranged from 5 per cent per month with security to 10 per cent in the absence of security. In exceptional cases the rate even goes up to 18 per cent. Of the expenses incurred by the father only a small portion consists of the belongings of the girl herself. Often even her jewellery is not in her control and it does not help her in times of crises. The household goods given at the time of marriage may not belong to her. In North India they may be disposed of by the in-laws, and even where they are utilized in her home, in the event of separation, nothing appears to belong finally to the woman.

The settlement of dowry has all the characteristics of a market transaction. What was originally intended to be a token *dakshina* for the bridegroom has now assumed enormous proportions. All over India, the committee heard the complaint that prevalence dowry is on the increase, and has penetrated communities and regions which did not practice it earlier. Its extent depends on the socio-economic status of the bridegroom and differs in different regions and in different caste groups. There are more or less well-defined grades of dowry for men in different professions. For example, men in the IAS and IFS in Orissa, Bihar, Uttar Pradesh and Punjab, belonging to well-to-do communities, can easily expect to get in cash and kind, at least a lakh of rupees. Business executives rank next. Engineers and doctors stand lower in these matters than the business executives. This class seems to expect that marriage would bring them not only a partner but also all the things needed to set up a modern household, such as a car, refrigerator, stereo system. These groups serve as pacesetters and naturally influence those below. Thus, a peon or a clerk would demand such things as a bicycle, a transistor and wrist watch. A scooter is a common item of gift to the son-in-law in the groups at the middle level. In villages too, there are similar demands.

Among Muslims of many regions the custom of giving cash to the bridegroom is prevalent. It is so in Kerala among patrilineal Muslims. In Andhra Pradesh this money is known as "Jode Ka Paisa", i.e. cash given for the bridegroom's outfit. In ordinary middle-class families this is settled in thousands. A general understanding is that this money is to be used for the expenses of marriage on the bridegroom's side. It is customary for the bridegroom to present sets of clothes and jewellery to the bride and give at least a feast after the bride is brought home. Socio-economic status of the families of the bride and the bridegroom and education and earning potential of the bridegroom are important determinants of the amount. In many parts of the country, the bridegroom is given cash after the 'Nikah' ceremony. This is called "Salami". The orthodox Christians of Kerala and the Catholics of Mangalore and Goa also have the custom of dowry, and expenses of marriage for both the parties are to be borne by the bride's people. The Christians of Mangalore follow their pre-conversion custom of *Kanyadan*, and their gift-giving puts heavy pressure on the bride's parents. It is reported that in Kerala the custom of dowry makes marriage near to impossible for many Christian girls belonging to large families. They may choose the ecclesiastical line or may leave the State in search of jobs, particularly opting for nursing. Many of them earn their dowry.

There is a distinct trend among middle-class girls to take up clerical or teaching jobs, nursing, or working as sales girls to earn their dowry in urban areas. The committee was told about it specifically in Kerala, Orissa, Bihar, Mumbai, UP and Delhi.

Dowry may also be demanded in the form of residential accommodation in places like Mumbai and Calcutta. Financial support for foreign education, or for setting up business is not uncommon. In a village near Delhi, we were told that motor cars were in great demand for ultimately to be put to use as taxis.

It is a disturbing trend that the girls themselves aspire to have their household set up in a grand style by the parents and to have clothes, jewellery, furniture and vehicle, etc. This is supposed to enhance the girl's status in the in-laws family. There is some truth in it for she has to face comparisons of gifts received by the brothers of her husband on the occasion of their marriages. A daughter-in-law's treatment is also related to the amount of dowry she has brought. This trend is spreading all over even among those do not practise dowry.

Desire for ostentation and sense of prestige and status have contributed to an increase in wedding expenses incurred by the parents. This works both ways; the parents of the girl try to excel in ostentation and the boy's party also make fantastic demands. The Committee encountered a most ridiculous situation close to the capital city of India in which the bride's parents had to spend thousands of rupees to satisfy the demand of the bridegroom's party that a helicopter must be arranged for them to come to the wedding.

Both in villages as well as towns parents offer certain justifications for demanding and accepting dowry. First, since they have to give dowry for the daughters, they are, in a way, forced to ask for dowry for their sons. Second, the fathers of educated boys like to get back the amount they spent on the son's education. Some also argue that owing to changed circumstances in which a son generally has a separate establishment and has a job somewhere away from home, the parents cannot expect much help from him, and so they consider his marriage as the major occasion on which their investment in his education can be recovered.

It is disconcerting to find that education has hardly had any liberalizing influence on the minds of the people in respect of dowry. On the contrary education has willy-nilly increased the scourge of dowry both in rural as well as in urban areas. An educated boy, and more so, one whose education and specialised training have helped him in acquiring a lucrative source of earning in life, expects a higher amount of dowry. The girl's parents on their part want to buy a good future for their daughter. It is often possible in some of these cases to delink the boy's parents' socio-economic status from the boy's status, and parents of girls compete among themselves for such a boy.

Education of girls also increases dowry, though indirectly. An educated girl aspires to marry someone who is better qualified; her parents also have similar aspirations. There is hesitation on the part of young men to marry better educated girls. In fact this is common expectation in an arranged marriage that a boy should be better qualified than a girl. Thus, the more educated a girl is, the more qualified a husband she needs. This necessitates greater dowry. In such situations, parents of the girls often feel almost cheated in educating their daughters. Of course, where the girl is allowed to earn and is capable of earning her own dowry, education may be an advantage, but it does not lessen the dowry. Only where a girl has taken up a career or has a permanent job will the boy's relatives be satisfied with a modest dowry. This clearly indicates the relation of dowry with economic dependence which is associated with women who are principally housewives. Dowry encourages the belief that regards the value of women's work in the home as non-productive.

Although, in the context of the family, dowry may appear to give a certain status to the woman who is fortunate enough to be able to bring more of it, the custom reflects upon and helps in perpetuating the inferior status of women in the society. In her natal home a girl is considered a liability, and consequently a drain on the family's resources. This has its effect on the socialization of children. There is traditionally sanctioned discrimination between boys and girls in the family with respect to food, medical care, etc. The enlightened sections may find this unimaginable but its truth cannot be denied. In the sphere of education, the middle classes all over India give more importance to boys' education and whenever a choice has to be made because of scarce resources, it is the boy who is likely to win in preference to girls, irrespective of the relative capabilities of the two. Undoubtedly, dowry is a big impediment in the progress of education of girls.

The present trend which comprises all kinds of objects of utility, comfort, and luxury (and also of obvious ostentation and false prestige) in dowry, the subtle demands for cash, assurances of 'decent marriage', and ways of conveying to the boy's people the direct and indirect gains that would accrue to them through a particular match, have all a strong flavour of market transaction. It is difficult to pinpoint what is bought and sold : a secure future and leisure for the daughter? Or transfer of responsibility of the girl who was hitherto a liability to her parents? What is more than clear, however, is that girls have to face an extremely unfair competition, in which their own worth is hardly recognized. The prospects of marriage produce considerable strain on the girls during their childhood and adolescence.

It is interesting to see how the values inculcated in the society operate to perpetuate the evil. A folksong of eastern UP says, "Let my daughter be married in a family where she will be swinging on a swing all the time". A rich girl's stereotyped ambition is that after marriage she should have nothing to do but sit on a comfortable mattress and chew betel. Most certainly these ideas set standards of desirability for others. It is revealing that the committee during its tour in Rajasthan found that in a girl's college, few girls could be counted on the tips of one's fingers looked forward only to a respectable and secure marriage so that they would not need to work for a living. With progressive standardization of lifestyles and greater communication between groups and communities, the values of a high consumption society, with its false ideas of prestige are influencing other sections also.

A notable feature of our society, which is closely related to dowry, is the involvement of man's prestige in the kind of work that the women of his house are required to do. That is how the norms for women of properties and business classes and also those belonging to the official class, include them to lead an almost parasitic existence. The farmers all over the country have been known to withdraw their women from the fields as soon as they become a little prosperous. Similarly the aspirant middle-class in urban areas are tending to withdraw their women from the area of gainful work, as soon as they have a stable source of income.

Dowry is an all-India phenomenon, but it is possible to identify its differential impact and working. There are some communities and groups (excluding those who follow the custom of paying bride-price) who have been relatively free from the menace of this custom. To give a few examples: most Muslim communities, the non-Catholic Christian groups outside Kerala and the Parsees do not practise the custom of dowry. The Nagar Brahmins of Gujarat, the Khatris of UP and the Mathur Kayasthas did not customarily settle marriage transactions in cash or kind. Several castes in Maharashtra also fall in this category. But today people belonging to these groups are also adopting dowry. It is rampant in Punjab, UP, Bihar and Rajasthan and to a lesser degree in Bengal, Orissa, and Madhya Pradesh. Here, as mentioned earlier, the flow of gifts is almost unidirectional. Aggarwals and other Vaisya groups in the Hindi-speaking areas, the Rajputs and the Kayasthas and the landowning castes of Bihar and UP practise dowry. Among the Kanyakubja Brahmins, the Rajputs, the Padidars and Anavil Brahmins of Gujarat and other communities, hypergamy has resulted in establishing high rate of dowry. In thc South the following groups are known for demanding and giving high dowries: the Reddis, the Kammas and the Velmas as also the traders and well-to-do Brahmins of

Andhra Pradesh the Naidus, the Brahmins, the Vellalas, the Mudaliars and the Chettiars of Tamil Nadu; Brahmins, Vaisyas and some Lingayat groups in Karnataka and the various Christian groups in Kerala. In Bengal all the upper castes practise dowry. Dowry among the Muslims previously consisted mainly of clothes, jewellery, and articles of household use of the daughter; and the other principal item of expenditure used to be entertainment of the bridegroom's party and celebration of the wedding. In North India and in the princely States marriage of a daughter had always involved substantial expenditure. But now, even among the Muslims dowry is demanded, though may be in a more subtle form. There is in fact no difference now in pattern and motives for conspicuous consumption and dowry, either religionwise or castewise:

Black money and unaccounted earnings have given a fillip to dowry during the post-Independence era. A new class of noveau rich has emerged that buys a daughter's future with dowry, to raise its own social status by entering into marriage alliances with families of high status. These people are keen to get rid of the black money, so they spend it lavishly during the wedding. In this process the level of expectation in the marriage market has changed altogether. Men of honest means and moderate income find it extremely difficult to remain so in order to compete with this class that has a free flow of black money. The committee received innumerable complaints from common people, who are fully aware of this situation and are also very bitter about it.

We would like to emphasize that the spirit of dowry and the transactions involved in it, particularly at the upper middle-class and upper class levels go against the goal of a socialistic society. Such value patterns of marriage expenses tend to influence other socio-economic groups. It is an undeniable fact that excepting a few rich, almost everybody has to spend beyond his means where dowry is involved. During our visits, women all over the country complained bitterly about the increasing burden of dowry and also told us that many girls had to remain unmarried because of this evil practice. The limited means of the parents and the abnormal demands for dowry impose a great strain on the minds of some young girls. In Orissa some doctors reported to us the increasing incidence of nervous breakdowns in this group. Elsewhere too we even heard of some cases of suicides by young girls who were faced with this problem.

Material considerations like wealth, jobs and professional opportunities have always formed one of the important incentives for marital unions even in countries where marriage is supposed to be based on love. What is deplored in the case of dowry is its compulsive character and material transactions in actual consideration for marriage. We require some concrete measures to do away with this state of affairs. The attack on dowry has to be multipronged. Our measures, though aiming at proximate ends, should take a determined step forward towards an egalitarian society. Social consciousness needs to be aroused particularly amongst women, to enable them to understand that by encouraging dowry they are perpetuating the inequality of the sexes. Reforms in marriage customs to simplify the ceremony, increasing opportunities for employment, condemnation of the ideal of a parasitic existence for women, a reassessment of the value of household work and home-making, as socially and economically productive, and the enforcement of the Anti-dowry Act, are some of the measures necessary to fight the increasing problem of dowry.

The problem of dowry cannot be solved only by educating the young. Therefore, it is necessary to examine the present law against dowry and do away with the loopholes which have made it totally ineffective. The present law may be regarded as only proof of the growing social awareness about the evil custom of dowry. It is essential that acceptance of money, property, or goods in consideration of marriage be made a cognizable offence. It will then activate social service organisations to take up the case and pursue infringements of the law.

In banning dowry it does not seem feasible to ban gifts for the daughter herself. The present law does not ban it, nor can future law prohibit it totally. This is likely to pose a difficult problem. This issue will have to be tackled at the level of mass education and social pressure. It will be necessary to keep record of things given to the daughter so that they remain her possessions and are not appropriated by the in-laws.

If public display of gifts is banned, it may hold unhealthy competition in check. It will spare the bride's parents much humiliation. This is not a minor issue. In Gujarat it is common practice to send round invitations to women to see the gifts being given to the bride and her in-laws. In many other areas, though not mentioned in such specific terms, there are a few occasions for which invitations are sent specifically meant for displaying the dowry. This must arouse strong social censure. We feel the women's organisations can play an active role here.

Ostentatious celebrations involving enormous expenditure on food, lighting and entertaining should also be banned. Viewed in terms of national interests, this is a drain on national resources and public amenities which are in short supply. Control over the expenditure on weddings should be viewed as an anti-inflationary measure. It is here that the interests of women and the nation converge.

Compulsory registration of marriage for all may gradually lead to simplification of rituals and would help eliminate occasions for gift giving. Further, it will be easier for the young to break the stranglehold of endogamy. During our tours, many persons, both men and women observed that intercaste marriage is one of the ways to fight the evil of dowry. For this it is necessary to build up strong public opinion in favour of such marriages. This would naturally go against endogamy and hypergamy wherever it is prevalent, and would lead to raising the women's status by undermining the importance of dowry.

It is necessary to devise ways and means to make women conscious of the limitations of their self-image. Whether they are transferable assets, as in the case of bride-price, or liabilities whose value has to be enhanced so that they become acceptable, women are demeaned. It is regrettable that women not only concur with but even encourage this practice. It is imperative that programmes on adult education and mass media should be purposefully framed to make the women understand the implications of both dowry and bride-price.

There is also need for a separate machinery to enforce the proper implementation of legal measures connected with marriage and dowry.

Widowhood

It is often mentioned that the problem of widow remarriage is the problem only of a section of society. It is necessary to ascertain how large this section is. In the absence of use of caste as a category for the collection of census data since 1941 onwards, population figures for 1931 census have been used to obtain some idea of the proportion of Hindu population which traditionally did not practise remarriage of widows. Population of these castes was added together and its percentage to the total Hindu population in 1931 was worked out. This is only an approximation. Our calculations show that at least 13.9 per cent of the Hindu population in 1931 did not customarily practise widow remarriage. This percentage is enough proof that the problem does not concern the whole of the Hindu society. But if we have a look at absolute figures (3,32,56,068) and think of the rate of population growth since 1931, it certainly does not appear to be an insignificant problem.

Furthermore, it is these groups who have served as reference groups for society, and have also been instrumental in bringing about legal reforms which are to affect the whole society. One example should suffice to bring this point home. There is enough evidence to tell us that only an infinitesimal number of widows in the general population were immolating themselves, that outside ruling and priestly families, the custom did not have a wide appeal. But in certain parts of the country reverence is shown for women who committed *sati* in the past. Commemoration stones of these acts can still be found in some regions. Newly married couples are sometimes taken to *sati* stone to show reverence and obtain blessings.

Even among those who allow widow remarriage, many groups do not look upon it favourably. At the most, it is accepted as a solution of the problem of maintenance of a widow. Among 'high class' Muslims too widow remarriage is frowned upon.

According to 1951 census there were 22 million widows i.e. 123 widows per 1000 females. According to 1961 census 10.8 per cent of total female population consisted of widows as opposed to 3.70 per cent widowers. The census of 1971 recorded 8 million widowers as against 23 million widows.

TABLE - 4.6

(A) PERCENTAGE OF WIDOWED PERSONS, 1971

Age Group	*Males/Females*	*Rural*	*Urban*	*Total*
All ages	Males	3.2	1.9	2.9
	Females	7.9	8.9	8.7
0—9	—	—	—	—
10—14	M	0.03	0.02	0.03
	F	0.07	0.03	0.06
15—19	M	0.18	0.05	0.15
	F	0.37	0.23	0.33
20—24	M	0.74	0.31	0.63
	F	0.95	0.71	0.90
25—29	M	1.40	0.69	1.23
	F	1.94	1.51	1.85
30—34	M	2.35	1.26	2.09
	F	4.06	3.46	3.95
35—39	M	3.09	1.63	2.77
	F	7.17	6.25	8.68
40—44	M	5.03	2.90	4.57
	F	14.34	13.46	14.18
45—49	M	6.45	3.94	5.92
	F	20.31	20.93	20.42
50—54	M	10.42	6.67	9.70
	F	36.28	27.73	26.53
55—59	M	12.50	9.07	11.87
	F	40.52	43.72	41.06
60—64	M	18.12	14.69	17.54
and above	F	62.21	63.98	62.50

Source: Census of India 1971 Series 1 - India Part II Special

(B) AGE-GROUP WISE PROPORTION OF WIDOWS TO WIDOWERS

Age Group	*Males per 100 females*
All ages	36
10—14	60
15—19	52
20—24	69
25—29	65
30—34	54
35—39	43
40—44	37
45—49	35
50—54	31
55—59	33
60—64	30

Source: Census of India 1971 Series 1 - India Part II Special.

This proportion has not changed drastically in the 1971 census. Tables 4.6 (A) and (B) make this clear. Presence of children is a positive deterrent to remarriage of mothers, particularly after they have crossed the age of 35 or 40 years. The fear of losing the children and not being able to have them with her is very real for a woman, and this applies to all women except those in matrilineal communities.

The condition of widows in our country may be examined from two angles : social and economic. These two are interrelated and are often indistinguishable from one another. Social attitude towards widows differs at different socio-economic levels with regard to details.

A change in the lifestyle of women after they are widowed is characteristic of Indian society, though there are regional and group variations at different socio-economic levels. Restrictions imposed on Hindu widows have been mentioned earlier. It should be emphasized here that with the conception of man as the breadwinner and the woman as his dependent, the married state for a woman is considered fortunate and conversely widowhood is associated with great misfortune. Lifelong mourning is imposed on them. The signs of the married state have to be removed from the person of the widow. In many communities this process is made specially painful. It emphasizes that her existence has been rendered worthless by the death of the husband. The Muslims of respectable families also follow regional practices of making a widow distinguishable. Other religious groups follow this behaviour pattern in varying degrees.

An important purpose of these restrictions on a widow is to make her unattractive. Reactions of the respondents in our survey to a question as to whether a young widow should be required to change her mode of dress are revealing. Combining partial and full approval we find that 59.52 per cent Hindus approve of such a change, whereas 61.49 per cent of Muslims, 62.16 per cent Jains and 52.94 per cent Parsees fall in this category. Though low in comparison to the above groups, the percentage of Christians (44.21 per cent) approving of such a change is not negligible. Only 30 per cent of the Sikhs expressed the same opinion. This low percentage among Sikhs may be due to the fact that most respondents belonged to Chandigarh which is a modern city. The lowest percentage is among the tribals, 27.78 per cent. Even today the social norm is that a widow should look different from a married woman in every manner. Even in educated circles deviation from this norm on the part of a widow is commented upon.

Association of inauspiciousness with widowhood still continues. Widows themselves avoid taking an active part in ceremonial occasions. For instance, among the Bohras, a widowed mother would not break the coconut for her son's birthday. Responses to our question indicate that there is some disapproval on the widow's participation in auspicious ceremonies. As many as 23.41 per cent Hindus disapprove of such participation while 10.14 per cent do so only partially. Over 22 per cent Jains, 13.13 per cent Muslims and 16.33 per cent Christians disapprove of widows participation. As against 58.87 per cent Hindus who approve, there are 71.94 per cent Muslims, 71.88 per cent Christians and 88.24 per cent Parsees who approve such participation.

A very interesting pattern is seen in the response according to caste groups : the percentage of upper caste Hindus approving of widows participation is the highest (63.45 per cent), next come the middle caste Hindu (60.43 per cent), then the lower caste Hindu (58.28 per cent) and last came the Scheduled Castes (50.66 per cent).

Thus, it appears that the distinction between a married and a widowed woman is kept more alive at the lower social levels; in fact there are definite ritual occasions in which widowed women are debarred from participating. However, these women, if young, are expected to remarry. Among Muslims if a son dies during the lifetime of his father, then his widow does not get any share of the property.

It is regrettable that though the condition of widows in our society caused such serious concern to the social reformers, and the Widow Remarriage Act was passed as early as 1856, societal attitude to this unfortunate group has not registered any appreciable change in all these decades. Immolation may have stopped, and cases of remarriage of child widows may have increased, but by and large, the condition of widows continues to be a blot on our society. The large group of widows, of all ages, whom we met in Varanasi, were in a state of destitution. Many of them had children. Only a few had any visible means of economic support. Allowances from the family were either negligible or non-existent. In the absence of any employable skills, most of them were depending on petty trades like making paper bags, packets of incense, selling *pakoras*, etc., earning an average income of Rs.15 to 20 per month. Some joined *'bhajan mandalies'* and earned about 37 paise in an evening and even that was not a regular income. Some were reduced to absolute penury.

The widows' scheme, adopted by the UP State Government, provides a small pension. According to the District Officer, only about 10 per cent of the recommended cases have received this pension. In their discussion with us, these women stated that though their lives were finished, neither they nor society had provided any protection or security for their children, whose future looked no less bleak than at present. We were informed by a member of the Gandhian Institute of Studies that some teenage daughters of these widows were employed as compositors by some of the small presses in Varanasi. They were mostly illiterate, and had to do their work by recognizing letters without being able to read which imposed tremendous strain on their eyes. He described their expressions as 'sightless' and 'vacant'.

Many of these widows had been sent by their families but family ties with brothers, sons or in-laws had gradually become tenuous. Some even said that they had run away to escape from ill-treatment by relatives. The older ones, no longer able to look after themselves, were prey to cheats. When they fell sick, the only care they could get was from some neighbours belonging to the same group who are in no position to look after others. Some of the worst cases are left before the Ramakrishna Mission Old People's Home. The latter, being already fully occupied, has stopped further admissions, hence even this avenue for care of these old and destitute women is now restricted.

According to the Gandhian Institute, which conducted a small investigation, there are approximately 5000 destitute or semi-destitute widows in the city of Varanasi. Majority of them come from Bengal but some were also from South India and Maharashtra.

We have recorded our impression of this group as a symbol of the status that our society allots to widows.

For those who have any property, however, legal reform securing the right of widows to a share of the husband's property has improved the condition considerably. The decision of the government to provide family pensions to widows of government servants during their lifetime, with additional allowances for children during their minority has also guaranteed a modicum of security.

Age at Marriage

Although the past few decades record a distinct rise in the mean age of marriage for women in India, the problem continues to be serious as is evident from the percentage of married persons (which would also include widowed persons) even in the age groups 10-14 and 15-19. Table 4.7 gives the percentage distribution of ever married persons according to sex and age during 1961 and 1971.

TABLE - 4.7
THE PERCENTAGE DISTRIBUTION OF EVER MARRIED PERSONS ACCORDING TO SEX AND AGE — 1961 AND 1971

Age Group	*Rural*				*Urban*			
	1971		*1961*		*1971*		*1961*	
	Male	*Female*	*Male*	*Female*	*Male*	*Female*	*Male*	*Female*
10—14	5.31	13.79	7.92	22.37	1.50	4.21	2.04	6.99
15—19	21.06	63.09	43.50	85.80	7.38	36.24	26.90	70.60
20—24	55.91	93.78	60.75	95.54	32.78	80.90	41.08	87.28

In rural areas in the 10-14 age-group, 13.79 per cent girls are already married, while in the 15-19 age group, 63.9 per cent are married. In urban areas this percentage is much less: 4.21 per cent in the age group 10-14 and 36.24 per cent in the 15-19 age group. According to another source, in the 12.5-17.5 age group, 45.21 per cent girls are married as compared to 13.29 per cent boys.

One redeeming feature of child marriage in India is that customarily the consummation of marriage takes place after the girl reaches puberty. It may be noted, however, that this age does not necessarily tally with the legal minimum age of marriage. The magnitude of this phenomenon is not easy to measure for the simple reason that people are not able to report their correct age in the census.

Low age of marriage is related with the near-universality of marriage in India. In a sense marriage is not an individual decision but a cultural one. Only 0.5 per cent of women never marry. Since all girls have to be married off, the thought of their marriage has to be entertained from their birth or early childhood. Early marriage is accompanied by seemingly easy solutions for a number of problems. Rules of endogamy prescribe that marriage should be arranged within a certain group and other norms of prescription, preference and proscription (such as close kin marriages, *gotra*, clan and village exogamy, and marriage within one's class) are best taken care of in the case of early marriage. Leaving the girl to decide when to marry may also mean her deciding whom to marry and her choice may not conform to the traditional norms and rules. Betrothals and early marriages are encouraged towards this end.

Closely connected with the concern for maintenance of group boundaries, is the desire to preserve the purity of women. The biological facts of gestation and lactation make repudiation of motherhood next to impossible. The emphasis on the purity of women springs from this. Chastity gets strong emphasis among Muslims also and with emphasis on purity of blood, early marriage appears to be the best solution, particularly for those who do not keep their women secluded. This concern for the purity of women was reflected in the compulsion of pre-puberty marriage among the Brahmins; for whom its violation results in ostracism. A father who could not get his daughter married before puberty was believed to commit a grave sin. In spite of strong opposition to early marriage from the reformers, it remained popular till the decade of twenty of the present century. Because of the ban on widow remarriage among the upper groups, early marriage was nothing less than a curse. Although not as low as among the Brahmins, age of marriage among the Kshatriya castes and trading castes was also fairly low. This is made clear by Table 4.8 presenting the mean age at marriage for the four groups: the Brahmin, the Kshatriya, the trading castes and the Scheduled Castes.

TABLE - 4.8
THE MEAN AGE AT MARRIAGE OF CENSUS SYNTHETIC COHERTS: INDIA AND SELECTED STATES AVERAGE FOR 1901—31

	Brahmin Caste		*Warrior Caste*		*Trading Caste*		*Scheduled Caste*	
	Male	*Female*	*Male*	*Female*	*Male*	*Female*	*Male*	*Female*
Assam	23.47	12.15	—	—	—	—	24.65	11.90
Bengal	21.53	12.16	—	—	19.92	12.51	18.46	11.20
Bihar & Orissa	19.57	11.77	21.10	13.24	21.32	14.30	13.81	11.14
Bombay	21.59	12.58	20.79	12.31	20.57	13.78	16.59	10.21
Hyderabad	17.06	11.82	16.96	11.45	—	—	15.90	12.30
Madhya Bharat	17.54	12.13	17.39	13.26	16.12	12.64	—	—
Madhya Pradesh	20.50	12.48	17.15	11.73	18.60	11.73	14.93	10.38
Madras	20.73	12.33	—	—	22.21	16.61	22.25	15.67
Mysore	22.00	12.12	25.31	14.82	22.36	12.70	24.37	16.42
Punjab	21.79	14.59	25.12	13.81	20.38	14.51	17.99	12.24
Rajputana	20.12	13.12	22.73	13.56	19.47	13,57	17.10	12.76
Uttar Pradesh	18.06	13.48	18.92	13.20	18.14	12.84	17.58	12.77
Travancore Cochin	22.43	15.63	28.32	17.22	23.20	16.62	23.82	18.76
All India (unweighted average) of reporting States).	20.49	12.80	21.38	13.46	20.21	13.80	18.95	12.98

Sources: Census of India, 1901, Vol.I, Part II, pp.353-366: Census of India, 1911, Vol. I, Part II, pp.242-283 Census of India, 1921, Vol.I, Part II, pp.108-167; Census of India, 1931, Vol.I, Part II pp.160-181 From Aggarwala, S.N. *Age at Marriage in India* (1962) p. 176.

It is striking to note that among the Brahmin and the Scheduled Castes, the age of marriage was the lowest. As pointed out earlier, since 1931, there has been a gradual but distinct rise in the age of marriage, especially among middle and upper classes in the urban areas but the rise is not so noticeable among the Scheduled Castes.

Census has stopped collecting data for marital status of girls below the age of 10. Therefore, it is not possible to know the incidents of child marriage between the ages of 0 to 10 years. But in our tours, we came across a number of children below the age of 10, who were already married. We were also informed of marriages where the bride had to be placed on a *thali*. In a village in Darbhanga, we saw a girl of three in a Balwadi, wearing *sindur* mark. (In a factory in Indore that we visited, a baby of 18 months in a creche was already married).

One of the important factors connected with early marriage is that onset of puberty is regarded as the right age of marriage, as the girl is considered ready for maternity. The notion that a girl can be married with proper rites only when she is a virgin is also an important factor accounting for early marriage. Thus, for those, whose girls cannot be confined to the house as they have to share in the work outside, early marriage is necessary in order to ensure their reputation and protect them from motherhood before marriage. This association between relatively free movement of girls, and early marriage is fairly clear. Some social scientists have related the continuance of the custom of early marriage among Scheduled Castes with their helplessness in protecting their women from the lust of men of upper groups who have economic power over them.

Scarce resources also constitute an important reason for early marriage. Since the girls do not support the family, the responsibility in respect of them is transferred to another family as early as possible. Another reason given for early marriage is to enable the proper adjustment of girls in their conjugal family.

Though not the only factor, low age of marriage is responsible for population growth, low standard of health of women, and high mortality in the child-bearing age. It is essential to take strong action in this regard. Compulsory registration of marriage would never help to curb the evil of child marriages.

Early marriage and lack of education constitute a vicious circle. A determined effort will have to be made to educate the girls in rural areas, and those from lower socio-economic groups in urban areas, if the age of marriage of girls is to be raised. Education of both boys and girls will inevitably contribute to raising the age of marriage. An important measure will be to educate the people so that they learn to delink onset of puberty with preparedness for maternity.

In urban areas and for the well-to-do in rural areas, education and the need for employment of boys has raised the age of marriage and this has contributed substantially to the raising of age of marriage for girls. Thus, education of girls is both a cause and an effect of raising of age of marriage.

In studies of attitudes regarding age of marriage which were conducted mainly in educated urban middle and upper classes, the desirable age suggested for the marriage of girls broadly ranges from 16 to 24.

Child marriages do not pose such a problem among the tribes. Among the hill tribes, few girls are married before 15. Only a few tribes like the Bhumia, Mahalis, Omnatya, Bajuras, Tharuas, some Koyas and some sections of Gonds practise child marriage. Banjaras hold the betrothal early but do not marry their girls before the age of thirteen which is the age allowed by their *panchayat*. Marriage immediately after puberty is fairly common and among many tribes of Central and Western India—in fact the onset of puberty is associated with maturity.

Customary Marriages

Customary marriages are normally coterminous with easy forms of divorce, and secondary marriages. Secondary marriage of a widow or a separated or divorced woman is accompanied by a nominal ceremony, mostly signifying the renewal of the "married" state for the woman. Depending on the region, the gifts by the man consist of things like glass bangles, vermillion, nose ring, etc. A feast announces and accords social approval to the union. But often the union may start with the man bringing the woman to live with him or the woman entering his house and starting to live with him. Feast and ceremony would follow much later.

While marriages among the dominant higher castes are performed by ritual ceremonies, since marriage is recognized as a sacrament, there have also been various forms of customary marriages practised by other castes, which do not involve any rituals, but are based on simple practices. These marriages are fully accepted by the community. Throughout the Himalayan tracts, *Jhajra,* which means putting a ring in the bride's nose is the customary form of marriage. In the trans-Giri territory of Simur, regular marriage is termed *Jhajrath*. Earlier, marriage according to Hindu rites was unknown but now the well-to-do and respectable Kanet and Bhat families have adopted them. In Maharashtra, the poor people practise *Mohutur*, which is shortened form of marriage, not as sacred but a completely legal union. In some parts of Madhya Pradesh, if an unmarried girl elopes she may be married only by a simple ceremony which is used for secondary marriages. In Manipur, however, cases of elopement, which are then followed by a proper ceremonial marriage, are of frequent occurrence, and not disapproved by the community. These are only illustrations of various forms of customary marriage.

Where a woman leaves one man and goes to another, payment of compensation to the previous husband may be said to be characteristic of the majority of those castes, among whom secondary union is permitted. In many areas there is no formal divorce; when a woman goes to live with another man, who is willing to pay compensation for her to the previous husband, with a fine and feast to the caste or village, the union is recognized.

It has been brought to our notice that in some of these cases, where a compensation has to be paid by the new husband, the woman's decision is not always voluntary. We were told in Himachal Pradesh that in the *Reet* form of marriage while the former husband must consent to the remarriage of his wife to another man, the wife's consent to this exchange is not essential. There have been cases where she is compelled to it by the former husband or by her father as the case may be. The women who met us, both in urban and rural areas, were outspoken in their criticism of this practice. Similar cases of compulsion have been reported from Madhya Pradesh.

The tribals are governed by the customs of marriage and divorce of their respective tribes. In the case of primary marriages most tribes have a preference for marriage by negotiation, but there are also provision to accommodate unions which are established by elopement. We were told by members of the Wanchoo tribe in Arunachal Pradesh that though negotiation is preferred, if a girl is emphatic in her refusal to accept the groom chosen by her family, then her decision is accepted. We believe this is common among most tribes.

A popular custom in the tribes of the plains is to get a boy to serve and help the girl's household for a few years to earn his bride. It is in the subsequent unions that individual choice gets exercised. Going to live with another man, who pays a compensation to the previous husband, is equivalent to divorce and remarriage. There is considerable variation in customs regarding marriage and divorce among the tribals, but an examination clearly indicates that the two partners are not at par with each other. There is compensation for the loss of woman, and the mother has to leave her children behind. There is, however, no stigma on divorce and remarriage. The average age of marriage is also higher among tribals, and no marriage takes place before puberty.

REFERENCES

1. Kapur, Promila, *Marriage and the Working Women*, 1970.
2. Kutty, A.K., *Marriage and Kinship in an Islam Society*, 1972.
3. Leela Dube,. *Matriliny and Islam*, 1964.
4. Ramu, G.N., *Women, Work and Marriage in Urban India*, 1989.
5. Schneider and Gough, Matrilineal Kinship, 1961.
6. Shah, A.M., *Household Dimension of Family in India*, 1974.

Five

Changing Milieu and Roles of Women

While granting equality of rights to men and women in the polity, Indian society implicitly accepts a sharp distinction between men's spheres and women's spheres and between masculine roles and feminine roles. Realization of true parity between the sexes granted by the Constitution will be possible only when conceptions and attitudes of the people are brought at par with it.

An overview of masculine and feminine spheres and roles in our society suggests that the inventory of activities considered proper for women and expected of them is not uniform all over India. Some basic notions about male and female roles, however, appear to be common.

Women are primarily associated with the home and man with the outside world. As home-makers women are expected to look after domestic chores, such as cooking and serving food, processing and storage of food, and cleaning the house. Woman's contribution to productive activities or to actual earnings of the family varies at different socio-economic levels and in different regions. Thus women, whether they work in the fields, factories or mines, or work at construction sites, or those who are engaged in household industries, or in white collar jobs, all of them are expected to be home-makers along with those who confine themselves exclusively to home-making activities. Housewives and mothers are the feminine roles. In the cultural understanding of the people, homemaking like childbearing and also childrearing cannot be distinguished from femininity. In other words these are sex-linked roles for women.

According to convention, participation in decision making for the community and the exercise of political power is regarded exclusively as the man's sphere. This is clear from the entirely male composition of the traditional Panchayats, either of villages or of caste groups including caste-like groups among Muslims.

By and large manual work for one's own house is to be done

by women, as they are considered derogatory for men. They may perform them only under special circumstances, for instance men may cook when women are disabled by illness or confinement. For community feasts cooking by men from within the group is a common feature at the lower socio-economic levels. Cooking, tailoring or sewing can be taken up as a vocation by men. Thus, suitability of women for these tasks appears to be a myth.

Broad regional patterns which show that there is no uniformity in the type and quantum of work expected of women also point towards this. What a woman does in one society or region is often dubbed as non-feminine in another. Weaving is the monopoly of woman in the North Eastern Hill areas, whereas in the lower parts of Himachal Pradesh it is a male activity. In Maharashtra and parts of South India it is done by men and women together and the woman is an indispensable assistant. *Phulkari* work of the Punjab is a women's craft whereas embroidery in Kashmir is done only by men.

In agricultural activities there are significant regional differences in the parts played by men and women. It is generally stated that men are supposed to do the heavier work. This is a supposition or belief which is not borne out by facts or by a cross regional survey of India. Men's tasks are not necessarily more arduous. What is more important is that men do work which is considered more prestigious. Ploughing and sowing in many parts and all the work of transportation by bullockcart and large-scale marketing of produce are the domain of men. In the hills, women's contribution to the economy is distinctly higher than that of men, in addition to household work which is very burdensome, for example, bringing water from far-off places, keeping a vigil throughout the night to scare the wild animals away. "In Bashahr, Chamba and Mandi women help their mates in wood-chopping. While men fell the trees women slice the timber. They carry the timber on their backs from the place where it is sawed to the place from where it is to be floated down the river. They have been seen carrying logs weighing anywhere between 200 to 300 pounds with perfect ease and equanimity". These are the unpaid family workers of rural India.

In the middle-class (which constitutes an extremely

amorphous category) the spheres of men and women are more sharply defined. Ordinarily all the work that women do is viewed collectively as being an important component of feminine roles and it is not forgotten that they are being performed by those who have a certain identity in the context of the family, i.e. as mother, as wife, as sister, and so on. Since women are mostly confined to the domestic sphere, their work falls into entirely different sectors. Where the family business consists of grocery, knitwear, embroidery, snacks, and other things which can be made at home, women are the main workers behind the scene. These are the unpaid family workers who may not be returned in the census under the category of workers. Most of the work that women do in the domestic set up is semi-skilled. There is a clear differentiation between work done for one's own household and that done for others, so the question of doing this category of work for others does not arise. It is only in unfortunate circumstances that women of middle-classes, who have no other qualifications and skills, may be forced to do these jobs as a means of earning a livelihood; crafts like knitting, tailoring and embroidery are in some cases adopted by women to make small personal earnings, sometimes without the knowledge of husbands. Ideas of personal and family prestige are strong at this level; people take pride in the fact that their women do not go out of homes to work for others.

This traditional concept of women's role is gradually changing as girls have started taking up white collar jobs. In some families, the earnings of the girl are set aside for providing her dowry and marriage expenses, but gradually, the inhibition of the parents to be supported by the earnings of a daughter are also breaking down. There are extreme cases of parents not wanting the daughter to get married, as it would deprive them of her earnings.

Amongst the well-to-do also the spheres of men and women are well-defined and separate. Eventhough with domestic help, the burden of drudgery does not fall on the woman, but she is still expected to run the home and bring up the children. Her precise activities would depend upon a rural or urban setting, level of education norms of segregation and seclusion, notions of purity and pollution. Homemaking is raised to a fine art and trifling details assume exaggerated importance, but even here there is insistence on a role differentiation, according to conventions.

On the question intended to evoke responses on the pattern of division of labour by sex in the family, 84.1 per cent respondents said that cooking is entirely a woman's job; only 3.84 per cent said that it is shared equally. As for sweeping and cleaning the house only 3.94 per cent said that the work is equally shared and only 2.14 per cent said that the work of cleaning the utensils is equally shared. These two activities were undertaken only or mainly by men in less than 1 per cent cases. Washing of clothes is shared by men to some extent. In comparison to this, only 50.74 per cent respondents said that care of children was in the hands of women, either entirely or mainly; 28.90 per cent said it was shared equally, and 10.05 per cent said that men did it entirely. Sharing in decision making about the household expenditure reveals a different pattern. Only in 28.18 per cent cases, expenditure on food was decided entirely by women. Decision making seems to have been largely shared (48.48 per cent) by men and women. In 33.96 per cent cases decision about expenditure on education is entirely in the hands of men, as compared to 9.66 per cent cases in which it is mainly in the hands of women. Responses clearly indicate a pattern in which, besides equal sharing in decision making, more women take decisions about the kitchen, other domestic matters and matters concerning the future of the daughters. Men, rather than the women, more often exercise their judgement regarding choice of school, type of education and job the son should take. As is to be expected, various sociological and anthropological studies of village and of urban localities and communities clearly point towards male and female spheres of activity. For example, in Gore's sample of Aggarwal families in and around Delhi, women were expected to remain at home and look after the kitchen. 80 per cent of the women were busy exclusively with household work. They did not handle the money. Desai's findings based on the replies given by 369 married women students tell us that a majority of men did not share the household work. A study of 500 college students of Jhansi in UP brings out a sharp contrast between the daily routine of boys and girls, between the restrictions on girls and relative freedom of movement for boys and between the range of exposure to the outside world and to their travel.

Notions of distinctiveness between the spheres of men and women, patterns of division of labour, and expectations of differential behaviour between the sexes have a direct bearing on: the process of socialization, on opportunities provided for the education and training of girls, on the kinds of ideals projected before them, on the kinds of expectations they come to have from life, and on the way they conduct their lives.

In the process of preparation for adult roles the spheres are distinct. However, amongst the enlightened sections this distinction may not be emphasized, but even here feminine tasks and over all abilities are assumed to be different. A girl has to be prepared for feminine roles as conceived by the stratum to which she belongs. Parents also have to take note of the attitude of the world outside the home, and special protection is needed for girls.

In the middle-classes, distinction between femininity and masculinity gets crystallized for the children in the pattern of domestic responsibilities, distribution of financial resources, and planning for the future. Domestic work is the domain of women and in very few families are the boys asked to share it. They may be asked to lend a helping hand in making purchases and running errands, bringing medicine, and escorting sisters, but household chores are beneath their dignity. Boys interested in cooking, knitting, or embroidery hardly ever get any encouragement from the family members, instead they are often ridiculed and discouraged.

Girls are sent to school but they are not sufficiently motivated to achieve excellence; neglect of studies and lack of interest is easily condoned. Very few parents visualize a career for daughters. Their main interest lies in finding a good match for them. Still many parents view education as security for unforeseen eventualities. Even where school or college performance is praised, lack of interest in household work is not condoned. Girls have to live a constricted life. In allocation of scarce resources, a daughter's education is often the first casualty. Parents are not inclined to undergo the inconvenience and strains involved in giving proper facilities to the daughter for better performance. At this level also girls may have to drop out because of family circumstances such as mother's illness or death. Attending functions like weddings and other ceremonies are considered more important than a daughter's education.

In the middle-class families there is a premium on boys' education for it is essential to enable him to get a job. Parents are ready to make all kind of sacrifices for the education of boys. Despite all the misgivings of modern times, they still hope that their efforts will bring them comfort in old age. Various sociological studies clearly bring out the fact that if the family does not have enough resources, even if the girl is brighter her brother will be sent for higher education and she will be told that ultimately she has to mind the kitchen. In fact, what is not always stated in so many words is the culturally determined attitude, that conservative parents cannot and should not depend upon a daughter for support.

It is necessary to note the effects of this emphasis of feminine roles on the development of personality and identity formation for girls. Girls receive informal education for roles which they are expected to perform in adult life. Many give up their ambition to take up career as these are regarded as incompatible with smooth and peaceful family life. They learn early in life that society expects greater flexibility of mind, capacity to adjust, and submissiveness from a woman. In respect of ideologies and values, girls feel that it is no use their committing themselves to any particular ideology because they may not be allowed to adhere to it after getting married.

Thus the constraints, visible as well as invisible, that are placed on girls have an effect on their personalities. Some of these girls join the workforce of the country as white collar workers, in professions and even take up challenging careers like politics. This is either before marriage or after marriage. When married women work outside the home they encounter problems of harmonizing their two roles. They have to evolve a pattern in which they can perform the two roles satisfactorily.

At the relatively lower economic level, both in the rural and urban sections, girls start their contribution to the running of household much earlier than boys. They take care of the younger siblings, help the mother in various domestic chores, and also participate in work of production which falls in the feminine sphere, or activities which fetch some extra income.

Both as preparation for adult roles and as a contribution to the work of the household, the girls' share is important. It is depressing to find that a fairly large proportion of girls are still out of school. In the rural areas there is a lurking fear that education makes girls less useful for adult feminine roles. If they get a little education they develop a distaste for the kind of work expected of them in the village and aspire to get married in towns. In fact, this problem is very real for the cultivators and artisans. It was voiced before the committee in very strong words in Himachal Pradesh and Andhra Pradesh. Education does alienate its recipients from their environment and creates a distaste for manual work.

Home and Work

In a discussion of the dual role of women we may first take note of the quantum of labour, both domestic and extradomestic. In the rural areas, even those who are confined in the home, because of *purdah* or other norms of respectability, contribute hard labour in activities such as running a dairy, processing and storage of grains and other foodstuffs, spinning, coir-making, preparation of cowdung manure, and so forth. It has been seen that a woman's direct contribution to the family economy and her actual control over many of the products gives her considerable power and initiative. Their economic value to the family and their own capacity to earn a living frees them particularly from rigid family controls, and bestows on them a certain measure of autonomy. In contrast the lower middle-class women of urban areas, who have little education and no independent source of income, are in a less advantageous position because of stricter norms of behaviour and almost total dependence on men.

In the social context, due to the low status attached to manual labour in our society and the cultural value associated with women's confinement to home, the work of rural and urban women as wage labourers, unskilled factory workers and menials is not conducive to a better status.

The average woman in rural areas can give little attention to the bringing up of her children. With dual roles and without any mechanical aids for housework, she is definitely overworked. So also are the women engaged in unskilled or semiskilled work in organised and unorganised sectors in urban areas. Overwork and more than a culturally acquired attitude of unconcern about public affairs, is responsible for the limited participation of women in activities like those of the trade unions or political parties. They may become vocal and assertive only when nonavailability of essential commodities, or escalating prices threaten to upset their household budget and routine.

It is necessary to assess the status of housewives of the middle and upper economic strata belonging to the urban areas, and also the urbanized rural families. Closely allied to this is the appraisal of the gains achieved in terms of status, by the women who have joined the workforce in white collar professions. The reform movements for the education of women in the late nineteenth and early twentieth century, along with the realization of the need for a measure of economic independence towards the late twenties and thirties of this century, helped to improve the position of women of this class to a large extent. The passing of Hindu Women's Right to Property Acts of 1929 and 1937 was an important measure to give widows some economic independence. Later, organised efforts were made to provide remunerative work to such women. As the number of helpless women with education upto higher secondary or graduation is increasing, need for work which suit their earlier status and which they can take up only after a brief training is also increasing. Desertion and widowhood in this class often result in a sharp fall in the composite social status of the woman.

Initially society accepted a widow's gainful employment and gradually a young unmarried girl's employment till she got married received approval. Post 1940, the Second World War gave an impetus to women's employment and even married women came forward to take up gainful employment. In the post-Independence period, the structure of opportunities expanded, education qualified more and more women for a variety of jobs, and economic compulsions increased.

The sociocultural environment of India has changed rapidly in the last five decades, especially in the quarter century after the attainment of India's independence. Forces of modernization continue to make a powerful impact and the society has to respond to the new needs and urges of the people. Mahatma Gandhi and other leaders who combined in them the roles of social reformers and political leaders projected the vision of a new society; the humble and the oppressed were to get a new deal and the women were to secure a measure of emancipation in the society visualized by them. It is true that their philosophy and action did not bring about an instant transformation in social attitudes towards the women but it did nevertheless have a powerful effect, and over the decades legitimized many of the new roles contemplated for women. A series of powerful forces are in operation today to bring about perceptible changes in the social milieu. Education, with all its inadequacies, has made a definite impact. It opens up an arena in which women can compete freely with men and prove themselves equally worthy. It also creates for them new avenues in the competitive employment market. The mass media, especially the film and radio, despite their faulty conceptualization and constricted reach have contributed towards refashioning social images and goals. The most significant impetus to change has been provided, however, by demographic pressures and economic compulsions. These have been responsible for women seeking to take advantage of the new structure of economic opportunities. Politicization and articulation of new ideologies has acquired a new meaning and a heightened significance in the changing economic context. In consequence, the legitimacy of the new roles for women is increasingly becoming a social reality. At least on the overt level, the attitude to women has undergone significant modifications, although on the covert level the alteration in the basic attitude structure does not keep pace with the more explicit changes. Thus we find that there is considerable role enhancement, or at any rate a role expansion for women. Beyond their traditional roles they are called upon to assume several new roles also. This is particularly true for the upper stratum of the lower class and for the middle strata of the entire society in which education has been taken up as a mark of social respectability and also as an instrument of economic gain.

. The persistence of traditional norms in regard to women's essentially domestic roles and the addition of new work roles in the wider society has created problems of adjustment for them. It has added to their burdens. Everyday domestic chores plus full-time employment imply a workload that cannot be managed easily by them. On the domestic front there is little help; they cannot neglect their responsibilities in this sphere. The in-laws and even the husband and the children do not extend to them the measure of sympathy and support they need. Added to this are the latest prejudices and built-in rivalries that are constantly at work in the home atmosphere. These contribute considerably to the psychological stress that a working woman has to undergo. The lot of the working woman, unless she has a really well-paid job and a set of educated family members who are attuned to her psychological needs and physical capabilites, is still deplorable. She has in fact to carry on two fulltime jobs leaving her little time for rest and leisure or for self improvement. The pattern for social interaction demanded by her out-of-home job cannot be smoothly worked out: the demands of the home and the built-in prejudices create impediments that cannot be managed easily.

New lifestyles of women are now visible. In pre-independence days some women had voluntarily decided against marriage in order to devote their life to the national cause or social service. Today in the professions, services, and in the field of social work, we have a number of successful unmarried women who enjoy high status. Along with married women, who are primarily housewives, there are women who combine housework and job, and there are also those who may return to their work or take up a job after their children have grown up.

The pace of change in attitude to women working outside the home or participating in public life has been slow and uneven. These attitudes are related to conceptions about women's inherent attitudes and capacities, her proper sphere of work, and man-woman relationships. Thus, education as a field of employment is more popular because the hours of work are more or less fixed, work at home and outside can be satisfactorily combined, and the work involves less contact with men. Even in mixed schools and institutions of higher education, contact with male colleagues does not have to be close. Work in the field of education does not conflict with traditional norms of femininity.

Although nursing does not conflict with the feminine ideal of service, the job involves contact with impure objects, contact with male patients, doctors and paramedical personnel, and odd hours of work, during night and day. It is only in recent years that nursing is becoming a more respectable and therefore acceptable calling in some regions.

Entry of women in films or the professional theatre had been frowned upon by almost all sections of the community. In many regions participation in domestic performances was associated with particular castes and communities whose women were professional dancers and singers. Now the situation has improved, though the prejudice still persists. In the past, dancing and singing were associated with courtesans only, but gradually with the cultural renaissance, they are becoming more acceptable to society. Giving a remunerative performance before an audience may be accepted in large cities, but it would still be considered unbecoming for the wife or daughter-in-law in small towns. The All India Radio had greatly helped in weakening this prejudice. Teaching music or dancing or organising music programmes is now acceptable. However, living by music or dance performances alone is laden with problems which a woman finds difficult to manage as a career.

In small towns and villages, young women, more so unmarried girls, find it very difficult to work because of the attitude of the people. A touring job is even more difficult. If a girl has been brought up on a traditional home she is likely to be handicapped by her own personality, and if she has been brought up in a modern atmosphere she is likely to create more misunderstanding.

In recent years women have done well in administrative jobs. But in this field the difficulties are of a somewhat different nature. At the utmost, men are prepared to accept a woman as an equal, but men still do not relish working under a woman superior. The traditional conception of women's limitations and her proper place were responsible for the well-known episode in Uttar Pradesh when the former chief minister Charan Singh stated that women officers should not be entrusted with administrative responsibility.

He thought that women were unfit for administrative jobs. The Press said that the chief minister was of the opinion that women were too 'delicate' to be entrusted with executive jobs. He also refused to meet a delegation of women officers wanting to convey their protest. Earlier, he had abolished the Mahila Yojana. According to press reports he exhorted the women to go back to their kitchens and look after their children.

This may be an extreme case but it does indicate a certain mind-set of thinking. There are many who share this view and relate the stories about the stupidity and failures of women in high positions, but who adopt a progressive posture in public. The view that women do not possess the essential attributes of an officer to function in high executive ranks cannot be attributed to male chauvinism or a conservative attitude alone. Even some women appear to assume it tacitly. For example, Shivani, a popular woman writer in Hindi, has portrayed a fictitious woman officer of the Indian Administrative Service in a manner that highlights the frailty of woman. Her novelette on this theme was serialized in a popular weekly and later issued in book form. The book leaves an unmistakable impression in the minds of the common reader that women do not quite measure up to positions of higher authority.

The problems connected with dual roles of women may be viewed as those of burden of work, interpersonal relations within the family, and of role conflict. Gainful employment of wives is often viewed with a degree of ambivalence by men. It is approved because it lessens the financial burden and raises the standard of living. However, it can be a source of disruption in the smooth running of the household. The other aspect is the economic independence of women, which is resented by many husbands. It is difficult to say how many women are in a position to take decisions regarding their own earnings. According to a study the freedom of association and movement which outdoor work involves, is not approved of in many homes and puts a stigma on working women. Even in those regions and communities which have had a long tradition of women working outside the home, husbands still do not tolerate women coming home late from office.

Most men do not want to give up their traditionally superior position in the family and do not offer any assistance to their wives in domestic chores. In middle-class families where they cannot afford domestic help and the husband does not share any work, the burden on the wife can become unbearable. A change in older attitudes and values is essential for achieving rationalization of the load of the work. During our tours, we were repeatedly told that men while living in the West helped their wives with domestic chores but when they returned to India, they stopped giving this practice.

Often women themselves do not like the idea of their husbands doing domestic chores as they consider that to be a feminine role. The attitude of relatives and neighbours is also unfavourable. They criticize working women as bad mothers and inefficient housewives. A study focussed largely on middle-class working women of Patna reveals that husbands of 131 respondents thought that it was the wife's duty to carry out household jobs and to look after children. Sixtysix were of the opinion that, since both were working, it was the duty of the husband to share some responsibility. Many women have to leave their jobs in order to be able to do their household duties satisfactorily. This, however, depends on the financial condition of the family.

Although the in-laws still tend to expect the same amount of attention from a working woman as they would from a non-working woman, there are positive indications that the situation is changing. When the woman's earning is an absolute necessity for the family or if the woman has a well-paid and high status job, she does get consideration.

It is often remarked that if the woman has to spend most of her income on servants and conveyance her employment is of no consequence. But it is seldom understood that a career in itself has its rewards and satisfaction.

The situation of women alternating between work and home leads to a role conflict. Some of them develop a feeling of guilt that they are unable to look after the children and home properly. Working women tend to pamper their children because they want to make up for what they consider to be lack of proper attention on their part. This is because of their role perception rooted in their socialization and the expectations of other members of the family. It is not realized that a child does not need the continued presence of its mother for its proper growth, nor is it realized that the other parent is as important for the healthy growth of the child. Role conflict makes working women tire themselves out giving personal service to the husband and attending to various tasks which are often beyond their physical capacity and endurance.

Besides the strains of shouldering the burden of dual roles and of facing a role conflict, there is often another kind of strain arising from a lack of adjustment between a woman's position at home and in the place of work. She may be better educated and lesser paid than the husband but he claims absolute superiority over her at home. According to Promilla Kapur (1970): "The husband's denial of the right of the wife over her own earned money or her privileges to relax or to move about freely... was found to be related to his patriarchal attitude towards husband-wife privileges and obligations."

But the problem of status inconsistency is deeper than this. Unfortunately our society is extremely status conscious and status-bound. If the wife enjoys a higher status in her work place, her circle of associates are also of higher status, and however the wife may try not to bring in her office status at home, the husband's adjustment with her becomes difficult. He tends to consider it a reversal of roles. Such a husband tends to become more domineering. Sometimes the wife is also to be blamed, for she too is a part of the status conscious society.

The situation in which the husband is employed in an inferior position in the same office or directly under the wife is perhaps the worst. Many wives are known to have deliberately refused promotions, in order to maintain peace in the family. Thus, when the position of the husband as not the principal breadwinner, as not superior to the wife, or his authority in the family being challenged is when serious problems can arise.

Another aspect of status inconsistency emerges in situations in which a wife has a relatively low status job with limited earnings. For example, nurses marrying doctors are found to leave their occupation mainly of reasons of status. Women working in low paid/status jobs generally leave their jobs after marrying businessmen or executives and thus waste their training, aptitude, and experience. It has been found that sometimes these earnings of the wife may be necessary for the household, and because of the presence of relatives or servants in the house, the wife may not be occupied fully at home, but still her working in low status jobs is not allowed, for it brings down the status of the husband. An idle wife attuned to the life pattern of the husband is more appreciated. It is seen that a woman is not allowed to work in low status positions even in an honorary capacity. By leaving their jobs women are forced to withdraw the support that they were giving to their needy parents or siblings prior to marriage.

It should be a woman's right to play a dual role. A woman should not be penalized for her important contribution as mother in the perpetuation of society. Childbearing is treated as purely a matter concerning women and hence the attitude that a woman must either give up her job or her right to bear children. A distinction between man's work and woman's work in respect of household jobs will have to be removed. If what are called woman's jobs come to be respected by society, men will cease to hesitate doing these jobs. This attitude needs to be built into the socialization process of children, both in the home and in the school.

It is necessary to make adequate provisions to give women opportunity to do both their jobs efficiently and satisfactorily. To this end, it is necessary to provide for creches, nurseries, and labour saving devices. Since all families cannot afford to buy gadgets it will be necessary to provide gadgets to do washing, vegetable chopping, preparing *chapati* and such other things which make household work a drudgery.

In the absence of many social and physical amenities like labour saving devices, easy transport, creches, inexpensive processed foods, as also conditions of service, such as transfers, many women will have to remain principally mothers and housewives. Some may have to confine themselves to the role of a housewife while the children are young. If family is important, home-making is so too. The inputs of household work and the mothers' role in rearing of children need to be recognized by the family and the society at large.

The housewife certainly contributes, even though it may be indirectly, towards a stable national economy by consolidating the economic structure of her own home. Her efficient management of her home alone ensures the saving potentiality of her earning husband. Recognition of her work for the purposes of 'national accounting' would certainly enhance the status of woman and acknowledge the debt of society to her.

Some Special Problems

In a rapidly changing and culturally differentiated society, a slow process of adjustment in its social value system and rigidity of its institutions, results in various forms of incongruous behaviour. The changing social patterns without restructuring or redefining social values and norms always cause deviant behaviour. Structural changes in the socio-economic system are needed for a smooth process of adjustment.

The problems of women discussed in this section cannot be tackled by legal methods of penalization and prevention alone but by providing institutional infrastructure for their reform and rehabilitation. The gap in the perception of their needs and available opportunities, is conducive to exploitation of the weaker section of society and cannot be offset by development programmes alone but by adequate understanding of the magnitude and intricacies of the problem and providing supportive institutional framework.

Prostitution

Prostitution is the worst form of exploitation of women and as an institution it speaks of man's tolerance of this exploitation on an organised level in society. Women are viewed solely as a sex object and as an outlet for man's baser instincts. The condemnation of the woman and not the man is the continuance of the standards of dual morality which prevail in most countries with regard to men and women. Some societies have continued to regard prostitution as a necessary evil and have tolerated it as such.

The social anthropologists' explanation of prostitution is that it has been in existence in some form or the other as long as society has attempted to regulate and control sex relationships through the institutions of marriage and family. Promiscuity or sexual communism preceded marriage and family, and sex was shared by all without any taboo or control. With the institutionalization of sex behaviour through marriage and particularly in society which lays great emphasis on the chastity of its women, prostitutes became an evil of necessity. In a way, they helped to retain the chastity and purity of women in society and hence performed a social function. Even now among certain tribal communities entrance of women into commercialized prostitution is a recent phenomenon and has only started with the advent of outsiders into the tribal community. In tribal communities which always enjoyed a certain degree of sexual freedom, the institution of prostitution did not exist. According to Rao and Rao in *Prostitutes of Hyderabad*: "In India, the emphasis on chastity value prior to marriage compelled women of deflowered innocence to court prostitution. Dowry among the upper castes has been a constraint in marriage and some frustrated women were forced to become prostitutes." Rao and rao further say: In parts of Andhra Pradesh, college girls, and young women practise prostitution and save their earnings. Some even have passbooks in which they indicate their savings which they say will form their dowry to enable them to make a decent marriage. "Child marriages and social discouragement of re-marriage of young widows have greatly helped in the recruitment of prostitutes from village in India. Caste inequality and sex exploitation by the economically well off castes are other factors."

In the 19th century, certain social customs were responsible for many women resorting to this profession, who were otherwise outside the hereditary and customary groups of prostitutes. The spread of child marriages, early widowhood, social taboos on widow remarriages, caste rigidity, dowry system and the practice of polygamy and polyandry among certain communities, the decay in the joint family system, and the generally low status accorded to women in society contributed to women being driven to prostitution as the only occupation for livelihood. At the same time, the beginning of industrialization and consequent urbanization in the latter part of the 19th and early 20th century, drew in large number of women other than hereditary prostitutes into this profession. One reason was the wide sex disparity in the big cities when the migrant worker who had to leave his family behind in the village for mainly economic reasons, became a customer for the prostitute.

Briefly, the following social and religious customs which may have contributed directly or indirectly to prostitution are enumerated as follows according to H.R. Trivedi from a survey on "Exploitation of SC Women" undertaken by the Harijan Sevak Sangh.

The Devdasi system which was so widespread in pre-Independence India that it necessitated legal measures such as the Madras Devdasi Prevention and Dedication Act of 1947 and the Bombay Devdasi Protection Act of 1954 is a system that continues today in parts of Tamil Nadu, Mysore, Andhra Pradesh and Orissa, practised particularly by the lower castes. A study conducted in Bombay in the mid sixties reported that as many as 30 per cent of the Bombay prostitutes were of Devadasi origin. In a study of the Bijapur district, girls are still dedicated to the temples amongst certain sections of the lower castes and enter the occupation with the consent of the parents. No social stigma is attached to this. The reason is mainly economic. These girls are also taken out of the town or village by an agent and a large part of the earnings of the Devadasis goes to the family members and agents.

Prostitution has been the traditional occupation among certain castes, for instance, the Naiks from the hilly regions of Uttar Pradesh where the woman is traditionally the breadwinner and the men have to marry from another caste, as their own womenfolk take to prostitution. The Uttar Pradesh Naik Girls' Protection Act was passed as early as 1929, but the practice continues even today and Punekar and Rao's study indicated that 43 per cent of the prostitutes were drawn from the Naiks of Uttar Pradesh.

Certain castes practise historical and traditional prostitution. A survey conducted in the Raipur and Raigarh districts for the Committee on the Status of Women found that very loose marriage ties in which adultery is scarcely regarded as an offence, encourage prostitution. "A woman may go and live openly with other men and her husband will take her back or two men each will place their spouse at each other's disposal". Women of the lower castes earn money and support themselves through prostitution which is carried on at the weekly bazaars or fairs. The women have historically been exploited by the higher castes, and are often handed over or mortgaged temporarily to creditors on return of loan. The men of such communities indulged in drinking and gambling and encourage their woman to earn money for them and also the emergence of the new industrial towns has encouraged commercialization of prostitution. The survey also found that agents and intermediaries come from outside the community and parents, in-laws and husbands take the initiative in getting women into prostitution for commercial gain. A large part of the income is sent back to the families. Prostitution is the only way open to women to earn a livelihood for the family. No stigma is attached to the woman if she brings wealth or income from prostitution to her natal or conjugal home.

A recent study of the immoral trafficking in women from the Purola Block of Uttarkashi district (UP) reveals that a large number of girls from the lower socio-economic communities go in for prostitution. In 1969, 45 women had entered and remained in this profession for three years. It was estimated that about approximately 500 families were dependent on this profession on account of extreme poverty. 60 per cent of girls from Rawain area were operating in Delhi and 77 agents were engaged in procuring women for prostitution. The causes for prostitution were the high bride-price and consequent indebtedness of the couple who were forced to work as bonded labour. The girl was then compelled to earn money to free the family from this debt through prostitution. In other cases, a man from a higher caste may pay bride-price and contract a marriage with one or more girls of a poor family and take her to Delhi and sell her into the trade. In other cases, Delhi brothelkeepers used girls from Purola to entice other girls or their cousins, etc., by showing them the easy life they could enjoy in the brothels. According to one report the history of this traffic in the Rawain area is about 60 years old, but it has increased recently, with the entrance of officials and traders.

Among the Bajgi caste in Purola region its occupation in service of the temple may be closely connected with the large number of women who go into the trade. Though the Devadasi system as such does not exist much now, certain castes closely connected with work of the temple are more prone to prostitution.

Families of majority of these prostitutes are landless and up to 75 per cent bonded for life to upper caste money lenders. Many of these communities belonging to lower socio-economic groups practise polyandry due to high bride-price. This may be sociological cause for the ease with which the women descend into prostitution. Women generally occupy a very low social position and labour incessantly in homes and in the field once they are bought or sold. Trafficking is on the increase in these regions and sometimes higher castes or powerful men in the village act as agents and are in liaison with procurers and brothelkeepers for taking young girls into prostitution.

According to a sociological analysis of prostitution in India, there are about 10,000 dancing and singing girls in India usually known as "Nautch girls". This community practises the occupation on an hereditary basis in different regions. The majority of 'Nautch girls' in Delhi are Muslims. The study also mentions a recent addition to the poor and customary army of prostitutes from the middle-class. These women practise prostitution often with the connivance of their parents or husbands in order to secure huge sums of money to keep up an appearance of affluence. Educated and outwardly respectable, these women are prompted to take to prostitution because of the undue emphasis on values of affluence. Middle-class prostitution can ultimately be traded to the economic factor, though it is the cult of consumption which encourages this pattern of prostitution. Large number of prostitutes also come from a group of women who have been deserted or abandoned by husbands and have no other source of income or employment open for them. According to a former commissioner of police, Calcutta, a large number of middle-class families are surviving on income from prostitution in the absence of alternative avenues of income. A number of these women are educated and quite a few are even graduates.

The causes of prostitution may broadly be classified into the following six groups:

(a) natural events such as death of father/mother/guardian/husband or relatives;

(b) economic causes such as ill-treatment or neglect by parents, husband, or relatives;

(c) domestic causes such as ill-treatment or neglect by parents, husband, or relatives;
(d) social causes such as kidnapping, seduction, deception, bad influence;
(e) causes of physiological significance such as sexual urge, illegitimate pregnancy, etc.;
(f) causes related to mental disposition of attitudes such as ignorance, desire for easy life and normal moral values.

Types of Prostitutes

The present practitioners of this trade can broadly be divided into two groups — hereditary class, where prostitution is the ancestral profession and the non-hereditary class who are driven to prostitution or introduced to prostitution due to number of reasons such as economic distress, desertion, destitution, lack of protection, family problems or pathological reasons, desire for easy life, etc. The report of the Committee on Moral and Social Hygiene of the Central Social Welfare Board in 1958 divided the prostitutes into four groups, namely: (1) hereditary (community, customs and social patterns), (2) religious or traditional, (3) victims of social and sociological conditions and (4) highly sexed, pathological cases.

Prostitution must be viewed not from the traditional or historical aspect, but as a form of exploitation of women and girls. According to Mahatma Gandhi, "Man is primarily responsible for the existence of these unfortunate members of society." Prostitution has now been commercialized and a number of intermediaries, the brothelkeeper, the pimps and touts for whom the profit motive has become the guiding principle, has increased the exploitation of women and girls.

Taking into consideration the three elements of prostitution, payment, promiscuity and emotional disturbances there can be two broad categories — professional and non-professional (clandestine). Professional or the public prostitute derives her sole and only livelihood from this profession in a brothel or in redlight districts in big towns. The higher type in this profession are street walkers and 'call girls' who find their clients in hotel lobbies, bars and luxurious establishments. Non-professionals are those who conduct their business in a clandestine manner.

Prostitution represents the exploitation of the poor by the rich and of women by men. If women have really to reach the level of equality with men, society should be in a position to ensure economic, social and psychological security for the traditionally exploited womenfolk. Prostitution is the worst form of women's exploitation and inequality.

What must be emphasized is the growing commercialization in the exploitation of women and girls. While the urbanization process and industrialization with its accompanying evils, particularly socio-economic insecurity, poor living conditions, etc., are important forces for the increase of prostitution in recent years, this profession like any other, operates on a commercial basis according to the law of demand and supply. The growing incidence of prostitution in metropolitan cities and urban areas is an indication of the growing demand on the one hand and poverty on the other. Some sociologists have emphasized the role of economic factors over and above the traditional and customary factors, such as poverty, low wages, lack of gainful employment, partial or complete unemployment which are contributory factors that constrain helpless women to embrace prostitution.

The increasing commercial aspect is represented in the host of intermediaries and allied trades which gather around prostitution. The most important ones are the procurers, pimps, landlords, musical instrument players, intoxicant sellers, *panwallahs*, hotelkeepers, flowersellers and the rough elements whose help is sought for protection. Some intermediaries work on a commission basis, like pimps. Procurers are engaged in the purchase and sale of women. The survey of exploitation of Scheduled Caste women has also emphasized that commercial prostitution has gained preponderance over the sacred or traditional prostitution, which used to be practised in the Bijapur region. An agent usually contacts a family and buys a girl or a fake marriage is declared and she is taken out of the town or village to practise this trade.

Once these girls have been lured or enticed, and in some cases forced into this profession, they are taken to a brothel. If the girls are unwilling, they are mercilessly beaten and punished and even locked up if they do not conform to the brothelkeeper or *gharwali*. Their status is that of an employee and their income is divided between the brothel keeper and as commission for the pimps and procurers. The rest is taken up for rent, lodging and food, while the remaining income is so small that the prostitute has hardly any savings or security for old age. They are fully exploited by the brothel keeper who enters into a bargain with customers and the prostitute has no choice, but to follow his or her orders. They are kept strictly under control and surveillance of the brothel keeper and his hired men. The prostitute is not permitted or encouraged to save or keep any valuables which are usually stolen. As she grows older, a prostitute desires to set herself up as a brothel keeper, if possible, or amongst some of the traditional communities like the Barias, the Bednies and Takyaies, they admit their daughters into the profession when they are grown up. She herself initiates her into the profession so that she may continue to support herself through the daughter's earnings. Amongst Deredar girls' they are given training in music and dance by their mothers from girlhood so that their *mehfils* and *mujras*, get large number of customers. In some cases, after a woman has been in the profession for 10 to 15 years, and is not able to attract customers, she is thrown out on the streets by brothelkeepers, and is reduced to beggary.

In certain tribal regions, particularly where new projects for construction, industry or mines, etc., have been established, contractors, traders and petty officials have seduced and then abandoned tribal girls. These girls have been forced into prostitution because they have been alienated and thrown out of their own tribal society. In Baladila (MP) For example, a serious situation was created, but the management forced the men to marry these tribal girls and thus saved them from drifting into prostitution. Generally such strong measures are not resorted to and the fact remains that a very large number of tribal girls are being lured into prostitution by unscrupulous men who have made this a very lucrative business for themselves.

The Suppression of Immoral Traffic in Women and Girls Act, 1956 repealed all previous enactments passed by the State and brought uniformity in the law. According to Beotra (1970): "The Act aimed at the suppression of commercialized vice and not at the penalisation of the individual prostitute, or of prostitution itself." In one case, the individual prostitute can be penalised. If she carries on prostitution "within a distance of 200 yards of any place of public, religious worship, educational institution, hostel, hospital, nursing home".

According to M.L. Sahney (1974), a senior police official, this section has severely restricted their powers for suppression of this traffic. He opines that:

"This restriction needs immediate amendment as the vice of prostitution has gone to posh colonies where the pimps have hired modern houses to run this profession. In the absence of these premises situated within 200 yards from the places as envisaged above, it is not possible to prosecute such women or girls soliciting their bodies for immoral purposes"

Another practical difficulty imposed by the Act itself is the provision for witnesses. Section 15(2) of the Act lays down that special police officers conducting the raid shall call upon two or more respectable inhabitants, at least one of whom shall be a woman, of the locality in which the place is situated, to attend and witness the search. Police officers have pointed out that this proves to be extremely difficult particularly in the case of a woman witness. Considering the social conditions existing today in our country, no respectable man/woman would like to help the police in the prosecution of sex offences. If anybody turns up for such help, he has to face harassment and even repent for his action, as the persons prosecuted are themselves criminals or are supported by them. At first these witnesses are lured with money, wine and women. If these tactics fail they are threatened with dire consequences with immediate danger to their lives and properties. Efforts were made to procure witnesses through welfare associations and agencies but all in vain. A letter was written to the Association for Moral and Social Hygiene in India for furnishing some names of social workers including lady social workers so that they could be contacted at the time of raids on brothels and places of disrepute. They have replied that although the members of the association were very sincere workers they were not certain whether any of them would be prepared to come forward during raids and face cross-examination in courts.

Social workers and police officers have repeatedly brought to our notice that the punishment imposed under the Act is inadequate to deter people from this crime particularly in view of the enormous income that can be earned from this traffic.

It has been realized that the Act was itself not sufficient to control this commercial exploitation and traffic in women. In fact the number of prosecutions under this Act have been very small in comparison to the volume of the traffic. A report of the Central Bureau of Correctional Services indicates that while the number of prosecutions under the Act has increased from 6428 in 1965 to 7573 in 1969, i.e. by 17.8 per cent, the rate of prosecution for the same period has gone down by about 10 per cent. About 58 per cent of these persons were only fined, 14 per cent acquitted and 8 per cent were released on admonition. Only 11 per cent were sentenced to imprisonment with a fine which is nominal (Rs. 200) and 4 per cent without fine. 78 per cent were charged under the Act for seducing for purposes of prostitution (Section 8 of the Suppression of Immoral Traffic Act). During the same period the number of such women rescued declined sharply. Only 7.2 per cent were charged under Section 4, which prosecutes persons over the age of 18 years for living on the earnings of prostitutes but exceptions are made in favour of mother, son, daughter and sister or other persons unable to support themselves on account of age or mental and physical incapacity.

The Department of Social Welfare set up an expert committee in 1968 to consider various proposals and suggestions for enlarging the scope of the Act with a view to make it more comprehensive; various amendments are under consideration.

It is important that certain changes be made in the Act to help eradicate this social evil. It is essential to prevent the women caught under this Act from returning to the profession by adequate rehabilitation arrangements. The persons who pay for their bail are invariably the procurers or brothelkeepers. Instead of sending the women and girls to jails, it is necessary to send them to protective homes. The age limit should also be lowered from 21 year to 18 years. Adequate arrangements should be made to give protection to girls and women in moral and social danger particularly destitute women, unmarried mothers and helpless young widows. At an orientation camp of the Association for Social Health in India held in March, 1974, one of the participants suggested improving the existing institutionalized services providing proper protection for abandoned and illegitimate children, especially girls, as a method that may help control prostitution. As far as the rehabilitative aspect is concerned, the Rama Rao Committee, 1954, had said that the after-care homes are not adequate and they should be associated with some programme to help prostitutes earn a decent living. Those who are detained under the Act require long-term treatment for rehabilitation. Special counselling service towards better understanding of the problems of prostitutes is important. The children of prostitutes should be prevented from entering the profession, especially the girls. They should be segregated from their mothers and institutionalized, but not in special homes which would put a social stigma on them. Women and girls, who do not wish to continue in this profession, but are compelled to do so for economic reasons should be rescued and engaged in remunerative work. There is, therefore, greater need for understanding the cause underlying prostitution and to make efforts to prevent more women from entering this profession as well as to rehabilitate those who are already victims of the trade.

These women need to be rehabilitated and their emotional and psychological problems are to be tackled with understanding. The most significant aspect is preventive. This applies particularly to women and girls in moral danger. An important segment of this group are women who are victims of family discord. Counselling services could help them and prevent their taking recourse to this profession. Counselling centres should also have homes for such women.

Women in Prisons

According to an estimate, women members constitute about 4.3 per cent of the convicts and 3.2 per cent of the undertrial prisoners, 73 per cent of female convicts and 54 per cent of undertrials are from Andhra, Maharashtra and Tamil Nadu. Since they constitute numerically a small segment of the total convict population, the condition of women prisoners has not received adequate attention. 72 per cent of the female convicts are between 21-40 years of age, and around 10 per cent are between 16-20. 12 per cent of women convicts are illiterates, 73 per cent of them are married, 15 per cent unmarried and 12 per cent are widowed. This means that a large section have children, who are either deprived of maternal care or in the case of very young children, are living with their mothers in prisons.

It has been found that more women serve short sentences as compared to men. Habitual proneness to crime is found to be less among them. This also means that a large majority of women prisoners are 'freshers' and are exposed to the influence of prison life for the first time. We would like to draw attention to the fact that the Law Commission has recommended that convicts on short-term sentences should not be sent to prison, where they are exposed to the unhealthy influence of hardened criminals.

Separate living quarters or wards with female wardens or matrons are provided for women as a rule. In rare cases child care services or creches for mothers in prisons are available in a few States. Training in skills such as *niwar* and *dari* making, tailoring, spinning, weaving, *bidi*-making, embroidery, etc., are not necessarily in tune with market labour requirements or conducive to self-employment.

The background of women prisoners studied by one or two experts reveals that their crime comes mainly from poverty or social helplessness. Most common are pickpocketing, attempted suicide, family feuds and domestic quarrels, questions pertaining to the custody of children, infanticide, destitution or vagrancy and murder of a lover.

The generally low level of literacy among women convicts, except for Kerala, where 45 per cent of women convicts were illiterate, reflects the lack of effort by prison authorities to educate them. In general, the women sections of the jails have practically no positive education or work programmes, presumably due to few prisoners; they cannot participate in the general routine of work due to strict segregation. Sometimes the women prisoners have dependent children with them for want of any family arrangement outside. Life for these young ones can be equally futile. Efforts to set up creches for children of women prisoners did not succeed due to very small number of children. Discrimination against women is prevalent, since they hardly share any of the privileges available to men convicts such as wage system, canteen, outdoor work, PT drill, library or prayer meetings or general recreation, or holidays. This is explained by the problems of segregation and inadequate staff to organise such activities for women.

It has been reported to us by senior officials of the police force that in some prisons, lunatics, both criminals and non-criminals, are housed along with other women prisoners. This appears to us to be not only unhealthy, but a dangerous practice. We fail to understand how any reform or rehabilitation of these convicts or the treatment of these lunatics is at all possible under these circumstances. Another problem that has been brought to our notice is that women prisoners are often sent to places away from their normal residence. This makes it impossible for their family, particularly children, to visit them. This isolation increases the difficulties of rehabilitation and readjustment to family life on their release.

The committee feels that the problems of women prisoners deserve special attention, particularly with regard to the care of the children if any, their rehabilitation and education. Since most of the women prisoners cannot return to their families or do not have families to return to after they are released, suitable arrangements for their rehabilitation needs to be considered along with after care programmes. While in prison, these women must be taught some activity or imparted training in a skill which would enable them to earn their livelihood on release. A suggestion made to us is to involve women's voluntary organisations for arranging useful educational, recreational and work programmes for women in prisons. Successful results have been seen in Maharashtra and Gujarat State where long-term women prisoners are released to the care of recognized women's institutions run by social welfare agencies.

Suicide

Suicide is a social problem affecting both men and women. However, a study of the causes and factors for committing suicide provide an indication of the status of women. Suicide is a 'reaction to problems that apparently cannot be solved in any other way — a final response which a human-being makes to inner emotional distress. Cultural patterns, socio-economic conditions, and group activities influence the extent of suicides and act as inhibiting or encouraging factors. In India, the medieval Hindu institution of 'Sati', which was finally stopped due to vigorous efforts of social reformers like Raja Ram Mohun Roy in the 19th century, was the earliest institutionalized form of suicide for women. Though it was thought to have had religious sanction, it arose out of a social system which had degraded and dehumanized the widows. Regardless of age, a number of those widows had to mount on the funeral pyre of their husbands forced by relatives and others. The prohibition of widow remarriage, the austerity imposed upon a widow and the cruel treatment meted out to her must have persuaded some of them to end their lives on the pyre in preference to leading a miserable existence. According to the vital statistics, deaths by causes and sub-causes prepared by the Registrar General's Census (Sample Registration System), suicides were reported to be the highest for women in the age-group 15-34, both in 1966 and 1969. The overall incidence of suicide for women was reported to be higher than males in 1966 and 1969, but it declined in 1967 and 1968.

In 1970 on an average 41.4 per cent of the persons who committed suicide were women. Among causes for suicide, the following were listed: (1) despair over dreadful disease 14.1 per cent (2) quarrels with parents-in-law 8.6 per cent and (3) quarrels with married partners 6.3 per cent as the major factors. An analysis of the percentage distribution of total deaths by the cause and sub-cause for women indicates that the maximum percentage of suicides occurred in the age group 15-34, the second largest being in the 35-54 age group.

In *Status of Women and Suicide* by Dr. Jyotsna Shah, it may be assumed that in this age group, "suicides committed by females were mainly due to quarrel with parents-in-laws and quarrels with married partners. The joint family system still prevails in India, therefore, the suicides by females may be taken to reflect the extent of oppression of the daughter-in-law in the joint family at the hands of the in-laws".

Though no national survey or indepth study on a national scale on the causes of suicides have been done so far, the report of the Suicide Enquiry Committee in Gujarat studied the problem of suicides between 1960-64 in the State. The study found that the number of women committing suicide for physical factors, mental factors and social and domestic factors, were larger than men, being respectively 514 males per 516 females, 431 males per 513 females, and 562 males per 1,192 females. As far as the economic factors were concerned, 256 men committed suicide as compared to 196 females.

A further analysis of the social factors indicates that out of 1,784 persons, 1,192 women committed suicide, and out of these the largest number were due to failure to adjust in matrimony, domestic unhappiness or ill-treatment at the hands of relatives. These were further cross-analysed with levels of education and a definite negative corelation between the educational level of women and the number of suicides was observed. The percentage of illiterate females constituted 61.9 per cent of the total cases of female suicides. As the educational level increased, the number of suicides decreased. Among the number of persons who committed suicide due to unhappy human life and other factors, the largest were from the illiterate group, next being literates below primary level, followed by primary, middle and higher categories. Significantly 1,058 married people against 95 single people commit suicide due to domestic unhappiness and out of these 836 were females which corroborates the statement about suppression of women in married life particularly by in-laws. The study established that more women in the 15-34 age group commit suicides due to domestic unhappiness.

This report pointed out the 'cultural lag' in our social institutions which have not kept pace with educational and technological advance as the basic cause behind the suicides. It listed as reasons, the lack of freedom in the choice of the marriage partner, changes in the family units and especially joint family relationships, child marriage, dowry and lack of education about sex and married life among others.

The report recommended homes for women to which they can resort in times of extreme hardship or family estrangement. Some voluntary homes have been established in Gujarat.

An earlier survey of suicides in Bombay State in 1954-57, indicated that the existence of suicide per population is 3.4 males and 3.9 females in Ahmedabad range, 4.1 males and 8.9 females in Rajkot range per one lakh of the population. The highest number of suicides was in the rural areas. 2,006 females who commit suicide out of 5,173 were in the 15-24 age group. The highest number of suicides was by women due to domestic quarrel. 75.8 per cent of females were from the literate group. The Suicide Enquiry Committee of Saurashtra in 1952-55 also bore out the fact that twice as many women commit suicide as men.

Though apart from Maharashtra and Gujarat, data on suicide and causes are lacking from other states, suicide remains a widespread social problem. There are various items appearing in the daily Press from time to time giving news of women who die to injuries received from burns, etc. Some of the reported accidental deaths due to burns, etc., may very well be self-inflicted. The majority of these women are housewives in the susceptible age group mentioned above. The causes have to be searched for... in our social structure, enjoining upon women an inferior status and position, socially, economically and culturally.

Another cause that in our opinion also pushes many women to end their lives is breakdown of family economy. In recent years there have been reports of women committing suicide along with their children. The burden of economic insecurity and grim poverty presses more heavily on women's minds particularly when she has children to feed. This increasing strain causes complete breakdown in many cases. The absence of social security or adequate employment opportunities leave a woman utterly helpless, in the absence of a breadwinner in the family. Rather than see her children starve, it is not unnatural for her to prefer ending her life. Suicides thus represent a serious malaise in social organisations, which will increase as life becomes harsher with increasing poverty and destitution.

Unmarried Mothers

Data on unmarried mothers is not available as there has been no attempt to examine the prevalence of this problem by any agency. Nevertheless it remains a social problem. Some indication is available in the Report of the Suicide Enquiry Committee which studied suicides in Gujarat between 1960-64. One of the causes of high rate of suicide among women was due to illegitimate pregnancies. Some time back, a leading gynaecologist had observed that there was an increase in the number of abortions asked for by unmarried girls after passing of the Medical Termination of Pregnancy Act. Social workers have long been aware of the problem of illegitimate pregnancies and unmarried mothers. Before the liberalizing of the Abortion Act these women and girls had either to resort to quacks for abortions and in the process a number of women may have lost their lives. The other alternative was to abandon such children in the destitute homes. Very often these unmarried mothers joined the ranks of the destitute women and were exposed to moral and social danger. Some of the women in the brothels may have initially joined the profession because of this stigma. While for some these illegitimate pregnancies may be due to rape, others were due to unhappy or maladjusted family life, broken homes, sexual maladjustment or even ignorance. A large number of women who were pushed into prostitution or into committing suicide did so because society does not accept an unmarried mother.

At an orientation camp held by the Association of Social Health in March 1974, some experts have advocated sex education since a great deal of confused thinking prevails with regard to sex. A medical expert citing case histories and research findings said, "there is either complete ignorance or complete misunderstanding about the role of sex and this results in social and sexual maladjustments. This calls for evolving an intelligent and comprehensive programme for sex education."

A medical expert at the same seminar cautioned against the alarming rise in veneral infliction among teenagers, due to profound socio-economic changes in society over the past few decades. They advocated sex education, health education to control this. Apparently prostitution accounted for only 20 per cent in the spread of veneral diseases.

The committee in the course of its tours met a few such cases in women's homes. Some of them had conceived as a result of rape, but the refusal of the family to accept them or assist them in any manner had wrecked their lives completely. In one instance, in Andhra, the father wanted to kill his daughter, but the mother, with the assistance of a school teacher, got her admitted into a women's home for safe keeping. The number of such homes are most inadequate and very little is known about them, particularly in the villages.

The problem of unmarried mothers is a result of rapid socio-economic change. The value system is changing and the struggle for existence brings out tensions leading to deviant behaviour. In Western countries it was found that the existence of this problem rapidly increased with increasing urbanization, growing affluence and the cult of materialism. The resultant breakdown of the moral order systems leads to the disintegration of traditional social values. Indian society even now practises segregation of the sexes and tremendous emphasis is placed on the chastity of women. Under such circumstances the tensions are often aggravated and problems become manifest.

We feel that this problem requires much greater attention than it has received so far from both official agencies and voluntary welfare organisations, particularly as the indications of its increasing incidence are already manifest. It is important to provide adequate assistance to these women for their rehabilitation and care for their children. Counselling services are essential to persuade families to take a more humane view of this problem.

Aged women

Traditional Indian society had through the joint family system provided for the care of aged persons. Even in the absence of the joint family, traditional norms of behaviour required the children to take adequate care of their aged parents and grandparents. The pressure of socioeconomic changes, the breakdown of the joint family and of traditional values have increased the significance of the problem of care of aged persons. It is easier for old men to live on their own but it is much more difficult for women. Most of them are economically helpless; even the minority, who may have some source of income are not in a position to look after themselves or protect themselves. This problem was brought to our notice by the Ramakrishna Mission in Varanasi which is running a home for old women.

The committee also visited an old-age home in Pune where all the inmates were from well-to-do families. Their relatives were paying Rs. 125 per month for food and lodging and some of them were paying for extra services like milk, etc. These women had been sent to the homes because they could not get along with their daughters-in-law. We also heard of cases where old women were living in destitute homes, not because they were destitutes but because there were no other homes available for them and the only way they could enter these homes was by declaring themselves destitute. It was also brought to our notice that these women, even if they had any family, are seldom visited by them.

A number of State Governments are operating schemes for old age pensions and the annual expenditure on such schemes is now about Rs. 10 crores. The reports received by us in most of the States indicate, however, that the amounts are very meagre, and the number of pensioners falls far short of applications or even recommended cases. We were also informed that because of their helplessness these pensioners have to give a share to the intermediaries, who assist them in obtaining the pension. This becomes a continuous process, because the women are threatened that without the commission the government will be informed of their death so that the pension will cease. We were also told that payments are not always regular causing great hardship.

In the changing social milieu the problem of aged women who are regarded as encumbrances by their families is going to increase. Greater attention to their assistance and care is necessary from the State and voluntary agencies.

Destitute Women

The number of destitute women has been increasing in recent years. According to one report, a large number of such women are found scrounging for small fish in the *nullahs* along highways leading out of Calcutta. A majority of them are elderly women. In a village in Birbhum we met a group of Santhal women who had been reduced to complete destitution because their ill health and age prevented them from obtaining any employment. They were agricultural labourers whom the landowners would no longer employ.

A large group of destitute women were widows and deserted women who have no means of support for themselves or their children. They swell the ranks of beggars and are exploited for immoral traffic. The Department of Social Welfare has estimated that about 1 lakh women, in the age group of 20 to 44, join the ranks of destitutes every year. We believe this to be very short of reality. Institutionalized services now available for them are highly inadequate, both in numbers and in the type of services provided for rehabilitation. Services for this group have only touched the fringe of the problem. It is imperative to obtain more reliable data to assess the magnitude of the problem and organise adequate services for their rehabilitation.

Conclusion

The reviews of the disabilities and constraints on women, which stem from sociocultural institutions, indicates that the majority of women are still very far from enjoying the rights and opportunities guaranteed to them by the Constitution. Society has not yet succeeded in framing the required norms or institutions to enable women to fulfil the multiple roles that they are expected to play in India today. On the other hand, the increasing incidence of practices like dowry, indicate a further lowering of the status of women. They also indicate a process of regression from some of the norms developed during the freedom movement.

We have been perturbed by the findings of the content analysis of periodicals in the regional languages, that concern for women and their problems, which received an impetus during the freedom movement, has suffered a decline in the last two decades. The social laws that sought to mitigate the problems of women in their family life have remained unknown to a large mass of women in this country, who are as ignorant of their rights today as they were before independence.

The changes in social attitudes and institutions cannot be brought about very rapidly. It is, however, necessary to accelerate this process of change by deliberate and planned efforts. Responsibility for this acceleration has to be shared by the State and the community, particularly that section of the community which believes in the equality of women. We, therefore, urge that community organisations, particularly women's organisations, should mobilise public opinion and strengthen social efforts against oppressive institutions like polygamy, dowry, ostentatious expenditure on weddings and child marriage, and mount a campaign for the dissemination of information about the legal rights of women to increase their awareness. This is a joint responsibility, which has to be shared by community organisations, legislators, who have helped to frame these laws and the government which is responsible for implementing them.

REFERENCES

1. Barbara Ward (ed.) *Women in the New Asia*, UNESCO, 1964.
2. Chandrakala Hate, *Changing Status of Women in post-Independence India*, 1969.
3. Gopal Krishan Gokhale in Rao R. and Singh, *Changing India*, 1934.
4. Kolenda, Pauline, Religion, Caste and Family Structure in Singer and Cohn (ed.) *Structure and Change in Indian Society*, 1968.
5. Leela Dube, *Women and Kinship*, 1997.
6. Majumdar, R.C., *British Paramountcy and Human Renaissance.*
7. Patrica Uberoi edited, *Social Reform, Sexuality and the State*, 1996.

Six

Women and Law

Women have been granted equality of status with men in our constitution. Founding fathers of the Constitution made it quite clear that in independent India women will enjoy equal opportunities in every walk of life. But large masses of women in India have remained unaffected by the rights guaranteed to them by the Constitution and laws enacted since independence. This chapter an examination of the subject in its various dimensions have been discussed in order to understand the legal problems of women and then possible future prospects.

One of the main characteristics of modern society is a heavy reliance on law to bring about social change. This is particularly true of countries which had been under foreign rule for centuries and attained independence after a long struggle. Inequalities and exploitation, generated or intensified by colonial regimes, cannot be eliminated by freedom from foreign rule only.

The tasks of social reconstruction, development and nation-building—all call for major changes in the social order and to achieve this legislation is one of the main instruments. It can act directly, as a norm setter, or indirectly, providing institutions which accelerate social change by making it more acceptable. The introduction of compulsory education can be sited as an example.

Like other colonial countries, independent India has also relied heavily on legislation in its effort to usher in a society where there will be no discrimination or inequality. It has sought to protect the interests of those who suffer from social and political disabilities by penalizing the practice of untouchability, eliminating caste distinctions and so on. By clearly emphasizing the principle of equality and removing all legal discrimination *inter-alia* between sexes, our leaders have shown their acceptance of the view that to achieve freedom there must be complete liberty for women, and "all legislative traces of inequality of women without exception must be removed".

Stress on removal of discrimination and special protective legislation for women was necessary because the British policy in the field of family law has a crippling effect on Indian women. Whatever the motivation was, the British adopted a policy of letting Hindus be governed by Hindu law and Muslims by Muslim law in matters of family relations. This policy of relying on age-old personal laws has been described as "another act of enlightened policy," but the aim was to encourage the feeling of separateness and prevent the unity of the two communities.

This policy achieved such success that modification of most of these laws has proved difficult even today. Coupled with this was another policy of non-interference or rather non-intervention in family law on the plea that 'as the British legislature cannot make Mohammedan or Hindu religion, so can it not make Mohammedan or Hindu Law'. This led to stagnation with the result that the two systems could neither absorb nor adjust to socioeconomic changes. Social tensions inevitably arise in situations when "law does not answer the needs arising from major social changes".

In early 19th century, due to efforts of our social reformers, some marginal adjustments were made in response to humanitarian considerations and social demands. Although female infanticide had been banned earlier, the most significant was the legislation which penalized the practice of *Sati*. The groundwork for this had been laid for a very long time, and this was an example where legislative legitimacy was given to an accepted social norm. The then Governor General, Lord Bentinck, referring to the proposed legislation, said that the government would be following and not going ahead of public opinion.

In 18th and early 19th centuries, the prevalence of child marriage leading often to early widowhood, was one of the major concerns of the social reformers. Their tireless efforts to curb this social evil finally resulted in "The Hindu Widows' Remarriage Act in 1856. Such social legislation stopped after 1857.

The social reformers realized that in the face of the government's refusal to legislate on social matters, the only way open was to spread education more widely among the people, particularly women. This, they felt, would help to eliminate some of the inhuman practices and also act as an incentive to women to organize and demand legislative changes.

As the national movement intensified, the early 20th century saw some activity in the legislative field. The plight of widows without any means of their own, depending entirely on the family, led to the passing of the Hindu Women's Right to Property Act in 1929, followed by another in 1937. These laws, while making the widow less dependent financially during her lifetime, stopped short of giving her any substantial rights of ownership since her right to property was only for life.

The success of the policy of division can also be seen from the fact that though demands for changes in the Muslim law to improve the position of women were also gaining momentum, the reformers of the two communities did not work together. A significant change that was made as a result of all the agitations for improvement among the Muslims was granting the right of divorce to Muslim women in 1939.

A byproduct of the policy of non-intervention in family law had been the diversification (due to customs) among the major personal laws in different parts of the country and varied interpretations of the sacred texts. These differences had hardened over the years. Among the Muslim schools of law—there were others besides the Sunni and Shia schools. This was partially remedied by the Shariat Act of 1937, which brought all Muslims under the Act and practically abrogated the customary practices which had grown over the years. Among the Hindus, where there were two major schools—Mitakshara and Dayabhaga—and other sub-schools, lack of uniformity posed a serious problem.

The demand for major changes, no longer marginal ones, grew as a result of the untiring efforts of Gandhiji, who did not want women to suffer from any social or legal disabilities. The inferior position of women in all matters—guardianship, inheritance and divorce—had an effect on the personality of the women. Under Gandhiji's leadership, the demand for improvement and modification of the law grew, and ultimately the government was compelled to move. A committee was constituted under the chairmanship of Sir B.N. Rau, whose terms of reference included suggestions for change and the Codification of Hindu Law, so that all Hindus would be governed by the same law. Even though the report was ready and Gandhiji's exhortation that 'women should not suffer from any disability or discrimination', had influenced India's national leaders, the resistance to change was so great that no effective steps could be taken for many years.

Only after Independence, under the leadership of Pandit Nehru, could this matter be taken up. Even so, the law had to be passed piecemeal owing to the resistance from those who believed in the *status quo*. It is significant that the same body, sitting as the Constituent Assembly, adopted the equal rights clauses in the Constitution without any debate, while functioning in its capacity as the Central Legislature and blocked the Hindu Code Bill, which attempted to provide only partial equality to women.

Women's participation in the freedom movement had greatly helped in the acceptance of the idea of their equality and the need for their emancipation. As a result, with independence, Indian women achieved political and some social rights and did not have to struggle for them like women in many other countries.

But legislation cannot by itself change the society. To translate these rights into reality is the task of other agencies. Public opinion has to be moulded to accept these rights. The judiciary and the executive also have a major role to play in this. But this effort has not always been forthcoming. Sometimes the judiciary has interpreted new legislation strictly but failed to give effect to the principle underlying the legislation, as for example, in dealing with cases of bigamy or the right of women to work. The executive branch of the government has seldom made an effort to set up the machinery to educate the people about the socioeconomic changes. The mass media used for publicizing certain measures taken by the government, has been conspicuously silent about social legislation. If legislation reflects the social values of a country the degree of women's emancipation is the natural measure of the general emancipation in any 'given society'. It is, therefore, necessary not only to pass legislation, but also to see that it is implemented. In the following sections, an effort has been made to point out the areas where the law is lagging behind the principles, which have already been accepted by our Constitution.

I. POLYGAMY

Polygamy and Law

Full equality of sexes can hardly be possible in a legal system which permits polygamy, and a social system which tolerates it. Though the institution of polygamy has prevailed traditionally in India, in the last five or more decades, it is on the wane and most marriages are today monogamous. The spread of Christianity with its concept of marriage "as a union for life of one man with one woman" marked the first step towards the legal recognition of the principle of monogamy. The advanced communities in the country like the Parsees and the Brahmos opted for the principle. The Parsee Marriage and Divorce Act, 1865 provided that any marriage during the lifetime of the wife or husband was void. The Indian Christian Marriage Act, 1872 lays down the condition that, neither of the persons intending to be married shall have a wife or husband still living. With the enactment of the Hindu Marriage Act, 1955, which lays down the principle of monogamy for all Hindus, 88 per cent of the Indian population are legally governed by the principle of monogamy.

The only personal law, which has remained impervious to the changing trend from polygamy to monogamy, is the Muslim law. Most Muslim countries such as Turkey, Iraq, Iran, Syria, Tunisia, Indonesia and Pakistan (including Bangladesh, which was then a part of Pakistan) have introduced reforms of varying degrees to correct the abuse of polygamy, but no legislative effort has so far been made in India to ameliorate the hardship caused to the Muslim women by the continuance of the institution of polygamy. According to an Urdu editor

> "...the law of polygamy is not an invention of the Muslims, but a part of the comprehensive religious code granted to them by God. And the Muslims have been exercising this right of theirs since the time of the holy Prophet to this day. To tamper with it would definitely amount to interference in religion. If some Muslim or non-Muslim administration force monogamy on Muslims, it would be a case of gross injustice; and the Muslims will oppose it as a religious duty."

During its tours, the Committee met with three different reactions. "In UP we found a positive hostility to any reform in the Muslim law, particularly among the educated middle-class. Among the poorer classes of the same state, we found a desire to have monogamous marriages and blunt denunciation of the inequities of polygamy. In Kashmir, the women uniformly and emphatically demanded that polygamy must be banned.

The seeming indifference on the part of the government in leaving only one section of the citizens to be governed by a law permitting polygamy and other inequalities was sought to be explained by the then Minister for Law and Justice, Mr Gokhale, when he said, "we believe that while we should do everything possible to build up and cultivate the consciousness for reform, the urge and the demand for the reform must come from the community itself".

Standardized Contracts

Marriage is regarded as a contract under the Muslim law for the purpose of procreation and legalizing of children. Some eminent jurists like Fyzee and Danial Latifi have, thereforew, advocated the device of standard contract of marriage, which would provide *inter alia* for stipulation like "The husband shall not take a second wife while the first marriage subsists, and if the husband has married or gone through a form of marriage with another woman after the date thereof", the wife shall have the power to divorce. As in Islamic law, marriage is regarded as a contract, the prevailing opinion of the jurists is that, generally such contracts become enforceable in courts.

Two subsidiary views exist regarding the technique : (i) to propagate the standard form of contract and leave it to the volition of the parties to enter into such contracts, and (ii) to provide an amendment to section 2 A of the Shariat Act *inter alia* that "every contract of marriage shall be deemed to include, unless otherwise expressly provided, the terms set out", which would contain a provision that the husband shall not take a second wife during the subsistence of the marriage.

The critical question for consideration is : What are the consequences of a breach of the contractual stipulation on the part of the husband that he would not contract a second marriage during the subsistence of the prior marriage ? Fyzee says that :-

(a) restitution may be refused to the husband;

(b) certain rights as to dower may arise; or

(c) the wife may have a right to divorce; or, in an extreme case

(d) the marriage itself may be dissolved.

Thus, the effective right of a Muslim wife having a standard contract is to get the dissolution of marriage or a right to live separately from the husband. This fails to provide a substantive relief to the first wife with children. As the second marriage is not invalidated, the position of the husband is not prejudicially affected due to the financial implications arising out of the step. The deterrence of the criminal sanction when a person intends to contract a second marriage is absent. Further, the solution of standard contracts is ineffective, in case of fake conversions to Islam from other religions to circumvent the prohibition against bigamy. The remedy is out of step with the position in the other personal laws in India and should be rejected.

Reforms to Correct the Abuse of Polygamy

The first approach to reform Muslim law relating to polygamy is to abolish it altogether. In Turkey, polygamy was abolished by law. The Turkish Civil Code lays down that no person shall marry again unless he proves that the former marriage has been dissolved by death, divorce or by a decree of nullity. The Turkish Family Law of Cyprus also provides that a marriage shall be declared invalid where at the date of the marriage, one of the parties is already married. The Tunisian Code of Personal Status in Article 18 provides : "Plurality of wives is prohibited. Any person who being already married and before the marriage is lawfully dissolved, marries again, shall be liable to imprisonment for one year or for a fine of 240,000 francs or to both even if the second marriage is in violation of any requirements of this law. The Muslims in the erstwhile USSR and the Peoples Republic of China are also governed by the rule of monogamy.

It deserves to be emphasized that in Tunisia the justification for the abolition of polygamy had its basis on a re-evaluation or re-interpretation of Islamic principles. Professor Anderson points out the following distinctive grounds :

> The first was the broadly based argument that there were certain institutions, such as slavery and polygamy, which were acceptable at a certain stage in human development, but which were repugnant to the civilised conscience today....
>
> The second argument was... that the Verse of polygamy itself allows plurality of wives only on two conditions, one of which is that the would-be polygamist should have no fear whatever, of treating them with less than equal justice. But experience, the President said, had proved that no man other than a prophet was capable of such a feat especially in contemporary conditions.

The second approach is to regulate the husband's right to contract a second marriage by rendering it necessary to obtain judicial or official sanction for a bigamous marriage. In most countries where Muslims constitute a majority of the population, this approach, with variations, is favoured. Iran, Iraq, Singapore and Syria provide that permission of the court is necessary for a bigamous marriage of the husband. The laws provide that in granting the permission, the courts should satisfy themselves about the financial capacity of the husband to maintain more than one wife. Some of these laws provide for additional grounds to be fulfilled like the capacity to do equal justice to the co-wives.

On the other hand, Sri Lanka, Ceylon and Indonesia confer the power to regulate bigamous marriage on institutions other than the regular courts. For example, Section 6 of the Muslim Family Laws Ordinance of Pakistan states that no male can contract another marriage during the subsistence of an existing marriage except with the previous permission of the Arbitration Council. The Arbitration Council may grant the permission if it is satisfied that the proposed marriage is necessary and just. If a person contracts another marriage without such permission, upon a complaint being made, he is liable for punishment which may extend to one years' simple imprisonment or a fine of Rs 5,000 or both. The legislation in Sri Lanka prescribes for the prior notice of the intended marriage and the display of the notice in the mosques and at the residence of the parties, that is, the husband, the first wife and the prospective second wife. In Indonesia, the Family Law Regulations of 1947 enjoin the marriage officials to clarify and explain the position of a bigamous marriage under Islamic Law and legal conditions and obligations relating to it, to the person intending to contract a bigamous marriage.

David Pearl studied the impact of the Muslim Family Laws Ordinance (1963) in Quetta (Baluchistan), Pakistan. Two points relevant for our consideration emerge from his study.

According to the first: "many men risk the penalties inherent in Section 6 (5) (a) and (b) of the ordinance, and marry a second wife without bothering to apply to the arbitration council for its approval."

The second relates to classification of marriages in the Muslim Law. A marriage is valid (*sabih*) if all the conditions and formalities relating to marriage have been properly fulfilled. A valid marriage confers on the wife the right to dower, maintenance, etc.; and creates reciprocal rights of inheritance between the husband and wife. Among the Sunnis, a marriage that is not valid may be either void (*batil*) or irregular (*fasid*). A void marriage does not create any rights or obligations among the parties. The children of the union are illegitimate. An irregular marriage has no legal effect before consummation and it can be terminated by worlds showing intention to separate. The children of the union are legitimate but the irregular marriage does not create mutual rights of inheritance between the husband and wife.

Pearl points out that the distinction between valid, void and irregular marriages was not eliminated and, therefore, "it was remarkably easy... for a girl under 16 to be married, or a man to ignore Sections 6 & 7 of the ordinance".

While the desirability of reform in Muslim Law is generally acknowledged, as mentioned, the government has taken no step towards changing the law for over two decades on the view that public opinion in the Muslim community did not favour a change. But this view cannot be reconciled with the declaration of equality and social justice. We are therefore of the opinion that ignoring the interest of Muslim women is a denial of social justice. The right to equality, in our view, like the right to free speech, is an individual right.

An Analysis of Polygamous Marriages among Muslims

An analysis of polygamous marriages among Muslims in India classifies them into four groups:

(a) The largest number of cases are of husbands who abandon their wives (and frequently children as well) and go off and marry somebody else. Frequently, the second wife remains ignorant about the earlier marriage and the children;

(b) Where the wives, finding the marriage unbearable have left their husbands, who, in order to avoid paying the deferred *Mahr*, refuse to divorce them;

(c) Wives who, because of economic dependence, acquiesce in the second marriage;

(d) Where a person of another religious persuasion deliberately adopts Islam to contract a marriage which could not be permitted under his own system of law.

Regulated Bigamy

The adoption of monogamy as a rule among the Hindus under the Hindu Marriage Act, 1955 has been criticised and an opinion has been expressed in favour of "carefully regulated bigamy." According to Derret (1970) :

> It is a serious question whether the sympathy which the public and courts seem to harbour for bigamous unions has no solid basis which we ought to recognise. It is argued that a carefully regulated bigamy i.e. popular marriages in cases of infertility, mental instability of the wife , and other cases where the good sense and humanity of the husband and his family recoils from divorcing her or annulling the marriage would not only be in accord with traditional Hindu religious sentiment and practice, but also much more realistic. It would savour less of "shop-window-dressing" with which the Hindu Code is charged. There is a small part of India which at present has controlled bigamy for Hindu husbands, namely the former Portuguese India (Goa, Daman & Diu)... This appears to work extremely well, and the parliament has had the good sense not to interfere with the modified Hindu Law still in force in those territories... Moreover, it was the opinion of Mahamahopadhyaya Dr. P.V. Kane, that polygamy should

> be tolerated for some classes on purely economic grounds... It is the health and happiness of Hindus that counts, and the rash abolition of polygamy in a euphoric moment is not working out satisfactorily.

As this view gives a misleading impression of being in the interests of women and as it is likely to be advanced in the context of Muslim Law also, it needs to be rebutted in full. We are not aware of a sympathy for bigamous unions or an opinion in favour of them in the absence of a systematic survey. A survey made some years ago showed 85 per cent of the men and 96 per cent of the women to be in favour of compulsory monogamy. While judicial decisions have rendered difficult, the enforcement of the penal provision against bigamy in Section 17 of the Hindu Marriage Act, 1955, it would only be fair to say that this stemmed not from a sentiment in favour of bigamy, but from a deep seated judicial attitude that penal provisions should be construed strictly. The 'economic grounds', in our considered view, equate women with beasts of burden and cannot be accepted. It is doubtful whether the advocates of controlled bigamy will also favour controlled polyandry as a general rule on the same grounds.

Long before the passing of the Hindu Marriage Act, monogamy in preference to controlled bigamy existed under the Marumakattayam Law in the State of Travancore-Cochin and in the Malabar District of the Madras province. It was introduced in the province of Bombay in 1946 and in the province of Madras in 1949.

We are of the firm view that there can be no compromize on the basic policy of monogamy being the rule for all communities in India. Any compromize in this regard will only perpetuate the existing inequalities in the status of women.

Enforcement Of Provision Against Bigamy Under The Hindu Marriage Act

While bigamy has been made an offence and the second marriage should be void, bigamous marriages are still prevalent among Hindus. Apart from the figures available in many of the states, a large number of such marriage exist. In Manipur, even though the women were very bitter about the wide prevalance of this practice, they were compelled to accept it as divorce or prosecution of the husband resulted in social ostracism.

The Government had failed to enforce the law. Even Government servants, who are forbidden under the Government Servants' Conduct Rules, were practising polygamy. The Committee was also informed that a Resolution in the Legislative Assembly calling upon the Government to enforce the law had been defeated by an overwhelming majority. It is interesting to note that most women of Manipur earn to support their families. In spite of their economic independence, they have been unable to assert their social and legal rights. Quite a few of them were living with their co-wives, some had separate establishments, but all of them contributed a part of their incomes to their husbands. Little social stigma seemed to be attached to such a situation.

In West Bengal, a training centre in Sriniketan for promoting self-employment had a number of women discarded by their husbands who had married a second time. We met two co-wives, whose husbands discarded them for a third wife taking the training. Similar cases were brought to our notice in some parts of Andhra Pradesh, Bihar, Uttar Pradesh and in the rural areas of Madhya Pradesh.

Under the present law, only an aggrieved person can initiate proceedings for bigamy, which means the husband or the wife. In the case of the wife, the complaint may be made on her behalf by one of her family members. Quite often an economically dependent woman who is also uneducated has neither the knowledge nor the means to go to court. Many of them are reluctant to appear in court and face social ostracism as brought our very clearly by Justice Sachar:

> We also cannot shut our eyes to the practical difficulties and problems faced by an Indian girl... Instances are numerous where Indian women have gone through a literal misery of marriage for years rather than go to a court of law and expose themselves to public gaze. The attitude of the parents and relations in most of these cases is also un-sympathetic.

Where social customs prevent a woman from appearing in public, the law permits some other person to make the complaint with the permission of the court. The question to be considered is whether the right to initiate prosecution for bigamy should be extended to persons other than the girl's family in all cases, in view of the general reluctance of her family members to lodge a complaint against the son-in-law or brother-in-law. The necessity of obtaining prior permission of the Court would provide adequate safeguard against undue harassment. In small towns and villages a social worker could fulfil this role admirably.

In our opinion such a provision is necessary to prevent the current widespread violation of a most salutary provision of the law which very clearly lays down the social policy of the country.

The existing penal provision against bigamy is further defeated in a considerable number of cases because of a technical construction placed on Section 17 of the Act. The Supreme Court in *Bhaurao vs. State of Maharashtra* held that the offence of bigamy was not proved unless it was established that the second marriage was celebrated with proper ceremonies and due form. This conclusion was arrived at on the basis that the section used the word 'solemnized'. They observe :

> The word 'solemnize' means, in connection with a marriage, 'to celebrate the marriage with proper ceremonies and due form' according to the Shorter Oxford Dictionary. It follows, therefore, that unless the marriage is 'celebrated' or performed with proper ceremonies and due form, it cannot be said to be 'solemnized'. It is therefore essential, for the purpose of Sec. 17 of the Act, that the marriage to which Sec. 494, I.P.C. applies on account of the provisions of the Act, should have been celebrated with proper ceremonies and due form.

As the law requires no specific ceremonies of marriage according to custom, it becomes extremely difficult to determine which ceremony or ceremonies were really essential. Whether the construction put by the court will subserve the policy and purpose of the Act, or the social objectives of the legislation was never in their contemplation.

The result of this interpretation is that a difficult burden is cast on the prosecution to show that the second marriage is performed with all due formalities. This burden in many cases cannot be discharged owing to the fact that second marriages during the subsistence of a prior marriage, are seldom performed with the usual pomp and show.

Even if it is not so, this judicial interpretation facilitates widespread evasion of law. As pointed out by Professor Derrett, the existing position will give rise to two types of devices being followed to evade prosecution for bigamy. First, a person intending to take a second wife, may deliberately undergo a defective form of marriage, to defend himself against a prosecution launched by the first wife or her relatives. Second, the relatives and friends of the second wife may commit perjury and say that the marriage is not properly solemnized and the first wife or her relatives would not be in a position to rebut it.

Shri M.B. Majumdar suggested that the words "solemnized" may be replaced by the words "contracted". But given the contemporary judicial attitudes, inherited from the English legal system, whereby the policy and purpose of an Act often are sacrificed to a literal construction of the Act, it is doubtful whether the suggested amendment will change the situation materially.

We recommend that words "solemnized" should be replaced by the word "goes through a marriage." Further, an explanation should be added to the section that an omission to perform some of the essential ceremonies by parties shall not be construed to mean that the offence of bigamy was not committed, if such a ceremony of marriages gives rise to a *de facto* relationship of husband and wife.

Injunction

As already mentioned there is often an inhibition against prosecuting a husband for his second marriage in the present social context. The easier remedy is to prevent such a marriage taking place, if there is prior knowledge of its impending celebration. The following two cases will show that though bigamy, including the attempt and abetment of it is an offence, the position is not as clearcut as we would like it to be.

In *Sankarappa Vs. Basamma,* the Mysore High Court held that the Hindu wife is entitled to a perpetual injunction restraining her husband from contacting a second marriage; that the suit is clearly permitted by Section 54 of the Specific Relief Act, 1877 (Sec. 38 of the Specific Relief Act, 1963).

On the other hand, a Division Bench of the Patna High Court in *Uma Prasad Singh vs. Smt Radha Devi* takes the view that a remedy by way of injunction against a second marriage is not available under the provisions of the Hindu Marriage Act.

The case seems to have been argued only on the basis of the Hindu Marriage Act, 1955 and the question of remedy under the Specific Relief Act, 1963 was not referred to by the parties or by the court. The only point for consideration is... Where the suit as framed and filed by opposite party 1 could be maintained under any provision of the Hindu Marriage Act, 1955.

Though the two cases can be clearly distinguished and there is no real conflict, it is desirable to clarify the matter. We recommend that a provision be introduced in Section 6 of the hindu marriage Act to the effect that nothing contained in the Hindu Marriage Act shall prevent a court from granting an injunction against a proposed bigamous marriage under the Act or under the provisions of the Specific Relief Act, 1963.

Laws in Former French and Portuguese Territories

After the merger of the former French and Portuguese colonial possessions with India, the laws in force prior to merger in these territories have not been abrogated and therefore they continue to be in force. A reference will now be made to these laws insofar as they affect the status of women.

Laws in Pondicherry

Prior to the merger, three different systems of personal law were applicable in Pondicherry. First, the Hindu Laws and customs applicable to Hindus and native Christians, (other than renoncants). However, in matters relating to marriage, divorce and allied matters, the Christians were governed by the French Civil Code. Second, the Muslim Law, which was more or less similar to that applied in India, governed the Muslims. Third, the French Law which was applied to the people of French origin and renoncants.

After the merger with India the categories of laws applicable increased and consequently the applicability of the Hindu Law became complicated. David Annoussamy categorizes the application of Hindu Law thus.

(1) Hindu Law prevailing in India applicable to migrants from the rest of India.

(2) Hindu Law applicable to Hindus of Pondicherrian origin consisting of Indian statutes (Applicable to Hindus).

(3) Hindu Law consisting solely of the Hindu local customs adhered to by Hindus who remained French nationals.

(4) Hindu Law consisting of customs of Pondicherry except in matters of marriage and divorce.

This category has been further subdivided into two groups, viz:

(1) India Christians who are governed according to their choice in respect of marriage, either by the French Civil Code or the Indian Christan Marriage Act and the Indian Divorce Act, and

(1) Indian Christians who are exclusively governed by the French Civil Code.

Laws in Goa, Daman and Diu

Even though these territories are now a part of India, no effort has so far been made to extend the Hindu Marriage Act to them. The result is that a section of Hindus today continues to be governed by a law which permits polygamy.

Districts of Goa and Diu

In the districts of Goa, polygamy is permissible among Hindus under the following circumstances :-

(i) when the previous wife is childless upto the age of 25 years;

(ii) When there is no male issue from the previous wife till her 30th year or when the previous wife who is below 30 does not conceive for ten years after her last conception;

(iii) in cases of judicial separation by wife and when there is no male issue.

(Note: In the case of Goa, previous wife's consent is required for the cases mentioned in (i) and (ii) above).

District of Daman

According to the Code of Customs and Usage of Non-Christian inhabitants of Daman, the male individuals are allowed to have many wives but Bramos of Modd Caste cannot have more than two wives.

However, there is no polygamy among Dhobis, Morai-Machines, Barbers, Salvia, Betelas, Porobias and Bramos except those belonging to Teloquia and Modd caste.

Note: For an individual to marry or re-marry more than twice-when his previous wives are living, an express consent of all of them is required previous to marriage, which shall be drawn by the 'Chief of Rancho' or by the Notary Public in the presence of four witnesses.

Judicial justification of any of the circumstances mentioned above is a condition precedent for polygamy.

In our opinion, the continuation of such diverse laws contradictory to our social policy, in these territories is totally unjustified. We recommend therefore, the immediate replacement of these laws by the Hindu Marriage Act 1955.

II. AGE OF MARRIAGE

Legal provision

Another major social evil which was sought to be curbed by legislation is child marriage. The disastrous effects of such marriages have been discussed already. One of the few areas where our social reformers had taken the initiative, even in the 19th century, was to curb this evil by legislation. The first legislation was the Civil Marriage Act which laid down the age of marriage to be 14 years. But as only a very small section of the people married under this Act, the problem continued.

One of the adverse consequences of child marriage, as realized by the reformers, was early consummation, with disastrous effect on the health of the young wives and their children. An effort was made in 1891 to prevent early consummation by the Age of Consent Act which prohibited consummation before 12 years. Due to lack of publicity and propaganda there was no impact of this provision. In 1925, the Age of Consent was raised to 13. This was the forerunner of the Sarda Act of 1929.

It was realized that legislation, while one of the major instruments of social change, is not sufficient by itself to fight against deeprooted prejudices and traditional practice. Thus, the legislators compromises this by leaving the validity of child marriage untouched by making such practice a penal offence. Parents of children, those 'performing, conducting or directing' as also the adult bridegroom, were all liable to punishment in varying degrees. The Act was further amended leaving untouched the structure of the earlier Act. The impact of this legislation and the present position regarding child marriage have been discussed already.

Apart from the Sarda Act, the various personal laws have their own minimum age of marriage. Not only do they vary in regard to the minimum age, but also in the consequences of violation of the law.

The Hindu Marriage Act, 1955 lays down as one of the conditions, the completion of 18 years and 15 years by the bridegroom and the bride respectively. Though passed in the post-independence era, the Act remains silent about the effect on the validity of the marriage and continues the earlier penal policy in cases of violation. Most writers hold the view that the validity on the marriage is not affected and this is also supported by judicial decisions.

The Parsee Marriage and Divorce Act 1936 on the other hand, lays down that no suit shall be brought to enforce a marriage between two Parsees or any contract connected with the marriage, if at the date of the institution of the suit the husband has not completed the age of 16 years and the wife 14 years. The Christian Marriage Act, 1872 provides that for a valid marriage under the Act, the age of the male shall exceed 16 years and that of the female 13 years. For a valid marriage under the classical Muslim law the parties should not be minors, that is, the parties should have attained puberty. Puberty is presumed in the absence of evidence to the contrary, at 15 and 19 in the case of girls and boys respectively.

Only the Special Marriage Act, 1954, a post-independence legislation which provides for a secular marriage irrespective of the religious affiliation of the parties, contemplates the solemnization of marriage between adults under this provisions, as it fixes the minimum age at 21 and 18 for males and females respectively.

The legal position noted above brings forth an important feature, namely, a lesser age of marriage is prescribed in the case of girls. No doubt, throughout the world, the laws generally provide for a lesser age in case of girls. For example, in the USA only eleven States prescribed the same minimum age for boys and girls. The remaining thirty-nine states permit girls to be married at a lower age than boys. As pointed out by Konowitz : "It (early marriage for women) can lead to premature removal from socially productive enterprise or lost opportunities.

When the legal age of marriage in case of a female is below the age of discretion, she cannot be expected to form an intelligent opinion about her partner in life. The policy of law which permits the marriage of a girl before she is physically and mentally mature, is open to serious question. As reported by the Pushpaben Committee, child marriage is one of the significant factors leading to the high incidence of suicide among young married women in India. Therefore, increasing the marriage age of girls to eighteen years is desirable.

In this context, it is necessary to point out an anachronism that exists in the Muslim law that governs some sects. After attaining puberty, a Muslim male in all sects and a Muslim female belonging to the Hanafi and Ithana Ashari Shirte sects can marry without a guardian. But a Maliki, Shafi, or Daudi or Salaymani Bohra virgin cannot marry without a guardian and her only remedy is to change over to the Hanafi School and marry according to its tenets.

In two recent decisions, viz. *Muhammad Haji Kammu vs. Ethiyumma* and *K. Abubukker vs. Marakkar*, The Kerala High Court struck a different note which mitigates this hardship. The parties in both cases were Shafis. In Abubukker's case, the mother who was divorced, sought the consent of her ex-husband to the daughters' marriage which he refused. On the marriage being solemnized, the father filed a suit for a declaration that the marriage was invalid as his consent was not obtained. The lower court declared the marriage to be invalid even though the girl was already pregnant. Reversing the decision of the lower court, Justice Pillai stated that under the Maliki and Shafi law the marriage of an adult girl is not valid unless her consent is obtained, and communicated through a legally authorised *wali* (guardian). As the father refused his consent, she could constitute any other relation or Kazi (in this case the Kazi) to act as her agent.

In our opinion a change in the law to remove the existing disability in these sub-schools and to bring them in conformity with the Hanafi law is necessary.

Aspects relating to Prevention of Child Marriages

As mentioned earlier the policy of the Child Marriage Restraint Act or other statutes is not to invalidate child marriages, but to punish their solemnization. The offences under the Act are, however, non-cognizable, and no woman is punishable with imprisonment.

There are large-scale violations of the Act particularly in the rural areas. The non-cognizable character of the offence is a serious hindrance to the effective enforcement of this law. The State of Gujarat amended the Child Marriage Restraint Act by making it a cognizable offence. Provisions have also been made for the appointment of a Child Marriage Prevention Officer. These changes have been welcomed by the Pushpaben Committee.

We recommend that all offences under the Child Marriage Restraint Act should be made cognizable, and special officers appointed to enforce the law.

Another effective approach to this problem is to render such marriages void. But in the present social and economic conditions, such rigorous measures may create more problems than it seeks to solve. We suggest, therefore, that it should be envisaged as a future goal.

As immediate measures to deter child marriages and to alleviate their consequences we suggest the following :

(a) to provide the girl the right to repudiate the marriage on attaining majority on lines similar to the "option of puberty" under Muslim Law;

Note: A Muslim girl married during her minority is entitled to a dissolution of marriage if the following facts are established:

(i) that she was given in marriage by her father or other guardian before she attained the age of 15;
(ii) that she repudiated the marriage before she attained the age of 18;
(iii) that the marriage was not consummated.

In our view the right to repudiate the marriage on attaining majority should be made available to girls in all communities whether the marriage was consummated or not.

(b) A general legal provision analogous to Section 38 of the Parsee Marriage and Divorce Act, 1865 which provides that "no suit shall be brought in any court to enforce any marriage between Parsees, or any connected with or arising out of any such marriage, if, at the date of the institution of the suit, the husband shall not have completed the age of 16 years, or the wife shall not have completed the age of 14 years." Under the Egyptian Civil Code, a marriage in contravention of the rule relating to age of the parties (completion of 18 years and 15 years in case of males and females respectively) though not invalid *per se* will not be registered. Under Article 99 of the Code such a marriage will not be recognized by the Court for the purpose of granting any relief, except a claim relating to legitimacy of issues.

We recommend legislation prohibiting courts from granting any relief in respect of a marriage solemnized in violation of the age requirements prescribed by law, unless both the parties have completed the age of 18 years.

Compulsory Registration of Marriages

Compulsory registration of marriage operates as an effective check on child and bigamous marriages, and also offers reliable proof of marriage. It ensures the legitimacy and inheritance rights of children. Section 8 of the Hindu Marriage Act, 1955, enables the State Governments to provide for compulsory registration of marriages and any person contravening the rule may be punished with a fine which may extend to twenty-five rupees. However it has been stated that failure to register a marriage will not affect its validity. Laws which provide for the voluntary registration of Muslim marriages are in force in the States of Assam, Bihar, Orissa and Bengal.

Among the Parsees and Indian Christians, the registration of marriages is compulsory. Registration is also compulsory for marriages solemnized under the Special Marriages Act, 1954. Section 16 of this Act permits voluntary registration of marriages celebrated under other laws. The figures given in Table 6.1 illustrate that the appeal of this secular law, though it ensures better legal protection to all parties, is still limited to a very small minority. Neither has the permission for voluntary registration attracted much response.

TABLE - 6.1

NUMBER OF MARRIAGES REGISTERED UNDER THE SPECIAL MARRIAGES ACT 1954

Years	*Bombay*	*Rajasthan*	*Delhi*
1968	601	11	148
1969	621	8	194
1970	766	13	229
1971	705	11	235
1972	816	6	212

TABLE - 6.2

NUMBER OF MARRIAGES CELEBRATED UNDER OTHER LAWS BUT SUBSEQUENTLY REGISTERED UNDER SECTION 16 OF THE SPECIAL MARRIAGES ACT

Years	*Bombay*
1968	19
1969	18
1970	43
1971	36
1972	26

The ultimate object should be to recognize registration as the sole and conclusive proof of marriage, irrespective of the religious rites under which it was solemnized. It may be mentioned here that India has neither signed nor ratified the United Nations Convention on Consent to Marriage, Minimum Age for Marriage and Registration of Marriage. Explaining the position of India on ratification, the Indian delegate stated "the Convention would impose an obligation to introduce legislation, and since that might not be feasible at the present time, he must reserve his Government's position on the question of ratification."

We regret that for over a decade no attempt has been made to introduce legislation to implement the objects of the UN Convention. This attitude indicates a casualness and lack of concern of matters affecting the status of women. We recommend that registration should be made compulsory for all marriages. We have a clear precedent for a uniform measure in the Registration of Births and Deaths Act.

III. DOWRY

The dimension and ramifications of the dowry system in its present form have been discussed in the previous Chapter.

We are compelled to record our finding that the Dowry Prohibition Act 1961, passed with the ostensible purpose of curbing this evil, if not of eradicating it, has signally failed to achieve its purpose. In spite of the rapid growth of this practice, there are practically no cases reported under the Act. During its tours of all the States, the Committee was informed of only one case that was pending before the court in Kerala, in which the father had filed the complaint only because of the ill-treatment meted out to his daughter.

During the debate on the Dowry Prohibition Bill, one MP observed. "But I feel the whole problem will be solved - very easily and more quickly, not by legislation, but by rousing social conscience. As soon as our women get economic opportunities and economic freedom, as soon as avenues of employment and other opportunities are opened to them, as soon as they become independent of their families, possibly there would not be any occasion for this law to operate."

The eradication of this evil by rousing social conscience is seemingly an attractive approach. The Committee's findings, however, indicate that there is hardly any evidence of social conscience in the country today. In Indore, at a fairly large meeting, the Committee was told of the case of a girl who was burnt in the legs and in the back by her inlaws as she had not brought an adequate dowry. The acceptance of this situation was indicative of society's indifference to this social evil. No one at the meeting mentioned the need to report the case to the police or even of socially boycotting the family. Many such cases were brought to our notice, but nowhere did we hear of any social censure being exercised.

An increase in economic freedom and job opportunities for women, to the extent that the practice of dowry becomes obsolete, under the existing economic conditions, will be a very long process. The educated youth is grossly insensitive to the evil and unashamedly contributes to its perpetuation. In our opinion, therefore, a stringent enforcement of the policy and purpose of the Act may serve to educate public opinion better.

A very small but significant step could be taken by the Government, by declaring the taking or giving of dowry to be against the Government Servants Conduct Rules. Such a lead was given earlier to prevent bigamous marriages and giving or taking of dowry should be similarly dealt with.

The major cause for the failure of the Dowry Prohibition Act, 1961 is that an infringement of the provisions of the Act is not made a cognizable offence. That the offences under the Act should be made cognizable was in fact suggested during the debate in Lok Sabha.

But the offence was not made cognizable, as it was apprehended that this might result in the harassment of citizens by the police and lead also to undue invasion of the individual's right of privacy.

In our opinion the policy of making the offence non-cognizable completely nullifies the purpose of the Act as it is unrealistic to think that the father of a girl who had paid the dowry (and who alone is in a position to adduce evidence of the fact that dowry was stipulated and given) would prefer a complaint against the interests of his daughter after her marriage.

We recommend, therefore, that the offences, under the Act, should be made cognizable. We are fortified in our conclusion by the recommendation of the Pushpaben Committee, to overcome the fears regarding harassment by the police and encroachment on the right of privacy. It is suggested that the enforcement of social laws like the Dowry Prohibition Act, the Child Marriage Restraint Act, should be entrusted to a separate administration with which social workers and enlightened members of the community should be associated.

In addition, two ancillary provisions should be incorporated in the Dowry Prohibition Act, 1961. It has been pointed out that one of the 'major loopholes' in the existing legislation is that anything is allowed in the name of gifts and presents.

Therefore, any gifts made to the bridegroom or his parents in excess of Rs. 500 or which can be so used as to reduce his own financial liability should be made punishable.

The practice of displaying the dowry by parents of the bride or the bridegroom, as discussed earlier, is prevalent in some parts of India. This naturally tends to perpetuate the practice as others follow suit. To curb this evil we recommend legislation of the lines of the West Pakistan Dowry (Prohibition of Display) Act 1967 which penalizes such display.

We suggest that an evaluation of the impact of the amended Dowry Prohibition Act should be made after five years. It will help in plugging loopholes which facilitate the evasion of this law. The next step should be to set a ceiling even on the gifts that may be made to the bride. This will help to improve the situation further because we have found that gifts given to the bride are often only a guise for dowry since generally she has little or no control over them.

REFERENCES

1. Archana Parashar, *Women and Family Law*, 1992.
2. Derrett, *A Critique of Modern Hindu Law*, 1970.
3. Derrett, A Round-up of Bigamous Marriages, *Bombay Law Reporter* Vol. 69 84 (s), 1967.
4. Fyzee, *Outlines of Muhammodan Law*, 1967.
5. Gurdit Singh V. Srimati Angrez Kaur *A.I.R.* 1968, S.C. 142.
6. I.B. Horner, *Women under Primitive Buddhism*, London.
7. Jahir Mahmood, *Family Law Reforms in the Muslim World*, 1972.
8. Kane, P.V., *History of Dharamashastras*.
9. Madho Prasad V. Shakumtala *A.I.R.* 1972, All. 119.
10. Rajani V. Prabhakar, 1957, 59, *Bombay L.R.* 11-69.
11. Rajkumari Agrawala, *Matrimonial Remedies under Hindu Law*, 1973.
12. Ranken, *Background to Indian Law*, 1946.

Seven

Divorce

The concept of 'union for life' or the sacramental nature of the marriage which renders the marriage indissoluble has gradually been eroded and through legislation the right of divorce has been introduced in all legal systems in India, but the same variations and unequal treatment of sexes characterizes this branch of law also. A monogamous marriage without the right of divorce would cause great hardship to both parties to the marriage.

According to the Census of 1971, the total number of divorced or separated women in the country is estimated to be 8,70,700 ; of which 7,43,200 are in the rural areas and 1,27,500 in urban areas. The ratio of divorced or separated women is 1630 per thousand males. The table 3.3 indicates the relative percentage of divorced or separated men and women to the total male and female population in 1961 and 1971. It is clear that the proportion of women who remain in this state is higher than men, in both rural and urban areas.

TABLE - 7.1
PERCENTAGE OF DIVORCED AND SEPARATED PERSONS

	1961			*1971*		
	Rural	*Urban*	*Total*	*Rural*	*Urban*	*Total*
Males	0.43	0.22	0.39	0.21	0.12	0.19
Females	0.53	0.43	0.51	0.35	0.25	0.33

Source: Country Statement- submitted to the World Population Conference, Bucharest (Romania) 19-30 August, 1974—Government of India, 1974.

Note: 1971 figures are based on 1 per cent sample data.

A survey undertaken by the Census in 1961 in 587 selected villages with a sample of 1,33,775 marriages covering a period of 50 years, had indicated a wide acceptance of divorce by the village community and some variations of incidence among the religious communities. Incidence of divorce was highest among the Muslims

(6.06%), followed by Hindus (3.21%). Among the Buddhists it was 3.7 per cent, among the Jains 1.68 per cent and among Sikhs 0.91 per cent. The incidence of divorce among Christians was considerably lower (0.41%). The causes for divorce show that adultery and barrenness are the commonest grounds for divorce in most of the villages studied. Extreme poverty is also found to be cause for divorce. In Rajasthan, sexual incompatibility and incapacity are recognized as grounds for divorce.

Hindu Law of Divorce

According to traditionalists, divorce was unknown in Hindu law. Even today, divorce is not a socially accepted norm among many sections.

We can take judicial notice of the fact that even today considerable sections of the Hindu society look with disfavour on the idea of dissolving a marriage.

Polygamy, without the right of divorce, caused tremendous hardship, in many cases.

Customary Divorce

Contrary to the general notion regarding the indissolubility of Hindu marriage, a large section of Hindus among the lower castes have traditionally practised divorce. These customary forms of divorce were recognized, both socially and judicially. The usual customary forms are :

(a) by mutual consent;

(b) unilaterally—at the pleasure of the husband or by the abandonment of the wife;

(c) by deed of divorce (*char-chitti*);

By Mutual Consent

The custom of obtaining divorce by mutual consent is prevalent among certain castes in Mumbai, Madras, Mysore and Kerala. In Madhya Pradesh it has been held that divorce by mutual consent is a valid custom among the Patwas of that State. A customary form of divorce by agreement (*chuttam-chutta*) amongst the Barai Chaurasiyas of UP has been declared valid by the Allahabad High Court. These are only a few illustrations to indicate the existence of divorce by mutual consent.

Unilateral Divorce

According to the custom prevailing in Manipur (Khaniaba), it has been stated that a husband can dissolve the marriage without any reason or at his pleasure. Among the Rajput Gujaratis in Khandesh, and in the Pakhali Community, marriage is dissolved if the husband abandons or deserts the wife. Among the Vaisyas of Gorakhpur in Uttar Pradesh, a husband may abandon or desert his wife, and dissolution takes place even without reference to the caste tribunal.

Divorce by Deed

This form is prevalent among certain castes in South India, also in Himachal Pradesh and the Jat community. Recently the Supreme Court has upheld a deed executed by the husband divorcing his wife.

Usually customary divorces are implemented through the intervention of the traditional Panchayats or caste tribunals. Therefore, in States where this has not been customary, the courts have not permitted Panchayats to take upon themselves the right to dissolve a marriage. Once the custom is proved, however, the courts will not interfere.

The courts have exercised a lot of judicial scrutiny and discretion in upholding or rejecting such customary divorce practices. In doing so, they have applied the strict test for the validity of such customs. In cases where the existence of a custom was not proved, or where the custom could be regarded as running counter to the spirit of Hindu law, or was against public policy or morality, courts have declared such customary forms of divorce as invalid.

Under customary law, there is no waiting period after divorce to remarry. But if divorce is obtained under the Hindu Marriage Act, then either party to the marriage can lawfully remarry only after a lapse of one year after the decree of divorce (Sec. 15). Retention of customary forms of divorce under the Hindu Marriage Act is advantageous because this process of dissolving the marriage saves time and money in litigations. The only difficulty that may arise is if the divorce according to customary law is brought at some stage to the notice of the court and the latter decrees that particular form of divorce to be against public policy or morality.

If one or both parties have remarried, such a marriage will be void and the status of the children will be affected. To minimize this, it has been suggested that the Ministry of Law should prepare an exhaustive record of customs relating to divorce found in different States and set up a panel of socio-legal experts to determine if any of these customs are invalid. Copies of the record should be made freely and easily available to the people and the Panchayats.

With the enactment of the Hindu Marriage Act of 1955, divorce became a part of the law governing all Hindus. The ground for this had been already prepared by the passing of the Hindu Women's Right to Separate Residence and Maintenance Act in 1946, which *inter alia,* permitted the wife to separate from her husband on the ground that he had married again. Following this, some of the States took the initiative and as with monogamy, legislated to permit divorce for Hindus.

Divorce Under the Hindu Marriage Act, 1955

The various grounds on which a husband or a wife can obtain divorce are (a) living in adultery, (b) conversion to other religion, (c) insanity, (d) incurable form of leprosy, (e) venereal disease, (f) renunciation, (g) where the respondent has not been heard of as being alive for a period of seven years or more by persons who would naturally have heard of it, (h) failure to resume cohabitation for a period of 2 years after the decree of judicial separation, and (i) failure to comply with a decree for restitution of conjugal rights. Two additional grounds have been given to the wife to obtain a divorce: (i) if the husband has more than one wife living, and (ii) if he has been guilty of rape, sodomy or bestiality. The former has a retrospective effect in the sense that when the marriages took place (i.e. before the Act), polygamy was legally permissible. This right can be exercised by either of the wives, and has obviously been provided to strengthen the social policy of monogamy. From the cases reported, it appears that many women have benefited from this provision.

Adultery

Since adultery is a very grave matrimonial offence, a very high degree or standard of proof is required. The courts have insisted that the offence of adultery should be proved beyond reasonable doubt. A husband or wife can ask for divorce only if at the time of filing the suit, the other party 'is living in adultery'. A single act of extramarital intercourse is not sufficient to dissolve the marriage, though it is sufficient for a decree of judicial separation. The Bombay High Court, therefore, rejected the petition of a husband as at the time of the petition there was no evidence that the wife was leading an adulterous life, though there was evidence that she had done so earlier.

Refusal to Resume Cohabitation

Another provision of, Act which is often taken advantage of is non-compliance with a decree restituting conjugal rights for two years or the lapse of the same period after a decree of judicial separation. One of the grounds for judicial separation is desertion, provided it is 'without reasonable cause.' It is in interpreting 'reasonable cause', the judiciary has often exhibited their inability to appreciate the socioeconomic changes and the Constitutional right to equality.

Whenever conjugal rights have come into open conflict with the woman's right of equal opportunity in education or employment, the attitude of the judiciary has often been rather ambiguous. Instead of guiding the conflicting parties towards a rational adjustment to the process of social change, the judiciary has either evaded the issue or thrown its weight on the side of the traditional view of the husband's authority. Two illustrations will suffice to demonstrate this tendency :-

(a) A husband's demand for his wife to resign her job as a teacher in city away from his place of employment, to join him, was upheld by the Punjab High Court, which ruled that it was the duty of the wife to remain under the 'roof and protection and submit obediently' to the authority of the husband.

(b) In a similar case, the Allahabad High Court took a step forward by opining that the concepts of protection and society are "inelastic and rigid rules which cannot be interpreted in the context of present day conditions and needs of society... In view of the altered social and economic conditions, both husband and wife may think it necessary to work and contribute to the family chest."

The Court, therefore, conceded the right of deciding the question to the wife where "in cases of economic stress for the sake of the family and children" the wife genuinely thinks it is necessary for her to work. The judgement, while conceding the right in cases of genuine economic necessity, totally evades the issue of the individual woman's right to decide whether to work or not.

We are of the opinion that difference in the place of work should not be regarded as a ground for a case of desertion or restitution of conjugal rights.

Cruelty and Desertion

Cruelty and desertion have not been made grounds for divorce though they are recognized as grounds for a judicial separation. It, therefore, follows that in these cases the innocent party to the marriage, against whom there has been cruelty, or who has been deserted, has to wait for two years before he or she can get a divorce. Uttar Pradesh has given the lead in this and amended their law to make these grounds for divorce. In our opinion these should be added as grounds for divorce in the Hindu Marriage Act so that persons are not compelled to follow the present circuitous route and undergo the expense of going to court twice.

Muslim Law of Divorce

Under Muslim law a husband has an absolute and unlimited right to repudiate the marriage at his will. This is known as Talaq. A Muslim wife had no such right to dissolve her marriage. Unwritten and traditional law tried to ameliorate her position by permitting her to seek dissolution under the following forms:

(a) *Talaqi Tafwid*: This is a form of delegated divorce. According to this the husband delegates his right of divorce in a marriage contract which may stipulate that *inter-alia* on his taking another wife the first wife has the right to divorce him. The courts have upheld these pre-nuptial and post-nuptial agreements as not opposed to public policy nor against the spirit of Muslim law. The Assam High Court has strengthened this right by declaring that such a power of Talaq given to the wife is irrevocable.

(b) *Khul*: This is a dissolution by an agreement between the parties to the marriage, on the wife's giving some consideration to the husband for her release from the marriage tie. The terms are a matter of bargain and usually takes the form of the wife giving up her dower.

(c) *Mubarrat*: This is divorce by mutual consent.

According to Hanafi law the inability of the husband to maintain his wife does not give her the right to dissolve the marriage. Following the Hanafi law the courts in India had refused the wife the right to dissolve her marriage on the ground of non-payment of maintenance. The Shafi and the Maliki laws, however, allowed the wife to obtain divorce on this ground.

Dissolution of Muslim Marriage Act, 1939

This Act took advantage of the law as enunciated by the Maliki and Shafi Schools and recognized the right of a wife to dissolve the marriage on the following grounds :

(i) that the whereabouts of the husband have not been known for a period of four years;

(ii) that the husband has neglected or has failed to provide for her maintenance for a period of two years;

(iii) that the husband has been sentenced to imprisonment for a period of seven years or upwards;

(iv) that the husband has failed to perform, without reasonable cause, his marital obligations for a period of three years;

(v) that the husband was impotent at the time of marriage and continues to be so;

(vi) that the husband has been insane for a period of two years or is suffering from leprosy or a virulent venereal disease;

(vii) that she, having been given in marriage by her father or other guardian before she attained the age of fifteen years, repudiated the marriage before attaining the age of eighteen years; provided that marriage has not been consummated;

(viii) that the husband treats her with cruelty;

(ix) on any other ground which is recognized as valid for the dissolution of marriage under Muslim Law.

Muslim women have benefitted by the Act. The provisions that have been resorted to most frequently are the 'option of puberty' and failure to provide maintenance by the husband.

Option of Puberty

According to traditional Muslim Law, when a minor girl had been given in marriage by the father or the father's father, the marriage was valid. She could, however, repudiate the marriage if she could show that the guardian had acted negligently or fraudulently. But if the minor had been given in marriage by any other guardian, she had the right to repudiate the marriage on attaining puberty. The present Act has modified the traditional law permitting her to exercise the right irrespective of who was the guardian who gave her in marriage. The courts in India have interpreted this right very liberally, often invoking the principles of equity and justice in favour of the girl. They have not rigidly applied the letter of the law in regard to the time when this right could be exercised. It has been held that a minor wife did not lose her right to repudiate the marriage within a reasonable time after she came to know of her right and not necessarily when she attained puberty. In such cases they have even waived the condition of non-consummation when such consummation was by force or before she attained the age of 15.

Right of the Wife to Dissolve the Marriage on Ground of Failure to Maintain

This right has been interpreted in two ways. One group of decisions, basing itself on the traditional 'fault theory', has denied the right to a wife to divorce where her conduct was such as to absolve the husband from his duty to provide maintenance. The other group has tended to uphold the right, irrespective of the wife's conduct.

These two groups of decisions clearly indicate that legislation alone cannot eliminate right traditionalism, with its desire to preserve the *status quo*. Without supporting judicial interpretation, even the policy of the law is negated. The decision of Justice Krishna Iyer is, therefore, significant as he has focused his observations on the right of the Muslim wife to divorce when her husband has failed to provide her maintenance for two years. He has used his erudition to support the theory of dissolution when the marriage has broken down, irrespective of the relative faults of the parties :

> There is no merit in preserving intact the tie of marriage when the parties are not able to and fail to live within the bonds of Allah, that is to fulfil their mutual marital obligations and there is no desecration involved in dissolving a marriage which has failed. The entire emphasis is on making the marital union a reality and when this is not possible..., the Quran enjoins a dissolution... This secular and pragmatic approach on Muslim law of divorce happily harmonizes with contemporary concepts in advanced countries.

We recommend that the right of the wife to divorce, on the failure of the husband to maintain her, irrespective of her conduct which may be the main or contributory course, should be clearly spelt out.

Muslim Law had always recognized that in some cases the wife may be able to get a divorce. To the uncodified law the Dissolution of Muslim Marriages Act 1939 has added further grounds. But the power of the husband to pronounce *talaq* unilaterally remains, and has in no way been curtailed either judicially or through legislation. As long as this absolute and unlimited right remains, the position of the Muslim wife will remain insecure and her status cannot be raised. We totally disagree with the view that with Justice Krishna Iyer's judgement and her right to obtain divorce by 'Khul', a Muslim woman's rights "are brought into approximation with those of the man." While the judgement is undoubtedly a great step forward, it has to be remembered that she still has to wait for two years without maintenance before getting her release. Also, a right to buy her release, as provided in the Koran can hardly be regarded as approximating the unilateral right of the man.

Legislation is the only instrument which can bring the Muslim divorce law into line with not only the needs of society but with the prevailing law in other Muslim countries. Turkey and Cyprus have completely prohibited unilateral divorce, while in Tunisia,

Algeria, Iraq and Iran the husband has to apply to a court. In Pakistan, Legislation has restrained the freedom of the husband to divorce his wife. He has to inform the Arbitration Council which will try and bring about a reconciliation. The husband's pronouncement of 'talaq' without informing the Arbitration Council has been declared to be an offence.

We recommend immediate legislation to eliminate the unilateral right of divorce and to introduce parity of rights for both partners regarding grounds for seeking dissolution of a marriage.

Christian Law of Divorce

All Christians are governed by the Indian Divorce Act, 1869. Under the Act, both husband and wife can obtain a divorce, but there is a great difference between the rights of the husband and the wife. The husband can obtain a divorce if the wife has committed adultery. The wife can seek a divorce on the following grounds:

(a) husband's conversion from Christianity and marriage with another woman;
(b) incestuous adultery;
(c) bigamy with adultery;
(d) marriage with another woman with adultery;
(e) rape, sodomy or bestiality;
(f) adultery with cruelty;
(g) adultery with desertion.

Thus, the wife has to prove two offences by the husband before she can obtain a divorce.

The law is so outdated that a need for revision has been felt for quite some time. The Government, realizing the need for reform, referred the matter to the Law Commission in 1960. The Commission prepared a Draft Bill. The Christian Marriage and Matrimonial Causes Bill, 1960, contains almost all the grounds included for divorce under the Special Marriage Act, 1954, such as desertion, cruelty, adultery, leprosy, venereal disease, conversion to another religion, and wilful refusal to consummate the marriage. Further, either party to a marriage can also obtain a decree of judicial separation on any of the grounds mentioned for divorce.

We regret that in spite of these preparatory steps, no action to enact this measure has been taken by the Government so far and recommend that no further time be lost to reform and amend this law on the lines suggested by the Law Commission.

Parsee Law of Divorce

The Parsees are governed by the Parsee Marriage and Divorce Act, 1936. Both the parties to the marriage can initiate divorce proceedings on the following grounds:

(a) continuous absence for 7 years without information to those persons who would naturally have heard of him or her;
(b) non-consummation;
(c) insanity;
(d) adultery, bigamy, rape or an unnatural offence;
(e) causing grievous hurt or venereal disease;
(f) imprisonment for 7 years or more;
(g) desertion for three years;
(h) non-resumption of cohabitation following a decree of judicial separation or restitution of conjugal rights;
(i) conversion.

In addition to these common grounds, the wife can obtain a divorce if she has been compelled by her husband to prostitution. The husband has the right to dissolve the marriage if the wife was pregnant by some other person at the time of marriage.

Jewish Law of Divorce

The Jews in India are not governed by statutory law but by their customary law. Originally, the *ghet* was the only form of divorce. In India, however, dissolution of the marriage can be done through the court on grounds of adultery or cruelty. The marriages are generally monogamous excepting in certain specified cases. Because they are a small minority, no effort has been made to codify or reform this law. We feel that this should be undertaken now and the principle of monogamy as well as the normal grounds for divorce as provided in the Special Marriage Act should be adopted for this community also.

Special Marriage Act, 1954

This Act provides for a secular form of marriage which can be taken advantage of by all persons in India irrespective of their religious faith. Persons who marry under this Act will be governed by the provisions of the Act and not by their own personal law, with respect to their matrimonial rights and remedies.

The grounds on which divorce can be obtained by either party to marriage are adultery, desertion for a period of three years, cruelty, unsound mind for 3 years, leprosy, venereal disease, continuous absence for 7 years without information to those persons who would naturally have heard of him or her, non-resumption of cohabitation for 1 year following a decree of judicial separation or restitution of conjugal rights. In addition to these, the wife can obtain divorce on the ground of rape, sodomy or bestiality. A special feature of this Act is that the parties can also dissolve the marriage by mutual consent. All that the parties need do in order to opt for divorce under this provision is, to present a petition to the court that they have been living separately for a period of one year or more, and that they have not been able to live together having mutually agreed to dissolve the marriage.

Grounds for Divorce

Conversion as a Ground for Divorce

In the field of personal law and particularly in divorce, the existence of various legal systems create a peculiar situation. The Constitution recognizes the right freely to profess, practise and propagate religion. Conversion, therefore, from one faith to another is an individual's right and the motive for the conversion is or should be beyond judicial scrutiny. But, when such conversion impinges on the right of another person, the question poses a problem. In India today as a legacy of the multiple systems, a person by his or her conversion also acquires the right to be governed by a different set of laws. Even after the Constitution, the codified Hindu Marriage Act has mentioned conversion as a ground for divorce. Is conversion then to be treated as a matrimonial wrong?

Under statutory Muslim law, a woman converted to a faith other than Islam or renouncing Islam has only the right to divorce if the husband has committed a matrimonial wrong-Conversion *per se* does not affect the validity of the marriage and is in no way a bar to its continuance. On the other hand, a man converted to Islam from another religion has the right to be governed by his new personal law, including the right to marry more than once. This is so even when his first marriage was a monogamous marriage. He is also entitled to claim that his new faith does not permit him to remain married to a Hindu and he can, therefore, proceed to divorce her by uttering 'talaq' three times. The Indian Divorce Act does not recognize conversion as affecting the validity of the marriage unless it is followed by the marriage of the husband to another woman. The Converts' Dissolution Act permits the convert to Christianity to dissolve the marriage provided the marriage has in effect broken down as a result of the conversion.

It requires to be proved clearly that cohabitation has been discontinued because of the conversion. Under the Parsee law, conversion is ground for divorce provided the suit is brought within 2 years. This thorny question is dealt with in many ways, but the problem remains of reconciling the right to freedom of religion with the possible impact of conversion on marriages. It has been suggested that the question of marital rights on conversion should be governed by principles of equity, justice and good conscience. The other is that no converted person can, for a period of two years at least, be able to affect any marital rights by resorting to the new religion. While the second suggestion has the merit of deterring people from easy conversion to solve their matrimonial problems, in our opinion conversion should not be a ground for divorce as it offers an easy way of evading matrimonial obligations.

Divorce by Mutual Consent

Our review of the different laws governing divorce indicates that both customary laws and the secular law, i.e. the Special Marriage Act, 1954 recognize mutual consent as a ground for divorce, but this is conspicuous by its absence in any of the statutory laws governing different communities. On the other hand, the religious laws and judicial interpretations of them have generally tended to emphasize the fault theory, being particular to prevent the party of a matrimonial wrong from obtaining a dissolution of the marriage. This leads often to the use of perjured evidence. There is even today an indirect way of getting divorce by mutual consent, by registering one's marriage under the Special Marriage Act. It is thus recommended that after celebration according to religious rites the marriage should be registeredand this ground should be recognized in all the personal laws so that two adults whose marriage has, in fact, broken down can get it dissolved honourably.

Prostitution as a Ground for Divorce

The provision in the Parsee Marriage and Divorce Act, 1936 which enables a wife to obtain a divorce if her husband has compelled her to prostitution, in our view, is a very desirable protection. We recommend inclusion of this provision in all other Personal laws.

As a general principle, we recommend parity of rights regarding grounds for both husband and wife. This already exists in some of the personal laws, and in our view is essential to guarantee equality of status for both partners. It may be noted that the findings of our survey on this question shows an overwhelming opinion in favour of parity. There are on an average 74 per cent of the respondents (72.9 per cent of males and 74.37 per cent of females) who have stated that the grounds for divorce should be the same for both husband and wife.

V. ADOPTION

"Adoption is the institutionalized practice through which an individual belonging by birth to one kinship group acquires new kinship ties that are socially defined as equivalent to the congenital ties. These new ties supersede the old ones either wholly or in part". It is the act of a person who takes upon himself the position of a parent to a child who is not in law his own child.

The origin of the custom of adoption is lost in antiquity. It has, however, been recognized in India for centuries and is also recognized in other South Asian countries, such as Burma and Thailand. Adoption forms the subject matter of personal law. In India the only personal law which recognizes adoption in the true sense of the term is Hindu Law which regarded adoption as the 'taking of a son as a substitute' in case there is no male issue.

Muslim Law of Adoption

Even though Muslim law does not recognize adoption, in India previously the law had permitted this right to Hindu converts to Islam, who had enjoyed this right prior to their conversion. This customary right was, however, partially abrogated by the Shariat Act under which a Muslim could make a declaration that he and his sons would in future give up all customary rights including that of adoption and be governed by the Act.

But the custom of adopting sons was in vogue in Arabia at the time of the Prophet Mohammad. The word *adia* used in the Holy Quran means adopted sons. Justice Ameer Ali held that a family Waqf could be made not only for the benefit of descendants of the founder but also of dependents, which would include an adopted child who has resided with the settler as a dependent relation. The Lahore High Court held the word 'family' to include an adopted child who had resided with the settler as a dependent relation. All these clearly indicate that adoption was not unknown among Indian Muslims.

Islam never gave any special significance to an adopted son, as it does not to a natural son. Islamic religion, unlike the Hindu one, does not associate a son, or any other relative, with the performance of the last rites of a deceased Muslim whether male or female. It, therefore, does not recommend adoption of son or a daughter for a person dying issueless, nor does it absolutely prohibit it. The Quranic verses having a bearing on adoption did not lay down a specific negative rule.

Parsee Law of Adoption

For the Parsees, there is no law of adoption as such or adoption recognized by custom. However, the widow of a Parsee dying issueless can adopt a *Palak* on the 4th day of the deceased's death, for the *ad-hoc* purpose of performing certain religious rites for the deceased. This adoption is only for a limited purpose and does not confer any proprietary rights on the *Palak*.

Christian Law of Adoption

The institution of adoption is not known in Christian Law in India. If Christian parents have no issue and desire that some child takes that place, the only way open for them is to approach the Court under the Guardian and Wards Act and be appointed a legal guardian. This is the procedure being followed today also by foreigners who want to adopt Indian children. In such cases if the Court has given permission for the child to be taken out of the country, adoption according to foreign law (i.e. law of the guardian) takes place outside the country.

Hindu Law of Adoption

The law relating to adoption has been amended and codified and brought in line with the principles of social justice. Previously, the object of adoption was to ensure spiritual benefit by performing the last religious rites and also to continue the line. The devolution of property was regarded as of secondary importance. It was because of this basic approach to adoption that Hindu Law did not recognize the right of a Hindu to adopt girls as she could neither ensure spiritual benefit nor continue the line of her father.

With the passing of the Hindu Adoption and Maintenance Act 1956, the whole basis of adoption has been changed. The Act makes three clear departures from the previous law of adoption:

(a) A Hindu can now adopt either a son or a daughter, since the religious purpose has given place to the secular idea of parents wanting a child.

(b) The husband can no longer give or take in adoption without the consent of the wife. In the case of an existing marriage, however, the primary right continues to be of the husband. The wife's right being confined to consent only, is in a sense, continuation of the 'Superior' right of a man which has been the running theme in Hindu Law.

(c) A woman can now adopt, if she is unmarried, widowed or divorced. Similar right is conferred on a married woman if her husband has completely and finally renounced the world, has ceased to be a Hindu, or has been declared by a Court to be of unsound mind.

The uncodified law did not recognize the right of a woman to adopt and even in the case of a widow, who adopted as the agent of her late husband, the rules differed and some schools prohibited it altogether.

The fundamental departure that the new Act has made, is in recognizing the right of a woman to adopt in her own right and no longer as the agent of her husband (dead or alive).

While the Act has certainly improved the status of women, we recommend that the right of adoption should be equal for husband and wife, with the consent of the other spouse.

We welcome the step taken by the Government in introducing a uniform and secular law of adoption - The Adoption of Children Bill 1972 - which is now before Parliament, since this would benefit the entire community.

The statement of objects of the Bill reads :

> In India there is no general law of adoption though it is permitted by statute among Hindus and by custom amongst a few numerically insignificant categories of persons. In recent years there has been a growing demand for a general law of adoption in India.

The growing demand was noticed by the Committee during its tours as a large number of women expressed their approval of right to adoption being extended to all.

We recommend the early enactment of the Bill as it will extend the right of adoption equally to men and women of all communities, and will be a step towards a uniform secular law.

REFERENCES

1. Journal of Indian Law Institute (different volumes).
2. Lenin Coll. *Works*, Vol 30.
3. Radha Kumud Mukerjee, *Hindu Civilisation*, 1936.
4. Ratna Kapur and Brenda Cossman, *Subversive Sites*, 1996.
5. Verma, B.R., *Muslim Marriage and Dissolution*, 1971.

Eight

Guardianship

In dealing with the question of guardianship of a minor child, two principles should be kept in view—the interest and protection of the child, and parental right. It was assumed, at one time, that both these principles coincided and there could never be a conflict. For example, the offence of kidnapping is committed when the minor child is taken out of the keeping of the lawful guardian without his consent. The motivation of the person who takes the child and whether such an act is in the child's interest, are factors which do not negate or even mitigate the culpability of the offence. Today, however, there is a shift and the interest of the child is in many cases of paramount consideration that law bears in mind. Therefore, legislation protects a person who reports and often takes to the police a child who is neglected. Such a child can be removed from parental custody and kept where his best interests would be served.

In earlier years, parental authority was synonymous with paternal authority and "social and legal thought rigidly adhered to the proposition that the father by his natural right is entrusted with the care and control of his children." Contemporary thought reflected in legislation of various countries has shifted to regarding the child's interest as of prime consideration and parental rights as being subordinate to it. But unfortunately our law does not clearly reflect this trend. In this branch of law, perhaps more than anywhere else, the judiciary has to set the pace in changing our prevailing norms.

A guardian may be natural, testamentary or appointed by court. While deciding the question of guardianship, two distinct things have to be taken into account—the person of the minor and his property. Often the same person is not entrusted with both. As in other spheres of family law there is no uniform law. Three distinct legal systems are prevalent, Hindu Law, Muslim Law and the Guardians and Wards Act, 1890.

Hindu Law of Guardianship

The Hindu Minority and Guardianship Act, 1956 has codified the law but as in the uncodified law it has upheld the superior right of the father. It lays down that a child is a minor till the age of 18. The natural guardian for both boys and unmarried girls is first the father and after him the mother. The prior right of the mother is recognized only for custody in the case of children below five, but even this right is qualified by the word 'ordinarily' It has, however, taken away the right of the father, which he enjoyed before, of appointing a testamentary guardian and thereby depriving the mother of the right. Under the present law, the father cannot resort to this device. In the case of illegitimate children, the mother has a better claim than the father.

Hindu law, however, makes no distinction between the 'person' of the minor and his property and therefore guardianship implies control over both.

The Act, however, directs that in deciding this question, courts must take the 'welfare of the child', as of 'paramount consideration'. It is under this principle that the judiciary has an important role to play, when there is a conflict between the paternal right and the welfare of the child. Recently, the Supreme Court held that in special circumstances the mother could be held to be the natural guardian even when the father was alive. Though the Supreme Court has used words like 'may be considered' and 'special circumstances' we hope that this judgement of the highest court will guide the lower courts, and prevent them from invariably upholding the father's right, even when it is against the interest of the child.

Muslim Law of Guardianship

Under Muslim law the father's dominant position is recognized and his rights are very wide, but there is a distinction between guardianship and custody. The term guardianship is usually used with reference to the guardianship to property. This belongs preferentially to the father and in his absence, to his executor. If the father had not appointed any executor, the guardianship passes to the paternal grandfather. Among the Shias the difference is that the father is regarded as the sole guardian but after his death it is the right of the grandfather to take over the responsibility and not that of the executor. Both the schools however agree that the father while alive is the sole guardian. The mother is not recognized as a natural guardian even after the death of the father.

There is some difference of opinion as to whether the right of the natural guardian extends only over the property rights of the minor or also over person. In the case of the father, there is no doubt that his right extends to both property and person. Even when the mother has custody of the minor child, the father's general right of supervision and control remains. The father, if he so desires, may appoint the mother as a testamentary guardian. Therefore, though the mother may not be recognized as a natural guardian, there is no objection to her being one under the father's will. When she is a testamentary guardian, she will have the right to control both the person and the property of a minor. The Shias however do not recognize the right of mother to be a testamentary guardian if she is a non-Muslim. Under both the schools, a mother has no right to appoint a testamentary guardian, except when she herself has been appointed as a general executrix under her husband's will.

Though a mother cannot be a maternal guardian, Muslim law recognizes that she has the prime right to custody of minor children (*hizanat*). This right is recognized by all authorities under Muslim law. "The mother is of all persons best entitled to the custody of her infant children." (*Fatwai Alamgiri*).

In the case of a woman custodian, the following qualifications are required:

(a) of sound mind
(b) of good moral conduct
(c) living in such a place where there is no risk, morally or physically to the child
(d) of such an age which would qualify her to bestow on the child the care it may need.

The last does not apply when the custodian is the mother. There is no general agreement however, about the qualifications necessary, if any, when the custodian is a man.

The mother's right of custody or *hizanat* appears to be an

absolute right and even the father cannot deprive her of it. Misconduct is the only condition which can deprive the mother of this right. There is however no unanimity as to whether this is a maternal right or a right in the interest of the child. The distinction though subtle, is relevant because if it is a maternal right then only her positive misconduct can lead to her deprivation of the custody; if it is a right in the interest of the child, then even when there is no misconduct on her part she may be deprived on the ground that some other person is more suitable as a custodian. This question still remains an open one. There has been no clearcut judicial pronouncement on this matter in India. In Pakistan it has been decided that *hizanat* is based on the presumption of welfare of the minor and therefore could be rebutted.

There is a difference between the Shia and Hanafi schools about the age at which the right of the mother to custody terminates. In the case of a minor son, the Shia school holds that the mother's right to *hizanat* is only during the period of weaning which is over when the child has completed the age of two. The Hanafi school, on the other hand, extends the period till the minor son has reached the age of seven. Both schools agree that the same age cannot be applied when the minor is a girl. The Shia Law upholds the mother's right till the girl reaches to puberty and the Hanafi school till she attains puberty. Both schools agree that only the mother has the right to the custody of a minor married girl till she attains the age of puberty.

The Muslim concept of *hizanat* is definitely an advance on the other legal systems, because it recognizes that for a minor child the mother's care and control is more desirable. The father, therefore, is required to pay maintenance to the mother for the child for this period.

Guardians and Wards Act, 1890

The supremacy of paternal right is the keynote of the Guardians and Wards Act which governs all communities other than Hindus and Muslims. It clearly lays down that the father's right is primary and no other person can be appointed unless the father is found unfit. However, as in the Hindu Law, the Act provides that the court must bear in mind the welfare of the child, though this is not mentioned as being of paramount consideration. In recent years, however, some of the decisions have broken away from the past attitude of looking upon the father not only as a natural guardian but as having "an inalienable right over his child". They now hold that "the welfare of the minor is of prime consideration and even the paramount right of the father should be subordinated...."

Recommendations

1. that the control over the person and property of a minor cannot be separated and should vest in the same person;
2. the question of guardianship should be determined entirely from the point of view of the child's interest and not the prior right of either parent;
3. the parent who does not have guardianship should have access to the child;
4. whatever the decision taken earlier, the child's choice of guardians should be obtained when the child reaches the age of 12.

We support the recommendations of the UN Commission on the Status of Women which are as follows:

(a) Women shall have equal rights and duties with men in respect to guardianship of their minor children and the exercise of parental authority over them, including care, custody, education and maintenance;
(b) Both spouses shall have equal rights and duties with regard to the administration of the property of their minor children, with the legal limitations necessary to ensure as far as possible that it is administered in the interest of the children;
(c) The interest of the children shall be of paramount consideration in proceedings regarding custody of children, in the event of divorce, annulment of marriage or judicial separation.
(d) No discrimination shall be made between men and women with regard to decision regarding custody of children and guardianship or other parental rights in the event of divorce, annulment of marriage or judicial separation.

REFERENCES

1. Basu, D., Constitution of India.
2. Dhagamwar Vasudha, Law, *Power and Justice*, 1992.
3. Paras Diwan, *Modern Hindu Law*, 1972.

Nine

Maintenance

The obligation of the husband to maintain his wife arises not out of any contract, express or implied, but of the status of the marriage. As in other branches of law, the right to maintenance forms a part of the personal law and therefore is not uniform.

Apart from the right given in the personal laws the Criminal Procedure Code, enacted in 1898, provided for right of maintenance. The right of the wife and dependent children to move the court for relief against the husband or the father who neglects or refuses to maintain his dependent family members is thus not confined to any particular religion but is given to all wives and children irrespective of their personal laws. In this aspect uniformity had been achieved in at least one sphere of family law. Considering the date of this law, the obligation was, understandably, confined to only the husband or the father, with no corresponding obligation being placed on the wife or the mother.

The Code has, however, been repealed recently and we are today governed by the New Criminal Procedure Code of 1974. In spite of the passage of 76 years, the new Code continues to reflect the old attitude to women. With some modifications like extending the right to demand maintenance to indigent parents and to divorced wives, the obligation to maintain continues to be that of the man. In the changed social context and particularly in view of our firm declaration of equality, it is irrational to place the obligation only on the man. However small the number may be, today there are economically independent women who can not only look after themselves but also their husbands and children. Similarly the duty to look after indigent parents cannot be restricted only to sons. As a matter of fact the exclusion of daughters from the obligation may be used as an argument to deprive them of their share in the father's property.

As we believe in equal status of husband and wife and of son and daughter, we recommend amendment of the law to provide for obligations expected of the economically independent woman:

(a) to maintain her dependent husband;
(b) to share with him the duty to maintain their children;
(c) to share with her brothers the duty to maintain their dependent parents.

The inclusion of the right of maintenance in the Criminal Procedure Code has the great advantage of making the remedy both speedy and cheap. The underlying principle of this is to prevent starvation and vagrancy, which usually leads to the commission of crimes. From this point of view, it seems unjustified to limit the total amount of maintenance for all dependent persons to Rs 500.

We welcome the extension of this right to divorced wives as earlier the implied financial deprivation in case of divorce was the only obstacle to a woman wishing to free herself from an unhappy marriage. But in extending this right to divorced wives uniformity has been sacrificed and no longer can all women claim to be governed by the same law which they had been governed by since 1898. An exception has been introduced, to deny maintenance to those divorced wives who have received a 'sum of money payable under customary or personal law'. This clearly excludes Muslim women who may have got the dower at the time of the dissolution. There is no scope even for judicial scrutiny to examine whether the amount paid as dower is adequate for maintenance or not. This exclusion of all divorced Muslim women defeats the purpose of the section to provide a speedy remedy to indigent women.

We, therefore, recommend that the ceiling placed on the maximum amount payable as maintenance should be removed and the term 'wife' to include divorced wife be made applicable to all women without any exception.

Hindu Law of Maintenance

Unlike the right given under criminal law, where the claim of the wife depends on the husband having. 'sufficient means', under Hindu Law her right is absolute and the husband cannot claim inadequate means to deny maintaining her. Even a previous order of the criminal court will not bar her right to seek further relief in a civil court. But she loses her right if she deviates from the path of chastity. Even a single lapse from chastity may alter her right detrimentally. Under criminal law, however, the right will be affected only if the wife is living in adultery at the time of her claim. Her past adultery will not affect her right but may be a factor in fixing the amount of maintenance.

The exacting standards are perhaps explained by the fact that both under the uncodified Hindu law as well as under the present law, the Hindu Adoption and Maintenance Act 1956, she gets a real maintenance. According to judicial opinion "just an adequate fare with nothing for clothing, residence as also for medical attendance and treatment falls short of maintenance: and these are "minimal in a civilised society. " While assessing the amount of maintenance, the court takes into account various factors like the position and status of the parties, the reasonable wants of the claimant and the obligations and liabilities of the husband. It also judges whether the wife is justified in leaving the husband. The justifiable reasons are spelt out in the Act.

The lacuna in limiting the obligation of maintenance to the man only has been remedied by the codified Hindu Law. *Maintenance pendente lite* (pending the suit) and even the expenses of a matrimonial suit will be borne by either husband or the wife if the other spouse has no independent income for his/or her support. The same principle will also govern the payment of permanent maintenance and the court will fix the amount taking the needs of the applicant into account. If necessary, the Court may secure the payment of this amount to the applicant, by securing a charge on the immoveable property of the respondent. Such a right will continue as long as the applicant for maintenance remains unmarried.

It is strange that while the question of maintenance as a real need and responsibility of either spouse was recognized on the one hand by the Hindu Marriage Act as early as 1955, the Criminal Procedure Code passed in 1974 should on the other hand have reverted again to the 19th century concept which regards woman as only a dependent.

Muslim Law of Maintenance

Maintenance of the wife is a precept in the Quran and the highest obligation of the husband. Maintenance (*nafaqa*) includes food, clothing and lodging irrespective of husband's means or on the wife's lack of possession of an independent income. She has, however, to be accessible to the husband and obey his reasonable commands. The Muslim wife also has the right to sue her husband under the Criminal Procedure Code, but under that law the sum ordered can never exceed Rs 500. Under the personal law, the court while fixing the amount, considers the rank and the circumstances of both the spouses. As already discussed, failure of the husband to maintain his wife for two years entitles her to get a divorce. Her right to maintenance lasts only as long as she remains a wife. If she is divorced, she loses her right of maintenance and is only entitled to it for three months (the period of *iddat*). After this period she has no further claim and it is this which has created a discrimination between the muslims and other Indian women. We recommend the removal of this discrimination and extension of right of maintenance to divorced wives.

Parsee Law of Maintenance

The Parsee Marriage and Divorce Act 1936, being a pre-independence legislation recognizes only the right of the wife to maintenance - both alimony *pendente lite* as well as permanent alimony. The maximum amount that can be decreed by the court as alimony during the time a matrimonial suit is pending in court is 1/5th the husband's net income. In fixing the quantum as permanent maintenance, the court will determine what is just, bearing in mind the ability of the husband to pay, the wife's own assets and the conduct of the parties. The order will remain in force as long as the wife remains chaste and unmarried. The right of the wife to be maintained by the husband has been regarded as being an inherent right. Therefore any contract by her, giving up future rights of alimony has been regarded as contrary to public policy.

Christian Law of Maintenance

The maintenance rights of a Christian wife are governed by the Indian Divorce Act, 1869. The provisions are the same as those under the Parsee Law, and the same considerations are applied in granting maintenance both alimony *pendente lite* as well as permanent maintenance. Apart from similar provisions in the Parsee Act, there are two sections in the Indian Divorce Act which reinforce the guilt theory on which the Act is based which indirectly affect maintenance rights. The first provides that if a divorce or judicial separation is obtained by the husband on the ground of the wife's adultery and the court finds that the wife is entitled to some property, it may on its discretion, order that the whole or part of the property should be settled for the benefit of the husband or the children. Conversely, the second provides that where the court has decreed damages to the husband against adultery, the court may while fixing damages make an order that the whole or part of the amount recovered should be settled for the benefit of the children, or used as a provision for the maintenance of the wife.

Suggested Amendments

While the right of maintenance is recognized in all the different laws, the common problem faced by most women even amongst the very few who know of their rights, is the expense and delay in first getting an order from court. Often a counter claim is made by the husband for restitution of conjugal rights in order to defeat or at least delay her right. Even when the order for maintenance is made, the husband very often fails to pay after a few months and this entails the wife's repeated visits to court and undergoing tremendous delay and expense. The arrears of maintenance are treated as a debt whose recovery is by the ordinary procedure on a par as laid down for all other debts. This is very often expensive and time consuming.

In order to minimize the hardship caused by nonpayment of maintenance, and to ensure certainty of payment, we recommend that all maintenance orders should be deducted at the source by the employer (as done in the case of income-tax). Where it is not possible to deduct at the source, as in the case of a business man or a self-employed person, the arrears of maintenance should be recovered as 'arrears of land revenue or by distress'.

As this procedure has been adopted in the recovery of income tax, extension of it in the field for recovery of a maintenance order should not pose any undue difficulty. An additional mode of execution of the maintenance decree may be, to adopt the same procedure as is done in the case of fines under the Criminal Procedure. This has the advantage of making the recovery both cheap and speedy.

The ultimate and the best solution however, lies in leaving a specialized court like the Family Court to deal with the entire question of maintenance. Apart from matters like the income of the respective spouses or the degree of financial dependence, a Family Court would be able to approach the question taking an overall view. The matters for consideration would be : (a) the husband's obligation to his divorced wife, as well as obligations incurred by him by a subsequent marriage; and (b) the divorcee's degree of dependence on the maintenance order and her efforts to become financially independent. A continuing process of assessment is necessary and only a specialized court (which will be free of the tremendous pressure of work and time an ordinary civil court has today) can exercise this vigilance.

INHERITANCE

Christian Law of Inheritance

As far back as 1925 the existence of a large number of statutes dealing with succession led the government to pass the Indian Succession Act. The object of the Act was to consolidate the large number of laws which were in existence and not to unify them. The laws governing succession of Muslims and Hindus were excluded from the purview of this Act. In the process of consolidating, two clear schemes were adopted — one dealing with the succession rights of persons like Indian Christians, Jews and the marriage under the Special Marriage Act (1955) and one for succession rights of Parsees.

In the first scheme, (persons who were not Parsees), when an intestate died leaving a widow and a lineal descendant, she would be entitled to a fixed share of one third of the property, and the children irrespective of their sex would share equally. This law was amended with the object of improving the rights of the widow and it was provided that where the intestate died leaving a widow and no lineal descendant and the net value of the estate did not exceed Rs. 5,000 she would be entitled to the whole of his property. Where the net value of the estate exceeded rupees five thousand, she was entitled to a charge of a sum of rupees five thousand (with interest at four per cent till payment) and out of the balance she was entitled to her intestate share. The section applied only in cases where the deceased had died intestate in respect of all the properties.

But inexplicably even this benefit has been denied to the following categories of persons :

(1) Indian Christians;

(2) Any child or grandchild of any male person who is or was at the time an Indian Christian; or

(3) Any Hindu, Buddhist, or Jain, succession to whose property is governed by the Indian Succession Act.

Since this provision seeks to give better rights to a widow without lineal descendants, the denial of the benefit to the above mentioned groups can not be justified on the grounds of policy.

But the Act confers no restriction on the power of a person to will away his property. Therefore the protection enjoyed by a Muslim widow to a share of the estate and by the Hindu widow to being maintained, is denied to other widows under this law. There is, therefore, a need to incorporate some restrictions, similar to that prevailing under Muslim law to prevent a widow from being left completely destitute.

Christians in Kerala

To add to the diversity of laws, the Travancore High Court held that the Indian Succession Act did not apply to the Christians of the State. The result of the decision was that Christians in Kerala and those outside are governed by different laws. The decision includes the multiplicity of laws which govern Christians within the State. The Travancore Christian Succession Act governs the succession rights of Christians in Travancore but the Act exempts those following the "Marumakkavazhi System" of inheritance. To add to this, certain sections of the Act are not applicable to certain classes of the Roman Catholic Christians of the Latin Rite and to Protestant Christians living in the five *taluks* mentioned therein among whom male and female heirs of the intestate share equally. The Cochin Christians Succession Act, generally governs the succession to the properties of Christians in the former territory of the Cochin State. The Cochin Act exempts members belonging to the European, Anglo-Indian and Parangi communities, and the Tamil Christians of the Chittur Taluk who follow the Hindu law.

A characteristic feature of the Travancore and Cochin Christian Succession legislations is that they are based on the former notions of the Hindu Law of Inheritance which discriminated against women. Therefore a widow or mother inheriting immoveable property takes only a life-interest terminable on death or remarriage. A daughter's right is limited to *Streedhanam*. Even in cases where she is entitled to succeed she takes a much lesser share.

Widow

Under the Travancore Act if the intestate has died leaving a widow and lineal descendants, the widow is entitled to a share equal to that of a son. If on the other hand, the intestate dies leaving a widow and daughters (or the descendants of a daughter) her share will be equal to that of a daughter. The nature of her interest (i.e. life interest) is the same when she takes the property in the absence of any lineal descendants. The widow's share is half when the intestate dies without leaving any lineal descendant but has left behind his father or mother.

According to the Cochin Act when there is a son or the lineal descendants of a son, the share of a widow is equal to two-thirds that of a son. If the intestate has left no son or the lineal descendant of a son, she is entitled to a share equal to that of a daughter.

Daughter

Even though she is mentioned as an heir along with a son in Group I of Section 25 of the Travancore Christian Succession Act, a daughter is entitled to "*Streedhanam*" only. The Streedhanam of a daughter, for the purpose of the Act, is fixed at one-fourth the value of the share of a son or Rs. 5,000 whichever is less.

The Cochin Act provides that where an intestate has left sons and daughters, each daughter shall take one-third share of a son. But like the Travancore Act, an important limitation in regard to a daughter's share is laid down in Section 22 of the Cochin Christian Succession Act. This in effect makes the right of a daughter to receive Streedhanam only. But the Cochin Act does not specify a limit on the amount of Streedhanam. Both legislations, however, provide that Streedhanam which has been paid, but promised by the intestate, will be a charge on his estate.

It is, therefore, apparent that the rights of inheritance of Christian women under the Travancore and Cochin Acts are meagre. Even these rights may be defeated as the testator has the absolute power of willing away his entire property.

We recommend that immediate legislative measures be taken to bring Christian women of Kerala under the Indian Succession Act as a first step to unify the law and as suggested above restrictive power be placed on the unfettered right of a person to will away his entire property.

Goa & Pondicherry Laws of Inheritance

The Christians of Goa were governed by the Portuguese Civil Code and continue to be so even today. The result is not only an addition to the multiplicity of laws but the prevalence of a legal system which is totally different from the ones prevailing in the rest of the country.

While the Portuguese Civil Code makes no differentiation on the basis of sex, it relegates the widow to a very low position. The order of the legal heirs of a person are—first sons and daughters who get the property in equal shares, failing them the parents inherit, followed by the brother and his descendants. The widow will inherit only if there is no heir in the above classes. But the widow will become the owner of "the agricultural commodities and fruits, called or pending, meant and necessary for the consumption of the conjugal couple". She will however lose even this right if she is divorced or separated from her husband.

Unlike the Christians in other parts of India, a person cannot will or gift away his entire property to the exclusion of his legal heirs. The portion over which a person has no control is known as 'legitim' and usually consists of half the property. But even this legitim can be denied to an heir under certain conditions, for example, if a child lodges a complaint against his parents for an offence which is not against his person or against his spouse.

But even a disinherited heir is entitled to maintenance. The recognition of equal rights for sons and daughters is undoubtedly to be welcomed but to relegate the widow to the fourth position and leave her with only the fruits and agricultural commodities needs to be remedied immediately.

The legal system for Christians prevailing in Pondicherry is extremely anomalous. During the French rule both Hindus and Indian Christians were governed by the Hindu law. After Pondicherry became a part of India, the Hindu Succession Act was extended to the State but as that Act only applies to certain categories of persons who come under the term 'Hindu', the Indian Christians in Pondicherry can no longer be governed by it. The Indian Succession Act has not been extended to the State, so the Christians there continue to be governed by the precodified Hindu Law, which relegates a woman to an inferior position and does not even regard her as being full owner even in the few cases where she can inherit property. The resultant position is anachronistic and should be remedied immediately. (We recommend extension of the Indian Succession Act to Goa and Pondicherry).

Parsee Intestate Succession Law of Inheritance

A feature of the rules governing the Parsee intestates is, that like the Hindu law and unlike the Muslim law, there are separate rules for the devolution of the property of male and female Parsee intestates. The rules relating to the intestate succession of males have the characteristic of Muslim law, namely, the share of a male heir is double that of a female heir of the same degree. For example, if a male Parsee dies leaving a widow and children, the property will be divided so that the share of each son and widow will be double the share of each daughter. Further, if a male Parsee dies leaving one or both parents, in addition to a widow and children, the property will be divided so that the father shall receive a share equal to half the share of a son and the mother will receive a share equal to half the share of a daughter. The inferior position of a mother in the scheme of succession thus becomes evident and the position is radically different from that which prevails under the Hindu Succession Act, 1956.

The above position may be contrasted with the rules applicable to the succession of a female Parsee intestate. If she dies leaving a widower and children, the property will be divided equally among them and if she dies leaving children only, among the children equally. Thus, while a son is entitled to an equal share in the mother's property along with the daughter, the daughter is not entitled to the same right when she inherits the property of the father along with the son.

It should be pointed out that the above provisions were enacted in 1939. At the time these rules conferred better rights on women than the then existing Hindu and Muslim laws. But with the passage of time, these rules have become out of step with the progressive trends in the society. The Parsee daughter's share remains half of that of a son as in Muslim law, but she is denied protection against disinheritance which is the beneficial feature of Muslim law.

Further, it is extremely doubtful whether Sections 5 to 56 of the Indian Succession Act govern the devolution of agricultural properties, as the Central Legislature was not competent to enact legislation relating to agricultural lands, in 1939. Therefore, it would seem that agricultural lands will devolve according to the rules in force prior to the amendment, according to which the son's share will be four times that of a daughter, the widow's share will be double that of a daughter; and father and mother are not entitled to any share.

Hindu Law of Inheritance

The problem of succession cannot be understood without reference to the law of joint family. Under the Mitakshara law, the law of succession is intimately connected with the special incidence of coparcenary properties. In coparcenary properties a son, son's son and a son's grandson acquire a right by birth. Thus only males can be coparceners.

The salient feature of a Mitakshara coparcenary is the existence of community of interest, unity of possession and the right of survivorship among the coparceners. So long as the family is undivided, no individual coparcener can claim that he is entitled to a specific share of the joint estate. His share is liable for increase by deaths and decrease by births. The properties are managed by the Karta who is usually the eldest among the coparceners. The share of a coparcener is ascertained only by partition.

Though the institution of joint family was common in most parts of India, there were two major systems prevailing in the country—Mitakshara and Dayabhaga—which dealt differently with the property rights. Added to these two systems was the matriarchal system which prevailed in some southern states. Pre-independence India, therefore, had a number of different systems of succession among Hindus and in most of them, the position of the woman was one of dependence with barely any proprietary rights. Even where they enjoyed some rights, they had only a life interest and did not enjoy full ownership. While earlier this may have been socially acceptable, with socioeconomic changes brought about in the 20th century this inferior position was no longer tenable. As discussed earlier, the rigidity that had crept into the law because of the British policy of non-intervention had made it impossible to adopt the legal systems to changes. The position, therefore, could only be remedied by legislation which would reflect the socioeconomic changes since our independence and at the same time fulfil the promise of non-discrimination guaranteed in the Constitution.

With the object of bringing in uniformity and in conformity with the norms of the post Constitution period, the Hindu Succession Act was passed in 1956 though after stiff resistance from the traditionalists.

The Act brought in some radical and fundamental changes, the most important of which was to introduce equal rights of succession between male and female heirs, in the same category, like brother and sister, son and daughter. It also simplified the law by abolishing the different systems prevailing under the Mitakshara and Dayabhaga Schools. The Act also extended to persons in south India previously governed by the Marumakkattayam law also. It recognized, however, that there had to be some differences in a system which was found in matriarchy. The hold of tradition, however, was so strong that even while introducing sweeping changes, the legislators compromized and retained in some respects the inferior position of the women. By yielding to pressure, it sacrificed the uniformity which had been one of the major aims in introducing this law. A close study of the Act discloses that there are still a number of different systems governing succession.

The most remarkable features of the Act, however, are the recognition of the right of women to inherit equally with men and the abolition of the life estate of female heirs. The Class I heirs of a man today are widow, mother, son, daughter, widow of a predeceased son, and sons and daughters of predeceased sons or daughters. These heirs take the property in equal shares and as absolute owners.

The one major factor which has attributed to the inequality between sons and daughters is the retention of the Mitakshara coparcenary. As mentioned earlier, membership of it is confined only to male members. No stranger can be introduced even by agreement of all the members and no female can be a member of a coparcenary. There are no succession rights in a coparcenary but the interest of a coparcener on his death goes to the remaining members. A number of decisions, as also legislation in the 20th century, like the Hindu Women's Right to Property Act, have made inroads in the concept of the coparcenary and in some ways it had really lost some of its important features. It would therefore have been quite feasible at the time of the 1956 Act to abolish it altogether. One point of view according to Mulla (1960) is that the "best solution would have been to abolish the ancient legal formula of acquisition of rights by birth and devolution by survivorship. Since the logical way was to assimilate the Mitakshara with the Dayabhaga, this could also have had the merit of equitable treatment of the nearest female heirs of a coparcener and of bringing about uniformity in the law in all parts of India." But there was strong opposition to this point of view and the institution was retained but an effort was made to make some provision for the nearest women members of a person i.e. Class I heirs.

The compromise arrived at was that if a male member of a coparcenary dies then for the purpose of ensuring that his heirs get a share of the property, his share of the coparcenary will be demarcated, as if there had been a partition and that share will be divided among his heirs. It means that, if there is a coparcenary of a father and two sons, the share a father would have got on partition would be one-third. This will be divided among his Class I heirs. The consequence of this is that the two sons in addition to their original interest as coparceners, will get equal shares of the father's property with the mother, grandmother and sister, etc. This naturally results in an unequal treatment between brother and sister. In a similar situation under the Dayabhaga system the daughter will get an equal share with the brothers as there is no right by birth for sons. The retention of the Mitakshara coparcenary, therefore, not only brings about inequality between the same class of heirs but also continues two different systems of inheritance.

The retention of coparcenary has also meant the continuation of two rights both of which affect the rights of female heirs detrimentally. The first is the right of a coparcener to renounce his right in the coparcenary. In order to do this, no specific formality is required beyond the expression of a clear intention. On such renunciation, the release is deemed to have separated him from the joint family though this will in no way affect the joint status of other members of the coparcenary. The result of this is that on his death, he will have no interest in the joint family which could be distributed among the Class I heirs. This deprives the female heirs of any share. A similar result can be achieved by a father who partitions joint family property during his lifetime without reserving any share for himself.

The second of such characteristics is the right to convert self acquired property to coparcenary property. The transformation of self acquisition into joint family property is frequently resorted to reduce the burden of income tax. But the effect of this is that the share of a female heir is reduced because in the self acquired property she would have had the right to inherit equally with the male members as Class I heirs.

Mitakshara coparcenary with its basic principle of right by birth of a male coparcener is the cause of unequal rights between the male and female heirs, though the Act accepted in principle the equality of the sexes. It should be noted that the Hindu Code

Bill 1948 as amended by the Select Committee, had, in fact, suggested abolition of the right by birth.

We recommend the abolition of the right by birth and the conversion of a Mitakshara coparcenary into a Dayabhaga one.

Another provision in the Act which contributes both to lack of uniformity as well as continuation of discriminatory treatment of female heirs is the provision excluding the devolution of tenancy rights under the legislation of the States, from the scope of the Act.

The apparent object is to protect the rules in State Legislations from the overriding effect of the Hindu Succession Act, which otherwise would have governed the succession to tenurial interests. The reasons behind this exemption, as they appear from the legislative debates are two-fold. First, that tenancy laws being property laws, apply to all whether a Hindu or non-Hindu. As the Hindu Succession Act is a personal law, it should not override the provisions of property law enacted in the interests of the agricultural economy. Second, that the States are responsible for agricultural laws and the Central Government is anxious not to encroach on the rights of the State Governments.

A serious objection is that the beneficial effects of the Hindu Succession Act can be denied by a resort to this provision. The bulk of the property in India is agricultural property and such an exemption detracts from the principle of uniformity. It may also be noted that the Act does not define the word "tenancy rights" nor is it defined in the General Clauses Act, 1897. Thus, on the question as to what constitutes tenancy rights, the last resort must be had to the specific legislation of the State itself, and it is quite conceivable that a State with dominant conservative groups could defeat the purpose of the Act by defining tenancy rights to include all interests arising in or out of agricultural lands.

No particular economic justification has been made out by the States or States concerned for having separate rules for devolution of tenancies. The fact that many States do not have special provisions for succession to tenurial interests and the fact that the exception protects legislations in some States in the North, gives rise to a suspicion that it was intended as a concession to the conservative elements in these regions. The argument that the Act is a personal law and that it cannot override a property law ignores two aspects: (1) in pith and substance a law providing for devolution of tenancies is a law relating to succession, and (2) the fact that these special laws may contain features which are more discriminatory than the existing Hindu and Muslim laws.

The legislation in Uttar Pradesh (Uttar Pradesh Zamindar Abolition and Land Reforms Act, 1950), a State which comprises one-sixth of India's population, furnishes an example of this kind:

> When a *bhumidar*, *sirdar* or *asami* being a male dies, his interest in his holding shall devolve in accordance with the order of succession given below :
>
> (a) The male descendant in the male line of descent in equal shares per stripes.
>
> (b) Widow and widowed mother and widow of a predeceased male lineal descendant in the male line of descent, who have not remarried.
>
> (c) Father;
>
> (d) Unmarried daughter.

The above scheme of inheritance shows that in competition with a son the widow of a deceased is not entitled to succeed. The claims of a widow and unmarried and married daughters are preceded not only by the lineal male descendants in the line of descent, but even by their widows who have not remarried. The exclusion of the widow and the daughters cannot be justified on any principle.

The seriousness of the problem is emphasized by the fact that the Act is likely to apply to all the agricultural land in course of time, in Uttar Pradesh. The Statement of Objects and Reasons of the Uttar Pradesh Zamindari Abolition Act says : "It is expected that the vast majority of cultivators will become *bhumidars*. The present intermediaries in respect of their *sir*, *khudkasht* and groves will be classed as *bhumidars* persons paying land revenue."

In order to achieve the social equality of women as also in the interests of uniformity, we recommend the abolition of the exception provided in Section 4 (2) of the Hindu Succession Act, relating to devolution of tenancies.

Suggestions have been made to the Committee that equality of sexes could be achieved under the Hindu Succession Act, if the law was amended to permit women to become members of the coparcenary and pending further legislation to permit them to act as a *karta* of the joint family. We do not feel that the situation will improve by making this recommendation as the present unequal treatment will continue as far as wives or widows of coparceners are concerned, who not having been born in the family cannot become members of it.

In all other respects, uniformity has been achieved among Hindus as the Class I heirs mentioned are the same for all. Similarly among the heirs of a female owner (with the exception of those who would have been governed by the Marumakkattayam and Aliyasantana law) uniformity as well as equality of sexes have been recognized. Sons and daughters (including the children of any predeceased son or daughter) inherit equally with the husband. A special provision however governs the property of women. In the event of her dying without leaving any children, her property does not automatically go to her husband. If the property in question has come to her from her father or mother it will go to her father's heirs, and if the property has come to her from the husband or her father-in-law it will go to her husband's heirs. For persons who were earlier governed by the Marumakkattayam law, the property goes first to the children and to the mother, and the father and the husband inherits only if there is no heir in this category.

Another discriminatory provision in the Act is the one relating to the right of inheritance to a dwelling house. It provides that where a Hindu dies intestate and his property includes a dwelling house wholly occupied by the members of the family, then the female heirs are not entitled to claim partition of it unless the male members choose to divide their shares in the dwelling house. Female heirs are entitled to only the right of residence. Even in this there is a discrimination as this right is restricted to unmarried and widowed daughters or those deserted by or separated from their husbands. A married daughter enjoys no such right.

Obviously in enacting this provision, the legislature intended to balance the familial with individual interest. The main object of the section is unexceptionable as it asserts the primacy of the rights of the family as against the right of an individual and therefore, the restriction against partition which is against the family interest is justified, and should be retained. But nothing justifies the invidious distinction between married and other daughters. We recommend the removal of this discrimination so that all daughters enjoy the same right.

Like the Indian Succession Act, the Hindu law i.e. both Mitakshara and Dayabhaga place no restriction on the power of testation. During the debates in Lok Sabha on the bill, the fear was voiced that this may lead to the rights of a female heir being defeated. But the Law Minister had brushed aside these fears by saying, "I believe that a normal father will never do any such thing and if at all he has to do it for any reason, he will surely make a provision for his daughter when he is going to deprive her of her share by will." But this is an over simplification of the question and as was pointed out during the debate in the Constituent Assembly, "an analysis of the inmates of rescue homes in this country will prove how many of these women are those who have been turned out of the joint family." The Committee's own experience in many places, particularly in Varanasi, more than proves the point that there are many women who have been reduced to destitution and beggary because their families have deprived them of all support.

We recommend that right of testation should be limited under the Hindu Succession Act, so as not to deprive legal heirs completely.

Muslim Law of Inheritance

A vast majority of Muslims in India follow the Hanafi doctrines of Sunni law and the courts presume that Muslims are governed by the Hanafi law unless it is established to the contrary. Though there are many features in common between the Shiah and the Sunni schools, there are differences in some respects. The Sunni law regards the Koranic verses on inheritance as an addendum to the pre-Islamic customary law and preserves the superior position of male agnates.

The heirs related to a deceased person by blood under the Sunni or the Koranic law are divided into three groups : (1) *Zav-il-Furuz* (the shares or the Koranic heirs); (2) the *Asaba* (agnates or "residuaries") and (3) the *Zav-il-Arham* (uterine relations). The heirs who are neither sharers nor residuaries fall into the third category. The sharers take the estate first; the remaining estate (or the whole of the estate in the absence of heirs of the first kind) is taken by the residuaries. If there are no sharers and residuaries the estate goes to the uterine relations.

Where there are sons and daughters they inherit as residuaries. Thus, if the deceased dies leaving a widow, son and daughter, the widow takes 1/8 as a sharer, the son takes 7/12 (2/3 of 7/8) and the daughter 7/24 (1/3 of 7/8). On the other hand, a daughter in the absence of a son takes the estate as a sharer; half the share if there is only one daughter and 2/3 if there are two or more daughters. Thus, if the deceased dies leaving father and daughter, the daughter is entitled to half the property as a sharer, the father to one-sixth as a sharer and the remaining one-third as a residuary.

One primary principle of Muslim law which grossly discriminates against women is that under the law of inheritance, if there are male heirs and female heirs of the same degree like a son and daughter, full brother and a full sister, the share of a female member is half that of the male.

Under the Hanafi, the widow, though a sharer in every case, is not entitled to take as a residuary. The share of a widow (or widows if there are more than one) is one-eighth. If the deceased dies without leaving a child, the widow's (or widows') share is one-fourth. The wife is not entitled to the *radd* (return). The social conditions of the present day necessitate that the measure of protection and security that a wife is entitled to, should be in no way inferior to that of any other member in the family, either during the lifetime of the husband or after his death. Therefore, a widow's position in the law of succession deserves particular attention.

Under the Shia law also, neither husband nor wife is entitled to the *radd* but if either of them is the sole surviving heir then they inherit the whole property.

If a Muslim dies leaving a daughter as his only close relative, she will not be allowed to take more than one half of his estate, the other half will go to some distant agnatic relative. Under the Shiah law the daughter would, in a similar situation, take one half as her share and the remaining half under the doctrine of *radd*.

Unlike Hindu and Christian Law, Muslim Law restricts a person's right of testation. A Muslim can bequeath only 1/3rd of his estate. The question is whether he has the power to correct any hardship that might arise under the law of intestacy in the exercise of his testamentary power (i.e. of one-third of his estate). It is beyond cavil that such hardship arises generally in the case of female heirs. But the Hanafi law appears to be particularly rigid in not permitting any device whereby the inequities of the laws of inheritance may be rectified.

A bequest to a stranger is valid without the consent of heirs, (if it does not exceed a third of the estate) but a bequest to an heir without the consent of other heirs is invalid. The consent of heirs to a bequest must be secured after the succession has opened, and any consent given to a bequest during the lifetime of the testatory can be retracted after his death. As the testamentary power exercised by a deceased in favour of an heir operates at the expense of their heirs, it is not an unnatural attitude to refuse consent to such bequests.

The Shiah law allows a Muslim the freedom of bequest within the disposable third and recent reforms in Egypt, Sudan and Iraq also permit this. If the rule is relaxed here it may be possible for a husband to make a bequest to his widow or widows which would help to make up for the inadequate share they get on intestacy.

Muslim law makes no distinction between moveable and immoveable property and though the right of a female heir like a widow or daughter has always been recognized and they have inherited absolutely (unlike the old Hindu law), we recommend that legislation be passed to give an equal share to the widow and the daughter along with the son as has been done in Turkey.

The medley of laws which govern the right of inheritance of not only female heirs of different communities but even of female heirs in the same community require immediate measures. Broad principles like equal rights of sons and daughters and widows, and a restriction on the power of testation so that dependent members are not left completely destitute are needed immediately.

But legislation cannot be an end in itself. Publicity of new legislation and educating women about their rights need to go hand in hand. Otherwise, like many other social legislations, the rights remain only on paper. During its tours the Committee found a large number of women completely ignorant about their rights of inheritance. Even whey they know, they have been so conditioned that many of them oppose sisters depriving their brothers of property. Our survey report confirms this finding, as 68.16% expressed their opinion against girls having some share with their brothers in property and 57.54% were against girls and boys having equal property rights. But in the absence of social security and inadequate opportunities for employment, a woman without financial security faces destitution in our country. It is true that in a country where a large section of the people are below the poverty line, measures for ownership of property will benefit only a limited section. However, for this section, ownership of property will make women independent and they will undoubtedly gain in status. Besides, this will effectively check "the feeling that women are a burden to the family."

General Recommendations

Matrimonial Property

The various personal laws in our country are uniform in recognizing the obligations of a husband to maintain his dependent wife. The right of a wife to a moiety of the husband's property on his death is, however, not an absolute right like maintenance (except in Muslim Law), as the husband under the present system can, if he chooses, deprive his wife completely under his will. Our recommendation regarding restriction of the right of testation, if accepted, will change the moral duty into a legal one. But neither of these two rights recognize the wife's claim to be a part owner of the property acquired and enjoyed jointly by husband and wife during marriage.

In the socioeconomic situation prevailing in our country, the contribution of the wife to the family's economy is not recognized. A large number of them participate in the family's effort to earn a livelihood as unpaid family workers. Even when they do not do so, the economic value of their effort in running the house and assuming all domestic responsibilities, thus freeing the husband for his avocation is not accepted in law, either directly or indirectly. Most married women do not have any independent source of income, many even give up employment after marriage or do not take up a job for many years, in order to be able to devote their full time to family obligations, particularly in bringing up the children. They are, therefore, economically dependent on their husbands. In majority of cases, property, both moveable and immoveable, acquired during the marriage, is paid for out of the husband's earnings. If a matrimonial home is acquired, it will be registered in the husband's name; if things are bought for the house the legal ownership will vest in the husband, as in economic terms the wife has not contributed anything. The principle of determining ownership on the basis of financial contribution is unjust and works inequitably against women.

While our personal laws recognize the right of a woman to own and dispose of her personal property without any control from the husband, our survey discloses that only 25.74 per cent have a regular salary and 7.14 per cent occasional wages, though 79.48 per cent believe that a woman should work to supplement the family income. In case of divorce or separation, this large group of women without any earnings or savings of their own, will be deprived of all property which they acquired jointly. Even property which she had got at the time of the marriage from the husband or his family, is denied to her in some communities. All these factors increase the dependence of the wife. The fear of both financial and social insecurity prevents her from resorting to seperation or divorce even when the marriage is very unhappy.

The demand for recognition of the wife's contribution in the way of house works is growing in many countries. England has passed the Matrimonial Proceedings Act in 1970 and the judicial decisions following, have emphasized the right of the wife to a share in the capital assets of the family. Lord Denning said that the wife "who looks after the home and family contributes as much to the family assets as the wife who goes out to work." He emphasized the importance of the home having been maintained by the joint efforts of both husband and wife and therefore "when the marriage breaks down it should be regarded as the joint property of both of them, no matter in whose name it stands."

It is necessary that legal recognition be given to the economic value of the contribution made by the wife through house work for purposes of determining ownership of matrimonial property, instead of continuing the archaic test of actual financial contribution.

We therefore recommend that in the event of divorce or separation the wife should be entitled to at least one third of the assets acquired at the time of and during marriage.

Family Courts

The statutory law in all matrimonial matters follows the adversary principle for giving relief i.e. the petitioner seeking relief alleges certain facts and the respondent in his own interest refutes them. In addition to this, as we have already noticed, most of the grounds in these statutes are based on the fault principle instead of the breakdown theory. The combined result of these two factors is that strong advocacy is often the determining factor in these cases. This is particularly unfortunate in the field of custody and guardianship, where the welfare of the child is often relegated to the background and the decision arrived at, is based on the well argued points of the lawyer. In the present system, the judge has no option but to give his decision on the point raised and argued. If he were to base his decision on social needs or in the interest of one of the parties, it may be considered as biased and hence reversed in the appellate court.

There is also no distinction drawn between matrimonial causes and other suits. This frequently leads to unusual delay which stands in the way of conciliation and further embitters the relationship of the parties. In a case filed for restitution of conjugal rights by the husband, the appellate judge referred to the "unfortunate fact that it has taken more than eight years for the appeal to come to me, such long delay...is extremely regrettable, because in such cases the time factor is of vital importance."

Conciliation which needs to be the main consideration in all family matters, is not a guiding principle in the statutes dealing with them. The legislators of the Hindu Marriage Act recognized the need but made only a half-hearted attempt to break away from the traditional approach. While they mentioned the need for conciliation, by emphasizing that the duty of the judge is to make 'every endeavour to bring about a reconciliation between the parties', they failed to provide the infrastructure necessary, like pre-trial investigation, specialized opinion of psychiatrists or social workers, which would help the judge to perform this role. The results, therefore, have not been satisfactory. The Parsee Marriage and Divorce Act, 1936, by its provision of special courts, also attempted to adopt a different procedure but that experiment too has not been a success.

The solution lies in establishing Family Courts for settlement of all problems dealing with personal law, where the role of the lawyer in adversary procedure is substituted by conciliation. The case of Japan which has successfully adopted this system is specially relevant as it is an Asian country and the emancipation of Japanese women, after the Second World War, almost coincided with the Constitutional recognition of equality in our country.

In Japan the proceedings in a family Court are informal. There are usually two conciliation commissioners of whom one is usually a woman, and the proceedings are not open to the public. A person having an interest in the case should appear before the Family Court and only under very special circumstances will the appearance of a representative be permitted.

The need for a Family Court in India has been expressed by many scholars. The Law Commission has also referred to it. The recent report of the Legal Aid Committee has strongly urged the need for such courts. In this connection, two institutions should be mentioned where the informal conciliation or compromise procedure has almost totally replaced the formal court procedure. In Rangpui (Gujarat) the 'Lok Adalat' deals *inter alia* with all family problems. Similarly, in Ahmedabad one section of the Jyoti Sangh work, dealing with all complaints pertaining to family problems, has acquired the status of a woman's court. They listen to both the parties and try to solve the problem by a compromise, failing which, other alternative solutions are suggested.

Indigenous system in India for settlement of disputes indicate that acceptance of this will be easier in our country. We, therefore, strongly recommend that the established adversary system for settlement of family problems be abandoned and established' which will adopt conciliatory methods and informal procedure with the aim of achieving socially desirable results.

Uniform Civil Code

Article 44 of the Constitutions states that "The State shall endeavour to secure for the citizens a uniform civil code throughout the territory of India".

During the debate in the Constituent Assembly, several members had expressed the fear that implementation of this article might lead to the abrogation of their personal laws. Shri K.M. Munshi had explained, that there was nothing sacrosanct about the personal laws, as they covered secular activities like inheritance and succession. Dr Ambedkar had also emphasized that India had already achieved uniformity of law over a vast area, and the only area of Civil law which continued to have diverse laws were the areas governing matters like marriage and succession. The other point which had been argued was that such diversity violated the principle of Fundamental Rights that there should be no discrimination between citizens.

These arguments remain as valid today when they were placed before the Constituent Assembly. The absence of a uniform Civil Code more than fifty years after independence, is an incongruity that cannot be justified with all the emphasis that is placed on secularism, science and modernization. The continuance of various personal laws which accept discrimination between men and women violates the fundamental rights, and the Preamble to the Constitution which promises to secure to all citizens 'equality of status', and is against the spirit of national integration and secularism.

Our recommendations regarding amendments of existing laws are only indicators of the direction in which uniformity has to be achieved. We, therefore recommend expeditious implementation of this Constitutional directive by the adoption of a Uniform Civil Code.

Criminal Law

The Penal laws of a country reflect more clearly the conditions of its society and its values than most other branches of law. It is, therefore, inevitable that the Indian Penal Code, enacted over a century ago would reflect values and protect interests which are out of tune with the norms prevailing today.

Certain penal provisions in the law are definitely influenced by the established patriarchal system, the dominant position of the husband and the social and economic backwardness of women. By amendments to the original Code, attempts have been made to reflect the socioeconomic changes in the country, but a major revision was needed. The Law Commission undertook this task and submitted the draft of a new Penal Code.

Criminal law has always given the same protection to men and women in respect of their personal safety, individual liberty, property and reputation. But along with this principle of 'equality before law', it has made special provisions to protect women *inter alia* against attacks on their modesty. Some of these measures require more stringent punishment to meet the present needs of our society, than the law provides today.

Rude or insulting behaviour by itself does not come within the purview of criminal law, unless such behaviour is likely to lead to a breach of peace. But an example of special provision is that it is an offence whenever anyone by words, sounds or gestures "intends to insult the modesty of any woman". When enacted, it was not necessary to classify this offence as a serious one, and therefore, the punishment provided was fine and/or imprisonment for a period which could extend to one year. Today eveteasing in most cities has become a social evil. But the offence in the last century was categorized as a noncognizable one and the police could not arrest without a warrant nor carry out any investigation without the specific order of a competent magistrate. This was one of the reasons why no effective steps could be taken to combat this menace effectively. The Law Commission took into account this drawback and recommended that it should be made a cognizable offence "so that in the changed social circumstances of the day, when women are coming out in larger numbers and taking greater part in various professional and business activities, they may have a sense of security." We welcome this change in the Criminal Procedure Code, particularly because, as we have discussed later, the lack of security of women acts as an obstacle to their taking up jobs away from home.

In all legal system, sexual intercourse with a woman without her consent or against her will is regarded as a serious offence.

Our law also does so by providing a punishment of imprisonment for life or imprisonment upto ten years, and fine for this offence of rape. Consent, which would negate the offence, is however very strictly interpreted and, therefore, consent, if given by the woman under duress or fraud, will be clearly disregarded by law. But under the present law, no provision is made for consent obtained by putting someone else in fear in the presence of the woman. The Law Commission has recommended adding this and the Indian Penal Code (Amendment), 1972 has included "anyone else present".

We welcome this change as a woman would, in order to save her child from a threat of injury, give her consent to sexual intercourse. This cannot be her consent as consent requires voluntary participation, not only after the exercise of intelligence, based on the knowledge or significance and moral quality of the act, but after having exercised a choice between resistance and consent.

Originally, the age of consent for sexual intercourse was 10 in the case of a girl, but successive amendments raised this to 16. The policy behind these changes was to protect girls of immature age from sexual intercourse.

The Medical Termination of Pregnancy Act 1971, however, holds that the termination of a pregnancy can be performed on a girl below 18 without her consent as long as the guardians's consent to the operation is obtained. In our view, consent to have sexual intercourse requires more maturity than to have an abortion, particularly when the girl is unmarried. The same age limit should be applied in both cases. In conformity with our recommendation made later, we recommend that the age of consent below which a girl's consent to sexual intercourse is not legal should be 18, permitting some degree of flexibility to the court in border-line cases to decide whether the girl is mature enough.

The offence of bigamy may be punished with imprisonment upto seven years and a fine. This indicates the seriousness of the offence. But as already discussed, limiting the right of initiating prosecution to only the aggrieved person, in our social context, defeats the purpose of the law. To remedy this we have recommended permitting any person to initiating prosecution for bigamy with the permission of the court. Apart from this, the present law restricts the jurisdiction of the court to the place where the bigamous marriage was performed or where the husband and wife last resided. This is likely to cause difficulties to the wife. On being abandoned, a wife will usually either go back to her natal home or if feasible take up a job, which may be away from where she resided with her husband. The present position, therefore, restricts her right to prosecute in many cases. We recommend that in addition to these two jurisdictions, provision be made for enquiry and trial for bigamy in a court within whose jurisdiction the wife is residing.

Retention of adultery as an offence is perpetuating the principle enunciated over a hundred years ago that the "dearest interests of the human race are closely connected with the chastity of women and the sacredness of the nuptial contract ... " The law today permits the husband to prosecute the adulterer' of his wife though it exempts the wife from punishment as an abettor. By doing this it brings out clearly the values of the last century which respected the dominant position of the husband and regarded the wife as his property. The Law Commission in its recommendation has only sought to remove the difference between the husband and wife by withdrawing the `privilege' a woman enjoyed earlier of not being punished under this provision. Adultery in our opinion is a matrimonial and not a criminal offence. The aggrieved is free to seek a remedy in divorce. Treating adultery as a criminal act, apart from reflecting outmoded values, sometimes deters the person of the opposite sex from giving help to a woman appraised by her husband. This was brought to our notice by several lawyers particularly in Andhra Pradesh. They mentioned many cases where lawyers, or houseowners were reluctant to assist a woman seeking divorce or separation from her husband because the latter had threatened to bring a charge of adultery against any man who gave her help.

We recommend that continuing to regard adultery as a criminal offence, is against the dignity of an individual and should be removal from the Penal Code.

Nationality

With the growing importance of human rights in the international sphere, the concept of nationality has come to acquire great importance. In Article 15 of the Universal Declaration of Human Rights 1948, the General Assembly of the United Nations declared that 'every one has the right to nationality and that no one shall be arbitrarily deprived of that nationality.' ·

Often the term Nationality and Citizenship have been used synonymously. The term citizenship refers to the relationship of an individual with the State from the internal aspect, while the term 'nationality' refers to similar relationship from the international aspect. Nationality is the status or quality of belonging to some particular nation or State. Therefore, the nationals of a State comprise all people who are politically members of the State but all of them may not possess full civil rights and privileges which are conferred on 'citizens.' Nationality gives the State a limited right to protect its nationals while they are outside the country. The State is also entitled to allegiance from its nationals even when they are abroad as also obedience to certain laws.

In India the matters of citizenship are governed by the Citizenship Act 1955 and the Rules 1956 as also certain provisions of the Constitution.

The Citizenship Act 1955 deals with the acquisition and termination of citizenship. Under Sec 5(1)(c), a woman married to a citizen of India does not automatically become a citizen, but may make an application and be registered as a citizen. An application by a woman for registration as a citizen under the provisions requires documentary evidence that she has either renounced her previous nationality or has lost it by operation of law. If she has neither lost nor renounced it, her application must be accompanied by an undertaking that she will do so on getting her Indian citizenship. This requirement is essential as our law does not recognize dual citizenship. But the question of whether an alien woman married to an Indian citizen will get Indian citizenship or not is left to the discretion of the Central Government and can not be challenged in a court of law. This provision of the Act is in accordance with the United Nations Convention of 1957 on the Nationality of Married Women. Under the Convention, all contracting parties agree that the alien wife of a national may acquire the nationality of her husband, through specially privileged naturalization procedures, but it must be at her request. The grant of nationality, however, may be subject to limitations imposed in the interest of national security or public policy. According to the information supplied by the Home Ministry, there were no statistics of the number of applications made by alien women married to Indian citizens or the number rejected, but '2151 alien women married to Indian citizens had been granted Indian citizenship under the Act'.

The lacuna in the Act is the absence of any provision dealing with the case of Indian women marrying foreigners. Her rights are governed by the general provisions which deal with renouncing Indian citizenship. Till she renounces it she continues to retain her Indian citizenship, even if her husband has renounced his. But it is in the interpretation of what constitutes renunciation that the hardship may occur. The provision which applies to all persons is that voluntary acquisition of citizenship of another country will amount to renunciation of Indian citizenship, as we do not accept dual nationality. On the face of it, the provision is unexceptionable but in practice this results in great hardship. If the law of the husband's country requires her to acquire her husband's citizenship by registration or any other way, her registration will be treated a voluntary act as it is not by operation of law. This is unfortunate as often an Indian woman marrying a foreigner requires special protection. Some countries specifically provide that a woman "shall in no case lose her nationality as a result of her marriage to an alien". If for some reason according to the law of her husband's country, a wife is deprived of her nationality, she becomes stateless as she had already lost her Indian citizenship the moment she registered for her husband's nationality. There is consequently no protection given to a woman marrying an alien to prevent this situation of statelessness.

According to the Home Ministry, "No Indian woman has yet lost her Indian citizenship by the sole reason of her having married a foreign national", though they agree that if she "acquires her husband's nationality by some other act, for example, registration, her Indian citizenship will terminate." The Ministry is however silent on the point as to how many of them have lost their Indian nationality by this process.

The right to determine whether the Indian woman's act acquiring her husband's citizenship is voluntary or not vests with the Central Government, which will apply rules of evidence specified in the Rules of the Act. One such piece of evidence is the obtaining of a passport from the Government of another country. Merely getting a passport from a foreign country should not be termed a 'voluntary' acquisition. Even the Supreme Court has expressed this opinion. Many jurists have also challenged the 'Rule' which lays down that getting a passport is a voluntary acquisition. In cases of emergency where time is important, many women would opt for getting a passport which is quicker but this can scarcely be termed a 'voluntary' act. 'From the practical point of view, an Indian woman married to a foreigner and living outside the country, may have to return for purely personal reasons like illness of a family member, and in such a case one would not hesitate to travel on any passport - the end being important and not the means of getting there.

Hardship to an Indian woman by arbitrarily applying the rules is best illustrated by the citizenship laws of Afghanistan. According to Afghan law, a woman acquires her husband's nationality by marriage. As long as this is the law, our law will accept the position that an Indian woman has both Indian nationality and Afghan nationality as she has not voluntarily acquired Afghan nationality. But the moment she returns to India on an Afghan passport, she loses her Indian nationality, because she will be deemed to have voluntarily acquired the citizenship of Afghanistan. Under no circumstances should she become stateless. We therefore recommend that the Citizenship Act be amended to provide a special rule for Indian woman marrying aliens, stating that she will in no case lose her Indian nationality as a result of her marriage to a foreigner. (a) Further, that her acquiring the passport of her husband's country should not be regarded as evidence that she has voluntarily acquired another nationality; (b) In the eventuality of her having been declared stateless, she should revert back to Indian citizenship automatically.

Another rule which operates against the interests of Indian

women marrying foreigners, is that their children cannot be regarded as Indian citizens, because the Act clearly states that a child will be considered an Indian citizen only if his father is one at the time of his birth. Explaining this rule the then Home Minister had said that this provision was to prevent dual or multiple nationality and not to discriminate against women, and in any case, the cases of Indian women marrying foreigners was very rare. This does not really explain the basis of the rule. Where the father and mother are separate and the mother is either *de jure* or *de facto* guardian, there is no justification to have the rule that child's nationality will be transmitted through the father. As a mother may be a legal guardian in preference to the father, if it is in the interest of the child, there can be no justification for this rule. We therefore recommend the amendment of Sec. 4(1) of the Citizenship Act to read as follows: "A person born outside India on or after the 26th January, 1950, shall be a citizen of India by descent if his father is married to a citizen of India at the time of his birth."

Under the modern day material pressures and industrialized world women are compelled to think of their legal right for their happy and peaceful life.

In good old days different social and religious traditions laid down certain norms of behaviour for women in India. But compulsions of changing human values and mass education programmes for women have brought about a changed outlook and a new angle of vision to the Indian women. They are now no longer content with their traditional roles and are not prepared to tolerate denial to them of the basic rights. Moreover it is now agreed that only a harmonious development of a regime of rights can provide the necessary conditions for peace and such a harmony is to be achieved not merely by declaring rights for women on paper but inculcating a culture of rights and responsibilities among the people. Women problem is a human problem and its future prospects are prospects of humanity at large and not of women alone.

Let us conclude this chapter with a recent article from *Hindustan Times.*

How Unfair to Fair Sex!

Article 14 of the Constitution of India guarantees equal rights to all citizens and equality before law. No discrimination can be made on grounds of sex, religion, race, caste, creed, etc. "The State shall not deny to any person equality before the law or equal protection of laws". The rule is that "like should be treated alike and not that unlike should be treated alike".

In the light of Article 14, the Government has been trying to help women find gainful employment. They work in government service and also occupy posts in the judiciary, the army, police and in other departments. And yet women are made to feel inferior to men especially around the time they marry. Demands for dowry are not unusual, keeping in view the social status of the bride-groom and his parents.

Husbands and in-laws further tend to harass women in numerous other ways. They resort to cruelty in their conduct and in the treatment they mete out to women. Thus, husbands cause harassment by forcing wives to do things that the latter may not like. The Supreme Court has held that cruelty in the legal sense need not be a mere physical assault. The Court holds that the conduct adopted by a married lady's husband or by any other relative, or treatment meted out to her which tends to undermine her health or reasonably affects her happiness can be termed 'cruelty'.

Even imputing unchastity to a woman is a very serious charge and, if established, may result in serious consequences. Such a woman would stand condemned in society, amounting to mental agony.

The Supreme Court has held that injury to reputation is an important consideration in determining the question of cruelty. Husbands and in-laws often level false accusations against a woman by questioning her integrity, resulting in extreme mental agony. They even institute false cases to terrorise women by greasing the palms of the law enforcement staff and many others.

Newly married girls often fall victim to the machinations of unscrupulous in-laws who create all kinds of trouble for them. Both husbands and in-laws cause such mental torture that they are left with no alternative other than committing suicide. When cruelty for dowry is *prime facie* proved by certain acts or documentary evidence, a case under Section 498A, 304B, IPC, and under the Dowry Prohibitions Act is registered. Though this Act has been amended from time to time, the unscrupulous manage to escape the clutches of law. It is therefore imperative to amend the law.

Some women suffer mental agony owing to polygamy. It has been argued whether a Muslim husband has a vested right to marry more than one wife and give universal divorce. It was held by the Supreme Court that so far as polygamy is concerned, the Mohammedan law is only permissive or optional in nature, and not obligatory. It levies a ceiling on wives and does not lay down that every Muslim should have four wives as a matter of right. It is in the form of an exception.

Divorce or judicial separation are sought in court on grounds of harassment, cruelty, misbehaviour, desertion, adultery and so on. Even court proceedings are unduly delayed, causing great harassment and financial losses to the aggrieved women. Poor women who do not have the means to spend on litigation are the worst hit. The police too does not usually move swiftly to secure justice for destitute women. Neither are the FIR's recorded speedily nor any prompt action initiated unless some pressure is brought on from higher levels.

The fact that women's problems are not attended to even when the complaints are lodged with the local police or with various women's cells needs no reiteration. (*Hindustan Times*, 27 Feb., 98)

Sectors Needing Reforms

Legislation represents national intent and policy and it is necessary that existing legislation and personal laws be reviewed, appropriately amended or new laws formulated, to ensure equality before law among sexes. Equally important is the need to provide free legal services to weaker sections including women in need. A great deal has been done in recent months particularly regarding equal pay for equal work and steps are being taken for providing legal aid, etc. Needless to add, as has been emphasized in earlier chapters, legislation in itself cannot achieve results, unless it is supported by socio-economic changes, an awareness of right and responsibilities by the weaker sections, effective legal implementation and follow-up machinery.

Marriage Laws

The legal system should ensure full equality of sexes even in terms of the personal laws. There should be no compromise about the objective of having monogamy as the rule for all communities in India. Any compromise in this regard will only perpetuate the existing inequality of the status of women. Towards this end, the following measures are suggested:

Reform in Law to Prevent Polygamy

Among some sections of the population, polygamy has legal sanction. However, before necessary changes in the law relating to polygamy are brought about, vigorous effort should be basically directed to generating initiative from among the affected groups so that by the end of the millenium it would be possible to have uniform legislation for all communities. For this purpose, the practices adopted in other countries with Muslim/Christian majority should be studied and made known widely.

Enforcement of Provision against Bigamy under Hindu Marriage Act

The right to initiate prosecution for bigamy should be extended to persons other than the girls family with prior permission of the court to prevent the current violation of this very salutary provision of the law which presents the socially accepted policy of the country. The approach should be towards making it a cognizable offence.

Registration of Marriage

Registration of marriages should be made compulsory for all marriages. For this to be operationally effective, suitable administrative machinery will have to be designed particularly in the rural areas. Enforcement of this could be made operational through amendment to Registration of Births and Deaths Act, 1969, to include compulsory registration of marriages.

Minimum Age of Marriage

The Child Marriage Restraint Act should be amended to raise the age of marriage for girls to 18 and that of boys to 21. However, for effective implementation proper machinery for enforcing the minimum age at marriage should be designed.

Prohibition of Dowry

Penalties for offence under the Dowry Prohibition Act, 1961, should be suitably enhanced to make the implementation of the Act more effective. To bring about greater awareness of the evils of dowry, socio-educational programmes should be launched by social welfare organisations.

Government servants giving or taking dowry should be treated as having violated the Government Servants' Conduct Rules similar to the Government Servants' Conduct Rules relating to bigamy.

Divorce Laws

Although there is right to divorce, but variations and unequal treatment of sexes, *vis-a-vis* divorce, characterize the various personal laws. As a general principle, efforts should be made to bring about parity of rights for both partners regarding grounds for seeking dissolution of marriage by 1985. Here too, vigorous efforts should be made so that there is a demand from the affected group for uniformity of legislation.

The Laws Relating to Inheritance of Property

Action should be taken in conformity with the broad principles or equal rights of sons, daughters and widows to ancestral property.

The Indian Succession Act is not uniformly applicable to all sections of women. Efforts should be made for generating the initiative from among the affected groups of women for bringing about necessary changes in the Succession Act so that by the end of 1985 it is possible to have uniform legislation for all communities by the end of the twentieth century.

On divorce and separation, the wife should be entitled to some part of the assets acquired at the time of and during the time of marriage.

Nationality Laws

The present rule prevents the children of such Indian women from being considered as Indian citizens. Where the father and mother are separated and the mother is the guardian, the justification for the applicability of the rule that the child's nationality will be transmitted through the father is required to be re-examined with reference to the relevant aspects which have a bearing in Private International Law. The Citizenship Act will, therefore, be modified if need be.

The procedures for regaining Indian Citizenship in the case of women of Indian origin, declared as Stateless are tedious and cumbersome. Efforts should, therefore, be made to design simpler procedure in this regard and what is more, there must be a sympathetic and helpful orientation at its implementation stage.

Bigamy Laws

The present law restricts jurisdiction of the court to the place where the bigamous marriage was performed or where the husband and wife last resided. This causes difficulties to the wife who may have to move on after being abandoned by her husband. Therefore; the provisions of the Criminal Procedure relating to jurisdiction should be widened to include trial for bigamy in a court within whose jurisdiction the wife ordinarily resides.

Adoption Laws

There is need to have a uniform secular and enabling law of adoption.

REFERENCES

1. Goonesekere Savitri, *Children, Law and Justice*, 1997.
2. Konowitz, *Women and the Law*, 1970.
3. Nijhawan Vs. Nijhawan, 1953, Delhi.
4. Please see Lok Sabha Debates.
5. Reports of the Law Commission of India.

Ten

Women in the News

Call for Women's Empowerment

Seminars, conferences and demonstrations by women's organizations marked the International Women's Day in the Capital few years ago.

Addressing a conference on "Development of women in Fifty Years of Independence, the First Lady, Mrs Usha Narayanan, said that very little had changed for the majority of women living in rural areas.

She underlined the need for greater co-ordination and interaction between governmental policy at the national level to tie in with the concerns and matters raised by women at the local government level.

The conference was jointly organized by the National Commission for Women (NCW), Department of Women and Child Development and Central Social Welfare Board.

Mrs Narayanan said that the women need to be empowered to take their rightful place on an equal footing with men. "They need to be liberated from discrimination and exploitation", she added.

She said that since Independence women have taken more and more initiatives to improve their condition by actively participating in Non-Governmental Organisations and Co-operatives.

For instance, she said that village level Mahila Mandals have taken up cudgels against rape, alcohol abuse by men and wife-battering.

Speaking on the occasion, the chairperson of NCW, Ms V. Mohini Giri, said that the concept of gender equality has become a crucial input to solve national and local problems.

She maintained that special attention was given by NCW to the condition of Scheduled Castes and Scheduled Tribes who were ignored so far.

She informed that four reports released by the commission to mark the occasion, were related to tribal development. She said that the NCW has undertaken special efforts to support the handicapped and disabled women.

She informed that the NCW forwarded a number of recommendations to the government to amend the discriminatory provisions in various laws relating to women.

Several women freedom fighters were honoured at the function. A special stamp to commemorate fifty years of universal declaration of human rights was also released.

Meanwhile, Pragateesheel Mahila Sangathan, a women's organization, staged a demonstration at Ferozeshah Kotla ground.

The activists of the organization also staged street plays to highlight the plight of the rural women. They also raised slogans against the government apathy to meet the basic requirements of the downtrodden.

Talking Point: Sex Workers Scoff at Legalization

They have more confidence in their music than in the government. Their working hours, conditions and most importantly, the compulsions which pushed them into their present profession qualifies for a human rights blacklist.

Their profession has no legality. And demands to make it legal only invite scorn. They are the children of a civilization's twilight zone. They are sex workers. And they don't buy the politician's sales pitch.

"*Sarkar ki baat mein dalali hai,*" says Radha Bai, a 35-year-old sex worker from Chatarpur in Madhya Pradesh. "*usko toh vote chahiye. Woh hamse kaam karate hain,*" she says. The others nod in agreement.

When it is election time, the politicians come with money and bribe their votes. After that, they are exploited and harassed mercilessly by the same persons, says Kalidasi, a veteran.

Radha has four children, three girls and a boy. "I have educated the children. I don't have property. But I don't want them to do what I did. *Kuch banna hai unko. Aur unko bhi is kaam se nafrat hai. Ab dekho ladki ki shaadi karni hai. Sarkar hamein 10,000 degi rupaiya toh aaj kal usse kya hoga? Shadi ke liye 2 lakh rupaiya mangte hain. Agar ladki padegi toh achcha rishta bhi chahegi. Jo hamne kiya woh kiya Rahne do. Hamara guzara hoh jata hai."*

Legalizing prostitution has no meaning for her. *"Jab school mein bharti karne jaate hain toh baap ka naam puuchte hain. Kyon puuchte hain? School main bacche bolte hain, 'Iski maa naachti hai.' Bacche rote hua humko aake batate hain. Hamare dil ko nahin lagta?"* is the poignant question Radha Bai raises.

Is it difficult for their children to get a good match? "It is not difficult to get a good match," says Kalidasi, *"par koi sukh nahin hai."*

Kalidasi and her daughter Aruna are from Muzaffarpur. Kalidasi's daughter married into a respectable family. The problem: They don't let the girl talk to anyone or step out of the house. She is prevented from talking to relatives. The dowry demands are enormous.

But Kalidasi had not left any stone unturned. The dowry she gave was substantial but she was not one to be cowed down by demands for more.

17 per cent Women Candidates Win in Lok Sabha Polls

Of the 255 women who contested the recently held parliamentary elections, 43 won giving them a winability rate of nearly 17 per cent. This percentage is nearly three times higher than their winnability percentage in the 1996 general elections when it was 6.68.

These details are included in a paper titled 'Women and their spaces in Indian politics' which has been written by Kamla Nath of the Centre for Social Research, Delhi.

The paper says there was a significant decline in the number of women candidates in Andhra Pradesh where it decreased from 174 in 1996 to 21 and Madhya Pradesh where the number came down from 75 to merely six. In Uttar Pradesh too, there was a decline from 103 to 60.

But the decline, witnessed among male candidates too, is attributed, among other things, to stricter criteria for nomination, a limit on poll expenses and stricter implementation of the code of conduct.

As for the States where the number of women candidates

this time was higher than in 1996, these are Gujarat, Karnataka and Tamil Nadu. In Gujarat, the number of women candidates doubled from the four who stood for elections in 1996. Similarly, in Tamil Nadu, the number of women nominees went up from three in 1996 to 12. In Karnataka too, the number of women contesting elections increased from five to eight. But in Karnataka, none of the women candidates managed to win a seat in Parliament.

In the case of Karnataka where no woman candidate has won this time, the paper notes that "this is rather unfortunate for a State which was the first to give reservation (to women) in local bodies and boasts of having 45 per cent of the seats occupied by women."

The paper also observes that women voters "seem to have played a role in the winning and losing of seats among candidates." For instance, the paper says in Rajasthan, the Bharatiya Janata Party government fell due to women voting against the Shekhawat government to protest against the government's inability to protect the dignity of women.

As for winning candidates, a study conducted by the centre in which 1,250 voters (60 per cent of them were women) were surveyed, 93 per cent supported the participation of women in politics.

Those surveyed felt that women are less corrupt, more humane, and address local needs rather than indulge in manipulative politics to stay in power.

The paper also notes that political experience is a major consideration for political parties when fielding women candidates. It says independent women candidates with a background in social work have not been inducted by political parties in their expanding base. It adds, "party women, with a few exceptions, are women with connections in the party structure."

Safe Motherhood Day will be Organized every Month

To educate and create awareness among pregnant women about the need for antenatal check-ups and to achieve a perceptible reduction in the maternal mortality rate, the Delhi government has decided to organize Matri Suraksha Divas (safe motherhood day) every month

The former Delhi health minister Harsh Vardhan said this will start from April 7, the WHO day on the theme "Safe Motherhood" with the slogan "Pregnancy is Special- Let's Make it Safe".

"However, in subsequent months, the date will be the 10th of every month," the minister says.

Dr Harsh Vardhan said maternal mortality rate in India is alarmingly high. The incidence varies between 400 and 800 per one lakh live births as against 1 to 3 reported in the developed countries.

"From this, it seems, for a woman to be pregnant in India is an invitation to death," Dr Harsh Vardhan remarked.

He said nearly one in four maternal deaths are due to haemorrhage and one in five are due to anaemia. Other causes include toxaemia, illegal abortions, sepsis and rupture of the uterus, he said.

"Most of these are avoidable and can be reduced by timely antenatal check-ups and proper treatment during pregnancy," Dr Harsh Vardhan said.

The government had organized safe motherhood campaigns earlier too, once in 1996 and twice in 1997. "Seeing its importance, the Union government also picked it up at the national level last year," the then Delhi health minister said.

The programme aims to:

- Provide antenatal care services to each and every pregnant woman.
- Acquaint every expectant mother with the location of the health facility nearest to her, where she could go for antenatal check-ups and delivery.
- Utilize the contact with the health provider to impart knowledge about contraception, neo-natal care, importance of breast examination and other relevant counselling.
- Give tetanus toxoid immunization whenever indicated and provide folic acid for prevention and correction of anaemia and elemental calcium as a supplement required during pregnancy.
- Provide facility of ultrasonography to needy pregnant

women, increase awareness about the benefits and importance of breastfeeding, and
- Identify high-risk cases and develop an appropriate referral system.

The former health minister said apart from all 500 static hospitals, dispensaries and mother and child health centres belonging to the Delhi government, Union government, municipal bodies, Centre Government Health Scheme (CGHS), Delhi government, etc., special arrangements for antenatal check-ups will be made in about 100 temporary centres to be set up exclusively in JJ clusters, resettlement and unauthorized colonies and underserved areas.

These temporary centres, attached to the static centres, would work from 9 am to 4 pm on Matri Suraksha Divas, said the minister.

He also said all available publicity media, including personnel interaction, would be used to spread the safe motherhood message and ensure the active participation of all pregnant women.

Magistrate Pulled up for not Recording Alleged Rape Victim's Statement as per Law

A sessions court, while deciding a rape case, has pulled up a metropolitan magistrate for not following the laid down procedure for recording an alleged victim's statement.

The woman had been produced before metropolitan magistrate B.S. Chumbak for legal proceedings under Section 164 (recording of statement or confession by a magistrate) of the Code of Criminal Procedure. But he did not record the statement as per law.

"His statement is most uncharitable. Instead of recording her statement under Section 164, which was part of the investigation and beholden duty of the magistrate, he perused the police case file and her statement recorded by police," said additional sessions judge J.D. Kapoor.

"The observations of the magistrate for not recording the statement of the prosecutrix (the alleged rape victim) and dismissing the investigation officer's application are uncalled for. The magistrate has observed since the prosecutrix had attained the age of majority, she was aware of the wrong and right about herself," noted the judge.

The judge added the magistrate "presumed any women having age of majority cannot be raped." "I cannot make any comment on such understanding of the magistrate then to advise him that in future he must not resort to such a step and record the witness' statement after satisfying himself the witness has made it voluntarily, without any pressure."

The rape case in question has ended in an acquittal. The prosecution had alleged the accused, Puran Chand, a shopkeeper, raped the prosecutrix after locking the Trilokpuri area shop on July 25, 1996.

The prosecutrix, distantly related to Puran Chand, had begun working in the shop only a month before the alleged rape. She was separated from her husband. The prosecution produced nine witnesses to support its case.

Defence Counsel S.P. Ahluwalia, assisted by Puneet Ahluwalia, in turn, argued the woman had allegedly stolen Rs 1,600 five days before the claimed incident. She was scared Puran Chand might lodge a complaint and pre-empted this by lodging the false rape case, counsel said.

Pointing out several contradictions and shortcomings in the case, counsel said there was also "an utter lack of scientific evidence corroborating even the commission of sexual intercourse". The prosecution had also failed to explain the "fatal" delay in registration of the case, he added.

After examining all the evidence, Mr Kapoor said several facts before the courts created "suspicion and doubt in the veracity of the prosecution case". One, the complete absence of any injury on the prosecutrix or the accused.

Two, lack of "scientific evidence to corroborate the factum of sexual intercourse". Three, delay in lodging an FIR. Four, Prosecutrix's failure to raise any alarm "during the alleged forcible sexual act". Five, her failure to bring the incident to the notice of neighbouring shopkeepers and the people present there.

"It is indigestible that a woman subjected to rape, would not raise any alarm... there was lot of rush in the market (because of a weekly bazaar on that day) but she did not tell anyone about what had happened... she straight away went to her cousin brother's house and then only telephoned the police from there," the judge said, acquitting the accused.

To hang or not: A woman's life in the balance

Though the Supreme Court has stayed the execution of Ram Shri, the first woman to be sentenced to death in independent India, the verdict has generated a controversy over society's right to kill another human.

Should capital punishment be abolished? If not, should extraneous considerations like the accused being a woman or mother of a small child be taken into consideration in determining the sentence?

These contentious issues relating to crime and punishment came to the fore recently as the National Council for Women took up cudgels on behalf of Ram Shri convicted of murdering her neighbour's family in 1989. But opinions differ.

Many have demanded abolition of capital punishment terming it as "barbaric." But others want it retained arguing that the very fear of death acts as a deterrent.

They, however, assert that the sentence should be given "in totality of all considerations and circumstances involving the accused."

The case of 37-year-old Ram Shri who was to be hanged with her father and brother on April 6, has necessitated a rethink of the country's criminal justice system, say women activists and jurists.

"The Supreme Court has made it categorically clear that the death sentence should be given only in the `rarest' of rare cases. So what is more important is that criminal cases should be tried very very carefully," says senior criminal lawyer Shanti Bhushan.

Former Delhi Commissioner of Police Ved Marwah, however, strongly opposes capital punishment saying it "brutalizes" society.

"Capital punishment has ceased to be a deterrent in our society. Mere statistics of crime in the capital are enough of an indication that the fear of death sentence no longer deters a criminal from committing heinous acts of crime."

"Moreover, there is an element of finality to death. If a mistake has been done in convicting an accused, it cannot be rectified once the execution is carried out," Mr Marwah, who is currently associated with the Centre for Policy Research, said.

Prof. Veena Mazumdar of the Centre for Women's Development Studies entirely agrees with this viewpoint saying "I am against any form of retributive justice."

But senior Supreme Court lawyer Kapil Sibal sees "absolutely no reason to abolish capital punishment."

"It is indeed a deterrent. Why should it be abolished when there is lack of value for human life in the urban society... Where crimes are committed at the drop of a hat," Mr Sibal asks.

But should there be discrimination on the grounds of gender? How does it matter if a murder is committed by a woman or a man? Should the court also be lenient to a man having a small child as the latter might be financially dependent on his father?

"The court should make judgements on the facts of each case. The accused being a mother is a relevant circumstance but again the court has to balance that with the nature of the crime. So the judgement should be made in totality of circumstances," says Mr Sibal.

"But again, if the accused is a man, the fact of him being a father should also be taken into consideration," he adds. (PTI)

Give women the right to conquer their fate

Mao-Tse-Tung had once said, "Half the sky, thou art woman." No society can advance without giving women their due recognition. Their status should be at par with that of men. But no matter how hoarse we cry ourselves, nothing constructive has been done to improve their lot, especially in the remote villages.

A woman's needs must, by no means, be neglected. For ages, India has been holding women in high esteem. It is India which had issued a proclamation to the effect that the mother and motherland are greater than heaven itself. However, this is only in theory.

For all practical purposes, there are very few instances which actually justify this contention. Women have been exploited and oppressed and injustice has been meted out to them.

Burning women in the name of sati, child marriage and dowry-deaths serve to show the extent to which they have been deprived in the past. Not forgetting their right to minimum basic education.

Instances of malnutrition and female infanticide abound. The school enrolment ratio for women is only 46. In India; a woman's earnings amount to only 19 per cent of the national income. This is because 90 per cent of them work in the unorganized sector.

In the agricultural sector, the work of a woman goes unpaid. Neither are home-based workers covered under Labour Laws or the Factory Acts.

"Why don't you give women the right to conquer their fate?" Rabindranath Tagore had once asked. A lot remains to be done in order to better their lot.

Formulating a national policy would certainly help but the need of the hour is a change in our attitude. Only this would help improve their lot, and result in the development and progress of our country at large.

Sandip Kumar Bose, Class XII, Hindu School
The Asian Age, 9 March, 1998

Woman's emancipation lies in equal rights and opportunities

I am a girl. In other words, a burden. I feel disturbed and ashamed of society's discrimination against women, more so, in the remote villages. Despite the progress made in various walks of life, violence against women persists. In most villages, women are tortured under the pretext of dowry or a modest protest raised against the male members of the family.

If the existing state of affairs continues, no village can develop. First and foremost, we should put an end to this discriminatory attitude. Women should be given equal rights of freedom. For the benefit of men in the country, a woman is a mother, daughter, wife, sister and above all, a sensitive companion. Then, why is she forced to lead a life of sordid imprisonment?

Right from her childhood, the girl child faces unfavourable circumstances. From the minute she is born, she is considered a burden especially in a poor family. Not without reason. The povertystricken parents have to save every penny for their daughter's dowry. She is not sent to school though her brothers attend school.

In course of time, the girl child realizes she has no right to education, desires and the good things in life. Before she grows up, she is sent to work as a maid in the city and at home, is taught to cook food. Before she blossoms into a woman, she is taught to please her future husband and in-laws. A demanding husband makes life miserable for her at her in-laws. To make matters worse, she is beaten or burnt to death for more and more dowry. Today dowry deaths have become so much of a regular affair that they no longer make headlines.

On an average, 17 dowry deaths are reported daily in India. In 1993, the number of deaths reported was 5,582. In 1994, there was an alarming increase to 8281 deaths. Even in Assam there is one dowry death in every 23 hours. Between 1989-90, dowry deaths saw an increase of 118.9 per cent, as far as registered cases were concerned.

Even if a girl is fortunate to be born into a good family and has an understanding husband, she is not spared. She possesses a body, in other words, is at a disadvantage. And hence she is raped. More often than not, she is betrayed in the dark, at waiting rooms, in trains or at home.

Sometimes she is even initiated into the sex trade to satiate the sexual appetite of men. Rape is a powerful weapon by way of which a woman can be demoralized and defeated. The recorded rape statistics say it all. In India, one in every 2000 women, is reported to be raped.

According to a recent article in one of the leading national periodicals, a woman is raped every two hours. Add to this the countless number of unregistered cases which make a mockery of the principle of freedom and human rights. Reported cases in India show an increase in areas where there is political unrest. For instance, rape became a burning issue in Assam during the elections in 1983.

This happens because women are a minority in every sense of the word. According to the census report of recent years, the sex ratio stands at 933 females per 1000 males. The literacy rate is 46.86 per cent for males as compared to 24.82 per cent for females.

The female work participation rate is 13.9 per cent while the male work participation rate is 51.62 per cent.

The aforesaid statistics present a clear picture of a woman's plight. However, despite the existing state of affairs, I feel, women themselves are somewhere responsible for their plight. Most women believe, ultimate happiness lies in marriage and procuring children. It is time a woman realizes that equal rights is the only key to true emancipation.

Vaswati Sarmah, Class X, St. Joseph's Convent, Tezpur, Assam
The Asian Age, 9 March, 1998

Hocus-pocus: When films project Eves as mere sexy sirens

A woman has several roles to play. The stereotypical image of Goddess Durga is worshipped worldwide. On the one hand, she is looked upon as a *pativrata nari* who believes in sharing her husband's sorrows and joys and, a mother, who bestows love and affection on her children. On the other, she is a ruthless woman who fears none when it comes to vanquishing the demon personifying evil.

It is evident from her dual persona that a woman is, any day, stronger than a man, if not physically, then mentally. We all know the hardships she undergoes in course of giving birth to a child. A woman is one of the most esteemed creations of God, despite the fact that she may have been created out of Adam's ribs.

But how much respect does our society have for her? Films are supposed to reflect the changes that come to characterize society. Yet, going by the manner in which a woman is projected on screen, it would appear that society at large has a very low opinion of her.

Women are reduced to being mere showpieces or sex objects. This is a reflection on the status she enjoys in society today. More than 80 per cent of Indian films have a man as the protagonist. The actress merely dances around trees and gyrates in the rain. There are films such as *Bandit Queen* and *Mother India* which show the hardships a woman has to face. But such films are few in number.

These days, a woman seems to have no privacy. Songs such as *choli ke peeche kya hai* may provide cheap entertainment for us men but, for a woman, it is a violation of her dignity. Eveteasers love to sing such a song when a woman walks down the streets.

A woman is beautiful and, perhaps, the prettiest creation of God. We must definitely admire her but we should never forget that she is a human being and not public property. Some of us tend to believe that a woman enjoys being eve-teased. I wonder if any of them have ever asked the women in their families if they like being looked upon as a *'Tu cheez badi hai mast, mast'*. Film-makers need to realize that the time has come when a woman should be projected as an entity with a mind of her own. As the adage goes, where there is no respect for women, progress for that nation is uncertain.

Tathagath Chowdhury, Class XI, The Assembly of God Church Scgool,
The Asian Age, 9 March, 1998

Women's Bill should be passed, says Mohini Giri

National Commission for Women the then chairperson Mohini Giri expressed hope that the constitutional amendment bill providing one-third reservation for women in Lok Sabha and State legislatures would be passed in the first session of new Parliament.

Addressing a function here on the International Women's Day, she said passage of the bill would mark an important step in the evolution of social and political order of the country. She said the concept of gender equality has become a crucial input in solution of not only global but also of national and local problems.

On relevance of NCW, she said "our endeavour is to act as a bridge between the broad-based constituency of women's organizations and the government as the 21st century is poised to be the century of women." Sensitization of judiciary and the police along with training to Panchayat women has become a cherished challenge before the commission in the last one year, she said.

She also appreciated the role played by women in anti-arrack movement in different parts of the country. As part of the celebrations, several women freedom fighters were also felicitated.

The four reports released by the commission were related to tribal development. Legal awareness had been launched by the commission to create identity and consciousness for women in the country.

Special efforts were being undertaken to support the handicapped and disabled women through social support measures, resources and appropriate experiment in the delivery of speedy justice had not only been cost effective but had also met with roaring success, the former chairperson said.

Justice Malimath, member of the Human Rights Commission hoped increased cooperation between the two organizations would lessen the problems of women. Minister of State for External Affairs Kamla Sinha also spoke on the occasion.

'Women don't need crutches'

Voicing the silence of millions, India's First Lady Usha Narayanan on International Women's Day rued that uneven development had left more people "untouched, unsung and neglected" and called for liberating women from discrimination and exploitation.

Declaring that women were "not in need of crutches or hand-outs," the wife of President K.R. Narayanan said they instead need to be empowered to take their rightful place on an equal footing with men. Inaugurating an open discussion on "Development of Women in 50 Years of Independence, organized by the National Commission for Women here, Ms Narayanan questioned whether Indian women had any cause to celebrate these 50 years. Observing that the overall picture was "of uneven development," she said due to this very little has changed for the majority of women in rural areas and among the poor in urban areas. As a result many million women have to still trek great distances to fetch water, blatant violations of women's rights occur in the name of traditions, rapes occur every hour, female child is seen as a liability.

Eminent sociologist-economist Rajni Kothari delivered the theme address, at the discussion. In the morning session freedom fighters from all parts of the country were honoured by activist Suman Krishna Kant, wife of the Vice-President, at the Vigyan Bhavan. A special commemorative stamp to mark 50 years of Universal Declaration of Human Rights was also released by secretary (posts) Rus Prasad.

Sewa: Ensuring security to marginalized women

Poor, self-employed women like vendors, artisans and labourers who don't get a regular salary constitute 94 per cent of the labour force in India. This large chunk of unprotected labour force that is unorganized gets no benefits like the salaried workers in the organized sector. Their survival depends on day-to-day earnings and in event of any economic, social and health risks they have to face more hardship.

The Self-Employed Women's Association, formed in 1972 by Ms Ela Bhatt, was meant to function as a trade union to ensure rights of this large, but invisible, section of the workforce. Ms Bhatt was head of the women's wing of the Textile Labour Association that was formed by Mahatma Gandhi and Anasuya Sarabhai.

"Our goal is to organize these marginalised women to ensure them full employment, food and social security keeping their self-reliance intact," says the Sewa General Secretary, Ms Mirai Chatterjee, who was elected to the top post in 1996 after Ms Bhatt decided not to stand for re-election to support and encourage new leaders in the organization.

Sewa is not just a trade union now, the movement has advanced a lot in the last 25 years to include a lot of sister organizations. Sewa, in the words of Ms Bhatt, is like a banyan tree that blows with the wind but stands rooted to the earth. The banyan tree grows branches which in turn sets roots and a new tree forms and with time no one can recognize where one tree begins and the other ends. "This is the way we grew and this is the manner in which we have to develop," says Ms Bhatt.

The women's movement is not just restricted to Gujarat alone where Sewa has 1.62 lakh members but has also spread to Madhya Pradesh, Bihar, Kerala, Delhi and Uttar Pradesh bringing the overall membership to 2.12 lakh.

At Sewa there is a great emphasis on self-management. "The organization must be owned and run by poor self-employed women independently. These women must be the decision makers as they should not remain mere beneficiaries but become owners and managers," feels Ms Bhatt.

The main challenge that Sewa faces is maintaining

momentum in a large organization made up of small decentralized units.

The Sewa has evolved a very democratic set-up where elections are held every three years and all Sewa members elect their representatives to the trade council, which consists of worker-leaders and they in turn elect an executive committee that coordinates activities of all the Sewa activities and organizations. The Sewa Academy trains women as organizers, so that as leaders they can mobilize more women to become a part of the movement.

Self-Employed Women's Association has started an integrated social security system for its members in areas of old age, family health insurance and family social services.

"We are trying to alleviate risks self-employed women face everyday. About 25,000 women are covered by this project and they save a small amount of money every month as a sort of insurance, which they can use in times of need," Ms Chatterjee said.

Sewa in collaboration with nationalized insurance companies and German Development Cooperation will support this Sewa project by providing assistance worth Rs 40,109,835 in the first phase. The women have to pay an annual premium of Rs 60 to get some protection against various crises. An additional Rs 15 ensures life insurance for their husbands. This is like a widowhood insurance which most of the women insisted upon.

Self-Employed Women's Association also helps self-employed women to organize themselves in sustainable organizations so that they can collectively promote their own development. About 87 independent women's cooperatives have been formed with support of Sewa.

However, the largest and most important cooperative is Swashrayi Mahila Sewa Sahakari Bank, which is owned by self-employed women as shareholders. The bank, first of its kind in India, was set up in 1974 with 4,000 depositors but within a short span of 24 years the number has risen to 1,25,000 depositors. The bank has also extended it's 790 rural savings groups after demand for this service grew in the State.

"We have very few defaulters because most of the times we allow extra time for repayments in case of any problems," said Ms Jaysree Vyas, managing director of the Sewa bank.

The Sewa Academy also organizes literacy classes for self-employed children and their children and it publishes *Anasuya* newsletter and has a video unit of its own, where trained poor women make films on their own and use them within Sewa to facilitate cooperation and understanding amongst its members.

Sewa, in Ms Bhatt's words, is still in its youth and to fulfil people's expectations, she wants laws for homemakers to be adopted by the governments, national policy for vendors and hawkers to be formulated and all different Sewa organizations have to involve more people and give better results.

Social consciousness of a different kind

He is only 27-years-old, yet, he has devoted almost a third of that life-span to children of sex workers in Varanasi and Delhi. When could he have started? "Seventeen," he answers with a beguiling smile.

And what could have inspired him?

"When I was studying in Hansraj College, my aimless walks would often take me to Delhi's G.B.Road, and the innocence of the children there, surviving in the midst of abjectly squalid conditions, would so tug at my heart, I eventually found myself involved in their affairs," he says with the same disarming smile.

Seems like the dogged smile did the trick. And charmed its way even into the coarsened hearts of the sex workers, because, today, the improving their children's quality of life has become Ajit Singh's life's mission.

Dropping out from the final year studies in M.A History at Hansraj College, Ajit decided to 'adopt' three illegitimate children of a sex worker from Varanasi.

Initially, it raised a storm at home. Later, witnessing his cast-iron-belt resolve, the parents also gave in and the three children were shifted to a hostel in Lucknow where they continue to finish their studies. Today, after several threats to his life, Ajit's involvement with the children of sex workers has grown so much, he has become their most trusted lieutenant, a one-in-a-million voice for the faceless multitudes who continue being exploited in the country's thriving sex industry.

His one-man outfit Guriya recently concluded a fourth two-day National Dance Festival for Women Sex Workers at Sri Ram Centre, in the capital. Over 200 women from Gaya, Muzaffarpur, Varanasi, Chatarpur, Raisen, Tirupati, Sangli, Belgaum, Mumbai, Calcutta participated, a few from as far-off as Bangladesh and Nepal.

He was assisted in this endeavour by the National Human Rights Commission (NHRC) and Child Relief and You (CRY).

Excerpts of An Interview With Ajit Singh

Why did you decide on a dance festival? Considering the stigma attached to them, why did you not organize some other vocational activity?

"Why not?" he counters. "Rehabilitation doesn't mean just stitching and tailoring. Most sex workers are talented classical dancers. It is only a question of putting their art in the correct slot. And, dance does not draw the suspicion of other criminal elements in the pimp-police-prostitute nexus, so it is easy for me to draw public attention to their plight through this medium. Dance has a ready audience, "he asserts.

Have you seen Meera Nair's *Salaam Bombay* that also features the condition of children in red light areas? Does it mirror reality?

"The true picture is even worse. A child's initiation into prostitution is so quiet, so subtle, it is often difficult to figure out when it actually happened.

What is it that you want to do for these children?

"Look, the women are already trapped in the vicious cycle. It is probably too difficult, or too late to extricate them. But, the children can still be retrieved. So, Guriya runs creches for them and lobbies for their education in reputed schools. I do not believe in isolation wards, so we try to place these children in the best public schools. We have so far managed to place 30 children. My concept of social welfare is different. I believe in introducing structural changes. That is why I focus my energies solely on children.

Should prostitution be legalised?

"No, I am firmly against that. Ninety per cent of the brothel prostitution in my experience, is forced. The call-girl racket may be exempt, but most others are lured into the trade through a flourishing racket of fake marriages and kidnapping. Even the

Immoral Trafficking in Women and Girls (Prevention) Act, 1986, that in spirit favours women, in actual implementation, is often used against them."

Women, a silent majority

Recently published *The Fiftieth Milestone* looks at India since 1947 through the eyes of women, edited by Shanta Serbjeet Singh and Jyoti Sabharwal and published by Sterling Publishers, it consists of 22 essays on a wide range of subjects.

Using the book as a sort of centrepiece, there was a panel discussion with Kiran Bedi, Neerja Chowdhury the Political Editor of the *Indian Express* and Padma Seth of the National Commission for Women, as well as Shanta Serbjeet Singh. It was certainly thought provoking.

All the panelists were critical of where women are today and felt they were in danger of becoming what Shanta called "the silent majority". Ms Bedi felt that women themselves were not doing enough in public administration, Ms Seth felt there was now a lack of leaders among women unlike the previous years and Ms Chowdhury felt the man had bonded together in Parliament to stop the Bill reserving 33 per cent seats for women.

All true, but wish there had been some recognition of the enormous strides women have made in these last fifty years in India. It is true their representation has come down in Parliament, but politics itself is no longer the pre-eminent mover of society it once was.

There are other dynamics and women are present in them. In any case the Panchayat reservations will see the imbalance rectified soon. If you ask what women have moved into in these last five decades, it might be simpler to ask what they have not moved into? And the answer is virtually nothing.

Some of it may well be a token presence, but women are present in large numbers and in all positions in numerous other areas.

Just look at the IAS, journalism, television, films, advertising, music, theatre, writing, the arts, publishing, social work, law, sports, medicine, the environment, education and this is just a partial list.

Someone should have pointed out that while it is true that women have a long way to go — and go they will — it is also true that they have moved a long way indeed. Much like India itself.

'Many teachers are unaware of gender discrimination'

India is a country where gender discrimination is still prevalent, mainly in the rural areas. The problem lies right at the outset when the children are sent to school, and that is where they first face up to situations arising out of their respective genders. The problem also stems from the attitudes of parents, and their respective outlooks towards society.

To counter this malady, the Delhi Commission for Women (DCW) felt the need to give adequate attention to this problem right at the primary and secondary school levels.

To discuss the role of the schools and society, in general, DCW organized three workshops involving teachers, students, the youth, educationists, parents and community leaders. The workshops were held at three different areas which represented the different cross-sections of society—South Delhi (literate and urbanised population), north and the old city (traditional attitudes) and outer Delhi (semi-rural populace).

The findings proved to be heartening and revealing. Heartening because all sections of the society were in favour of introducing life-skills courses in schools, and revealing as many teachers were found to have a stereotyped mentality, not giving much thought to the gender bias which exists in society.

The recommendations of the workshop included suggestions to involve the boys and girls equally in all sorts of extracurricular activities, including NCC/NSS. Also, it was suggested that teacher should be trained to orient themselves to changes in societal attitudes and the progressive times. The celebration of International Women's Day in every school was widely recommended to further the cause of women's progress and gender equality. The workshops felt the need to make screenings of documentaries on gender equality a part of the school activity, as also the need to organize discussions among parents, teachers and students on gender issues a regular feature in schools. The recommendations are to be presented to the Chief Minister.

Peace prayers and seminars mark women's day in city

Addressing an open discussion on "Development of women in 50 years of Independence," First Lady Usha Naryanan called for greater coordination and interaction between governmental policy at the national level to tie in with the concerns and matters raised by women at the local government level as also sensitizing people to the plight of poor women.

The then chairperson of the National Commission for Women Mohini Giri expressed the hope that the 81st Constitution amendment bill providing one-third reservation for women in the Lok Sabha and Assemblies will be passed in the first business session of the new Parliament.

'Education rather than reservation'

New Delhi, March 8: "Empowerment of women consists in education and universal entitlement and not reservation and sweet words," said Ms Amola Pathak, chairperson of the Sulabh Women and Child Welfare Association, addressing a conference organized on the eve of the International Women's Day.

A large number of women, especially from scavenger families, attended the conference.

Asserting that the time had come for women to be treated as equals, Ms Pathak added, "Far too long women have been living on sufferance of men who have treated women as chattel and products and not as equals in the making of a new India. Of the estimated seven lakh scavengers, about 60 per cent are women and, hence, their liberation and rehabilitation is of supreme concern". Among those who spoke on the occasion, was Ms Veena Nayyar of International Women's Political Watch.

Plight of Muslim Women

Ishtiaque Ahmed on their status

A feminist agenda is forcing its way to newspaper headlines across the world. In India women are fighting for 33 per cent reservation in Parliament and legislative assemblies. Muslim women in the repressed Arabian societies are clamouring for change. In Iran, a beginning has been made by President Mohammad Khatami appointing a woman to an important position. Women's participation in diverse fields has been increasing in most democratic nations. But the insignificant participation of Muslim women in Indian and in Muslim societies, particularly in the Islamic countries, is a matter of concern.

A leading feminist wrote "Politics means collective endeavour for social transformation that empowers women to fight any form of oppression, exploitation, injustice and degradation." Muslim men have curtailed most of the rights of their women. According to the orthodox 'Ulema', the primary duty of a conservative Muslim woman is to look after her husband and children. She is not allowed to venture outside her home except with the permission of her husband or father. This provision is strictly enforced in Saudi Arabia and now in Afghanistan. Why have the self-proclaimed guardians of Islam, the Taliban, forgotten that women in Islam have been valiant warriors and able rulers? Where are Aisha and Khadeja in Taliban's Afghanistan?

In the time of the Prophet, women participated freely in the affairs of war. *Shahihal Bukhari*, an authentic collection of edicts, records how Muslim women actively helped the wounded in the famous Islamic battle of Uhud. Aisha, the Prophet's wife and others were seen removing the dead and wounded from the battle field. The status of women in Islam deteriorated with the passage of time. In Islam proper dress is suggested and not veiling to avoid indecent exposure. Ms Lila Ahmed writes in *Woman and Gender in Islam* that veiling was essentially a non-Arab practice prevalent in those areas dominated by the Roman and Persian empires. It was probably more prevalent in countries like Syria and Palestine. It was connected with social status and was used among Greeks, Romans, Jews and Assyrians, all of whom practised veiling to some degree.

The challenges faced by women in Islamic countries are known. The Quran allows them to earn their livelihood. Taliban bans women from working, and bars girls from schools. Islamic history shows that Khadeja, the first wife of Prophet, ran her own business, engaged her own employees and chose her own husband. There can be no role model better than Khadeja for the sad world of Muslim women today. Women have been put under a strict dress code in Iran after the revolution. It is a reality that this strict *purdah* is not liked by all. They are forced to obey the dress code in the name of Islam.

However, major changes are taking place in Iranian society today. The process began last year when the daughter of the former President of Iran was elected to the male-dominated *majlis* (parliament). These changes signify that women's liberation in Iran is gathering momentum. The election of Khatami is a protest vote against the conservative forces in Iran. Women in Iran feel that their assertive role from their houses to parliament will give new substance to the women's movement in Iran. The religious clergy will never take the initiative for granting them a place in society and governance without strong efforts made by the women themselves.

The twentieth century has been an era of vigorous re-awakening in the areas of political thought, literature and knowledge. Hoda Shaaraawi is recognized by historians as the first leader of the women's liberation movement in Egypt. She founded the first women's federation in 1923 with women from the upper and middle classes. They fought to abolish the veil, to raise the age of marriage for girls, to prevent polygamy, to diminish the absolute right of men to divorce and to give women the right to vote.

This organization worked hard to bring women's rights to the forefront as part of the national struggle for liberation in Egypt. Doreya Shafik was a brave fighter for women's rights, and organized a political party for women in Egypt in 1953, called Hisb Ben El Nil. She led a demonstration to parliament demanding the right to vote for women, but failed to achieve her objective and committed suicide.

Despite the severe curtailment of democratic liberties, the women in all Arab countries including Algeria, Palestine, Lebanon, Syria, Iraq, Sudan, Yemen and Tunisia have organized their struggles in various fronts, whether military, political, economic, social or cultural. The Arab Women's Solidarity Association fights for freedom and human rights inside the family, nationally and internationally. If the patriarchal class system is global then resistance must be global too. In Pakistan, the "Muslim girls' lot is reduced to *chadar, choolha aur chahardivari*" lamented Fehmida

Riaz, the hapless poetess who was exiled by the then President of Pakistan, Zia-ul-Haque for her bold views.

In Pakistan and Bangladesh women are in the forefront of the movement for women's as well as human rights. It is for this reason that even Zia-ul-Haque, despite his zeal for Islamization, could not remove the Muslim family ordinance of 1962 enacted by President Ayub Khan guaranteed certain rights to women. In Malaysia, there are a number of women's organizations actively campaigning for their rights. Sisters-in-Islam work for creating awareness among the Muslim women. In Dhaka, reformist groups are campaigning for the reinterpretation of Muslim personal law to bring it in line with modern social values. In India efforts are on to involve women in the governance of the nation. In the recent Panchayat elections, about one million women participated as candidates.

In Indian society Muslim women are pushed to the wall, particularly in rural areas. They are the victims of, first, the selfish interpretation of Islamic laws by the religious class and, second, of the low literacy level. In November 1995, when 45 Muslim women filled their nomination to participate in the civic bodies' election from the area in the vicinity of Darul-Uloom, Deoband, the Ulema became alarmed. They issued a *fatwa* barring Muslim women from participating in elections as it will bring them into contact with men. Their *fatwa* hardly had any impact on women and conscious Muslim voters. It was rejected by them. The Ulema must change their approach, otherwise the Muslim masses will declare a *fatwa* against them.

Illiteracy is another problem. The literacy rate for Muslim women is a shocking, 19 per cent, which is less than half of that of women from other communities. The national literacy rate for women is 39 per cent. There is a need for paying greater attention to education than to *talaq* and uniform civil code. Muslims should not also stick to the traditional forms of education.

The Hindustan Times, 4 March, 1998

Rape rate of minors rising, conviction figures remain low

New Delhi: She was only four. Until it happened. She went to play with Rakesh Bhaiyya in the Trilokpuri neighbourhood. He smothered her cries with a quilt. It hurt. And she came back bleeding and crying. Rakesh was caught. But it was too late. Her life had changed.

They had gone to the temple. They were still in school — Class VII and IX. And sisters. It was 8 pm. Early for some cities but in Delhi, definitely late. Sunil Tiwari, Inderjeet, Sandeep and Somu took them to an empty room after threatening them. They knew the four but that didn't matter. Locked up in a little shed in lonely Najafgarh, they were raped. The boys were arrested.

But the Najafgarh nightmare hadn't ended. The next day, it was same case. Two sisters aged 15 and 17. Four boys and one of them Jitender, a distant relative, followed by Nizam, Raju and Shashi. Traumatized by their brutality, the 17-year-old jumped into the Yamuna as Jitender was taking them back. To be saved only by a fire brigade crew searching for corpses.

In numbers, the minors rank highest among rape victims while conviction rates are low.

The maximum sentence a rapist can get under Section 376 of the Indian Penal Code is life imprisonment—14 years. Just a handful of years compared to a lifetime of living in trauma.

In 1997, 111 cases of victims below 12 years of age were reported to be topped only the 176 cases in the 13-16 age group. This is followed by 93 in the 17-18 group. Of the total 526 cases reported, only 485 were worked out. The three cited cases are of February. It is March now and total rape cases in Delhi is already 543 and rising even as experts claim that the rate of rape cases in Delhi is double the national average. The statistics are depressing. But then so is the crime, devastating.

Ms Yamin Hazarika, deputy commissioner of police, Crime Against Women Cell, says, "The rape cases are on the rise because of increased population and also increased reporting. In such cases, the accused are normally held in jails for a long time as undertrials and the courts don't give them bail easily. The trials are in camera, so many times, it is not followed up in court."

With low conviction figures, most rape cases often peter out without having reached a logical conclusion in court. The victim is frequently ignored and the police claim that the attackers were acquaintances. Not the ideal atmosphere for discouraging potential offenders.

Ms Hazarika explains, "Most of the times, the case is settled as the complainants deny their claim. In others, the accused is married" and says, "This will ruin my life". In some other cases, the complainants just disappear and don't turn up for cases." The victims are usually from the slum area in the outer fringes of Delhi. The children normally belong to the lower middle-class families. "It is usually a migrant population. One day they are here and the next, they are there because they are a floating population anyway. They don't even inform the police before the shift or phone up to find out what is happening to the case," says Ms Hazarika. Faced with an erosion of bonding or accountability to community peers, it is the minor girl who is the unfortunate victim of the stresses of living in urban cities. Most parents scared of the social stigma attached to rape, prefer to sweep it under the carpet. The problem manifests itself in other ways. It doesn't disappear.

"Bojh": Indian women caught in a web of rigid tradition

New Delhi: Throughout the nineteenth century, the focus was on women and women power.

Discussions, conferences and workshops concentrated on the strengths and weaknesses, nature, capacities and potential of women from all walks of life across the world. In India, the "wrongs" began to be deplored after "renaissance,", albeit the Indian version, which swept the country in the 18th and 19th centuries.

Almost two centuries later, as the world celebrates the International Women's Day, it is time to take stock of the plight of the Indian woman — aptly depicted in the film *Bojh* screened at India Habitat Centre to mark the occasion.

Starring Uttara Baokar and Chandra Bisht, the film explores the position of women in society and attempts at explaining their character. It tries to prove that women are their best friends as well as their worst enemies.

The film is on the relationship shared by two women — the docile wife of a brahmin pandit and her dominating sister-in-law.

Nimuli, the protagonist, juggles her life between the kitchen and looking after the elderly sister-in-law. Her sister-in-law, a widow, relives her past and tries to impose the same rules and regulations on Nimuli as she encountered in her life.

There is reservoir of frustration borne out of the rigid social customs that are imposed on widows. As the plot unveils, an intense rivalry emerges between the two women, one trying to impose herself on the other. The role of the husband portrayed is also very traditional.

However, the story though on a familiar theme, could have been presented in a better manner. The characters are restricted and unable to "live" their roles. And there remained the question whether change could only be brought about from the upper strata of the society?

"Even though people in the cities assume they understand our problems, they don't. Problems are steeped in tradition and there is no way out of it," observed a woman tending the garden outside the auditorium when asked for her opinion of Women's Day.

A pessimistic view, but she has probably voiced the opinion of many women sharing a plight similar to hers. And this shows where the work for uplift has to be taken up all over again.

Minor girls abducted, sold

Ghaziabad: Two minor girls of Shaheed Nagar in Sahibabad were reportedly kidnapped and sold for Rs.1,000. In two other cases, two minor girls were kidnapped.

Savitri (15) and Suneeta (14) of Shaheed Nagar were lured to become dancers and were kidnapped, alleged their father Dalchand in the FIR. His neighbour Mrs Shabana, wife of Jamil Ansari of E-Block, Shaheed Nagar, used to visit Dalchand's house.

She is alleged to have been luring the two minor girls to learn dancing and live a luxurious life. After the two girls were kidnapped, an FIR was lodged with the Sahibabad police.

Shabana is reported to have admitted to the kidnapping and having sold both the minor girls to one Pappu of Shastri Nagar Park's jhuggi cluster for Rs 1,000, the police said. Pappu allegedly took them to Mumbai on the promise of getting them trained as dancers there, police said.

Birbal Saini of Mohalla Gurdhar Garhi, in Kavi Nagar, alleged that his daughter Indrish (13) was kidnapped when she went to fetch water from a neighbouring house on March 27. He alleged that initially the police did not register his case. Only SSP Daya Shanker Singh did intervene, then a case was registered. Birbal has named Sheru, Anil and his wife Leela of Shekhri and Naresh of Govindpuri, Modi Nagar in the FIR for the alleged kidnapping.

In the other case of kidnapping under Garh police, one Chiranjilal has alleged that his 15-year-old daughter Meena was kidnapped on April 18. He has named Ishwar, Munilal, Vijinder and one more in the FIR. A case has been registered, but no arrest has been made so far, the police said.

Two women, 16-year-old girl found dead

New Delhi: Two women and a 16-year-old girl died unnatural deaths in different parts of the city. One was a murder, the second a suicide, and the police were unsure about the third.

A 55-year-old widow, Som Devi, was reportedly found murdered at her first-floor New Ranjit Nagar flat, in Patel Nagar area of west Delhi.

The victim's body was found by her 12-year-old grand daughter Kavita when she returned home from a night-long Jagran in the colony at about 6 am.

"The victim and Kavita, whose mother stays in Faridabad, used to live in the flat. There was no apparent ransacking in the flat...Kavita is in shock. We will come to know if something was taken from the flat only later," said an area police official.

"Kavita had left for the function on Saturday night and returned in the morning to find her maternal grandmother bleeding from the nose. The victim could have been smothered to death," he said.

"Things will be clear only after the autopsy report comes in. A murder case has been registered in the Patel Nagar police station and further investigations are in progress," added the police official.

In the second case, a 35-year-old woman, Kamla, reportedly committed suicide by setting herself ablaze at her Dakshinpuri home in south Delhi around 10 am on Sunday. "She doused herself with kerosene. We are trying to ascertain what led her to commit suicide," said an area police official.

In the third incident, 16-year-old Rajni succumbed to her 90 per cent burns at Safdarjung hospital. The police said the girl, engulfed in flames, had suddenly come out of a room in her Palam Colony house. It is not clear whether the girl committed suicide or had been killed by someone.

"At that time, her mother, who is ill, was lying on a bed and her father was sitting outside. Her younger brother Kamal (12) saw her and raised an alarm. Her father Kishan Pal came running and then wrapped her in a blanket," said an area police official. "Rajini had left her studies around two years ago. We are investigating what led to the sudden fire. The exact cause is yet to be ascertained."

55-year-old killed for being a 'witch'

Jaipur: A 55-year-old woman was killed at Jhali Jee Ka Barana village in Rajasthan, the police said. Kesar Bai Regar, 55, was killed on March 25 allegedly by Bhanwar Lal Meghwal who suspected her of being a witch and responsible for the illness of his sister. Meghwal's three sisters had died due to illness. The fourth was also unwell and was being treated by occult methods.

3 widows shot dead in Bihar

Patna: Four people, including three widows of a family, were shot dead in separate incidents in Sitamarhi and Nawada. Official sources said three widows were shot dead by some anti-socials, allegedly with an intention to grab their landed property at Jamua village under Bairagania police station in Sitamarhi.

Why Should a Woman Be Like a Man?

Dilip Raote

Recently I was stuck with three tickets for the Dresden Chamber Choir concert. I looked around for company, but none of my friends had any particular interest in Western music. So I went to the All Saints' Home in Mumbai's Mazagon area and made a date with two Anglo-Indian ladies, Louise and Joy. They are older than I in age but young where it matters — the heart. The concert was superb and the conversation lively.

Louise and Joy are not really inmates of the home. Louise's

house, where she lives alone, is under repairs and she has sought temporary shelter in the home. Her children have flown the nest. She has travelled abroad extensively, but she does not indulge in the "them and poor us" comparative idiocies of travelled Indians. When she was in a London pub, the racist bartender was rude to her son. Louise intervened to end the clash with this comment: "Son, these people haven't travelled after they lost the empire. They don't know their geography. Leave them to their ignorance." I loved that. Louise smokes cigarettes as if Marlene Dietrich were her model. The long cigarette-holder is missing, of course. Joy is a former nurse and YWCA warden. At the All Saints' Home, she is in a post-retirement posting. She too has relatives all over the globe.

Civilising Influence

When you have mature, cosmopolitan company, the conversation is catholic — ours travelled from politics to the theft of grave stones to the decline of courtesy and civility in Mumbai. Joy and Louise took me back to the graces of Jane Austen's world. I clicked my heels and bowed. I opened and shut taxi doors for them. I stood until they were seated. It was so civilising.

It is this civilizing influence that I miss with younger girls. They are so uncouth. They don't know to stand, how to sit, how to walk. They don't have the table manners for a formal dinner. College girls spit on the road with as much aplomb as any male lout. They pick their teeth and noses in public places. And their language, oh their language! There too they are aspiring for equality with men. It is embarrassing to hear anyone use four-letter words or narrate scatological jokes. It's doubly so when young women do it. And their laughter reminds me of a P.G. Wodehouses' comment, "She had a penetrating sort of laugh. Rather like a train going into a tunnel". India's educated young women are acquiring the gracelessness of the lower middle classes portrayed in American films. The consequence is an absence of sensitivity. Without sensitivity there is no grace.

When women had a secondary role, they were keen observers. From their vantage backseat points, they saw, noted and acted on their observations. Women learned to anticipate the demands of their men and children. They developed sensitivity. They observed families higher up the social order and sought to polish the rough edges of their own families. The ambition was to acquire 'style' and 'grace'. The overwhelming fear was that a graceless act would shame the family. Women were the civilizing influences.

Better Role

Social and economic freedom should have heightened sensitivities. Instead, they have fuelled ambitions to acquire more possessions. The democratization by consumerism had deadened aesthetic sensibility. 'Style' has come to mean merely 'more expensive'. So you have these graceless women using foul language at home with their equally graceless husbands in the presence of children. The TV or music system blares and everyone speaks in shrill voices. It's 'in' to be loud.

Women now have the opportunity to be better than men. But they are striving to be just like them. It is poor ambition. It is also economically and culturally self-defeating. When this realization hits women, there will be a revulsion against vulgarity. And then there will be coaching classes to inculcate grace in globalizing managers, housewife hostesses, college girls. Grace will be a crucial job and marriage requirement. Graceful writers in all languages will be back. There will be larger crowds at classical music concerts. Romance, wooing, dancing will be stylized again. It was thus at the end of the 19th century. It will be so again. This time, however, women will have to set the rules. Young women must prepare for a better role than a crass imitation of man. It is they who must set the new civilizing standards.

Index